Lecture Notes in Artificial Intelligence 3067

Edited by J. G. Carbonell and J. Siekmann

Subseries of Lecture Notes in Computer Science

Springer
Berlin
Heidelberg
New York
Hong Kong
London
Milan
Paris
Tokyo

Mehdi Dastani   Jürgen Dix
Amal El Fallah Seghrouchni (Eds.)

Programming
Multi-Agent Systems

First International Workshop, ProMAS 2003
Melbourne, Australia, July 15, 2003
Selected Revised and Invited Papers

Springer

Series Editors

Jaime G. Carbonell, Carnegie Mellon University, Pittsburgh, PA, USA
Jörg Siekmann, University of Saarland, Saarbrücken, Germany

Volume Editors

Mehdi Dastani
Utrecht University, Institute of Information and Computing Sciences
P.O.Box 80.089, 3508 TB Utrecht, The Netherlands
E-mail: mehdi@cs.uu.nl

Jürgen Dix
Technical University of Clausthal, Department of Computer Science
Julius-Albert-Str. 4, 38678 Clausthal, Germany
E-mail: dix@tu-clausthal.de

Amal El Fallah Seghrouchni
University Paris X and LIP6 (University Paris 6 and CNRS - UMR 7606)
8, Rue du Capitaine Scott, 75015 Paris, France
E-mail: Amal.Elfallah@lip6.fr

Library of Congress Control Number: 2004106947

CR Subject Classification (1998): I.2.11, I.2, C.2.4, D.2, F.3, D.3

ISSN 0302-9743
ISBN 3-540-22180-8 Springer-Verlag Berlin Heidelberg New York

Springer-Verlag is a part of Springer Science+Business Media

springeronline.com

© Springer-Verlag Berlin Heidelberg 2004
Printed in Germany

Typesetting: Camera-ready by author, data conversion by Olgun Computergrafik
Printed on acid-free paper   SPIN: 11011576   06/3142   5 4 3 2 1 0

Preface

Recently, the area of autonomous agents and multiagent systems (MAS) has grown into a promising technology offering a credible alternative for the design of intelligent and cooperative systems. Several efforts have been made by academic researchers, by industrials and by several standardization consortiums in order to provide novel tools, methods and frameworks to establish the necessary standards for a wide use of MAS as a technology in its own right and not only as a new paradigm.

However, until now the main focus of the MAS community has been on the development of *formal and informal tools* (e.g. MASIF as OMG specifications, FIPA), *concepts* (e.g. concerning mental or social attitudes, communication, cooperation, organization, mobility) and *techniques* (e.g. AUML, modal languages, verification techniques) in order to *analyze and specify multiagent systems*.

We are convinced that the next step will concern the development of programming languages and tools which can effectively support MAS programming and *implement key concepts of multiagent systems in a unified framework*. The success of agent oriented system design is guaranteed if we can bridge the gap between analysis and implementation, and thus develop powerful and general purpose programming technology such that the concepts and specifications for multiagent systems can be easily and directly implemented.

This technology should include *agent based programming languages, tools and techniques*: these were the themes of the Dagstuhl seminar *Programming Multi Agent Systems Based on Logic* (see [2] and the recent [1]), where the focus was on logic-based approaches. During the seminar, the idea came up to broaden the scope beyond logic-based frameworks and thus ProMAS came into being.

ProMAS 2003, the *First International Workshop on Programming Multiagent Systems: Languages, Frameworks, Techniques and Tools*, was held in July 2003, in Melbourne (Australia) as an associated event of AAMAS 2003: the main international conference dedicated to autonomous agents and multiagents systems. ProMAS 2003 (http://www.cs.uu.nl/ProMAS) was the first international workshop dedicated to MAS programming and it will be followed this year by ProMAS 2004, which will also take place within AAMAS 2004 (July 2004 in New York City, USA).

ProMAS 2003 was an invaluable opportunity that brought together leading researchers from both academia and industry to discuss the design of programming languages for multiagent systems. In particular, the workshop promoted the discussion and exchange of ideas concerning the concepts, properties, requirements, and principles that are important for future programming technology for multiagent systems.

This volume of the LNAI series constitutes the official (post-) proceedings of ProMAS 2003. It presents the main conclusions of the ProMAS event. Besides eight high quality papers selected among the (fifteen) submitted papers, we also invited three leading researchers working in industry. While the workshop papers represent mainly basic research, the invited papers describe work that is applied in various industrial applications. The eleven papers in this volume can be roughly divided into the following three groups.

Programming MAS: This section consists of three papers. *Keith Decker* describes in his paper a new vision for programming multiagent systems and presents a toolkit for MAS applications: DECAF. *Rick Evertsz et al.* describe how to implement industrial applications of MAS using their system JACK. *Jörg Müller et al.* relate the problem of programming software agents with designing executable business processes.

Languages for MAS: This section consists of three papers. *Rafael Bordini et al.* relate AgentSpeak, a planning language for autonomous agents, to a general purpose Java model checker. They consider the important problem of verifying multiagent programs. *Amal el Fallah Seghrouchni et al.* describe a computational language for autonomous and intelligent mobile agents. *Mehdi Dastani et al.* introduce a programming language for cognitive agents that have beliefs, goals, plans. The syntax and semantics of this programming language are presented.

Principles and Tools for MAS: This section consists of five papers. *Paul Scerri et al.* present a proxy architecture and team oriented programming method that allow effective coordination between large teams of heterogeneous agents. *Shamimaby Paurobally et al.* consider methods and tools to develop agent interaction protocols. They can be used to bridge the gap between intuitive developments and formal specifications. *Martin Kollingbaum and Timothy Norman* are concerned with agent architectures and aim to bridge the gap between analysis and programming (or theory and practice) of agent systems. *Martin Dinkloh and Jens Niemis* present a graphical tool which helps in integrating the design and implementation of agent conversations. Finally, *Bruno Mermet et al.* introduce a method for designing and validating multiagent systems.

We would like to thank all the contributors, PC members and referees for their outstanding contribution to the success of ProMAS 2003. We are especially thankful to AAMAS 2003 organizers and Simon Parsons for their technical support and for hosting ProMAS 2003.

March 2004   Mehdi Dastani
                                                                     Jürgen Dix
                                                     Amal El Fallah Seghrouchni

References

1. J. Dix, M. Fisher, H. Levesque, and L. Sterling, editors. *Logic Based Implementation of Agent Systems*, volume 41 of *Special Issue of the Annals in Mathematics and Artificial Intelligence*. Baltzer Science Publishers, 2004.
2. J. Dix, M. Fisher, and Y. Zhang. Programming Multi Agent Systems based on Logic. Technical Report Dagstuhl Seminar Report 361, IBFI GmbH, Schloß Dagstuhl, 2002. URL: http://www.dagstuhl.de/02481/

Workshop Organization

Organizing Committee

Mehdi Dastani	Utrecht University (The Netherlands)
Jürgen Dix	Technical University of Clausthal (Germany)
Amal El Fallah Seghrouchni	University of Paris 6 (France)
David Kinny	Agentis Software (Australia)

Program Committee

Rafael Bordini	University of Liverpool (UK)
Jean-Pierre Briot	University of Paris 6 (France)
Mehdi Dastani	Utrecht University (The Netherlands)
Yves Demazeau	University Joseph Fourrier (France)
Virginia Dignum	Utrecht University (The Netherlands)
Jürgen Dix	Technical University of Clausthal (Germany)
Amal El Fallah-Seghrouchni	University of Paris 6 (France)
Michael Fisher	University of Liverpool (UK)
David Kinny	Agentis Software (Australia)
John-Jules Meyer	Utrecht University (The Netherlands)
Oliver Obst	Koblenz-Landau University (Germany)
Julian Padget	University of Bath (UK)
Leendert van der Torre	CWI (The Netherlands)
Cees Witteveen	Delft University (The Netherlands)

Additional Referee

Birna van Riemsdijk	Utrecht University (The Netherlands)

Table of Contents

Section I: Programming Multiagent Systems

Section II: Languages for Multiagent Systems

Section III: Principles and Tools for Multiagent Systems

A Vision for Multi-agent Systems Programming

Keith Decker

Dept. of Computer & Information Sciences
University of Delware, Newark, DE 19716
decker@udel.edu

Abstract. In order to increase the number of agent applications in practical use, it is a given that we need to incease the rate at which problems are conceptualized and specified using MAS-based approaches. However, we must also address two other problems: moving from specification to actual implemented systems without programming from scratch, and the training of people to carry out such work. In this paper we examine four desiderata for practical development tools – a focus on programming as opposed to architecture; programming at the multi-agent level; "value-added" architectures; support for persistent, flexible, robust action. We also examine observed training shortfalls of graduate students attempting to implement technically complex multi-agent applications. These desiderata and observations are made in the context of DECAF, an MAS development toolkit developed at the University of Delaware and based on early versions of RETSINA.

1 Introduction

MAS research has moved into its second decade, and along with the vast increases in computer power and interconnectedness that have occurred is the growing realization that distributed, open, and dynamic computational systems are becoming the norm. Whether MAS solutions to the development of such complex distributed systems will be widely adopted remains to be seen. There are many technical and social roadblocks to widespread adoption, two of which we will describe here. The first is the technical problem of moving from specification to implementation, and the second the social problem of training programmers to specify and implement such systems.

Since the early days of DAI (Distributed Artificial Intelligence) experimental researchers have created implementations and demonstrations of their ideas, but rarely with industrial applications directly in mind. As MAS (Multi-Agent Systems) became the focus in the '90's, more concerted efforts on toolkits that could be reused began to appear. Long running conference series such as ATAL (Agent Theories, Architectures, and Languages) (from [1] to [2]) detailed numerous agent architectures and toolkits for experimenting with architectures. Agentlink.org lists over 100 available toolkits [3]. The question then shifts to exactly how each toolkit actually supports the transition from application specification to application implementation. We postulate four desired areas of support for application programmers.

M. Dastani, J. Dix, A. El Fallah-Seghrouchni (Eds.): PROMAS 2003, LNAI 3067, pp. 1–17, 2004.

1.1   Avoiding APIs: Focus on Agent Programming, Not Architecture

Too often, in order to retain architectural generality, a toolkit provides a set of common services/classes that can be integrated in many ways. Application programmers are better served by a focus on agent programming, and not on architectural design (which better serves researchers exploring next-generation agent-based systems) Certainly APIs for agent communication, ACL (agent communication language) message construction, directory service/agent name server access, etc. are useful and necessary. However, they still leave a huge gap for the agent application programmer: how should they be chained together? Given an API for retrieving incoming communications, how should it be used? Retrieve one message at a time before processing; retrieve all periodically; interrupt to retrieve; retrieve in a concurrent thread, etc.? Hundreds of such decisions need to be made and have little to do directly with the actual domain actions of most types of agents (although some decisions can be crucial – that's why agent architectures are of such intense research interest). For this reason we advocate the construction and use of relatively "complete" architectures for the use by application programmers, possibly indexed by important application features that are supported (i.e. upper-time-bound guarantees on the processing of an incoming message in one architecture, automated non-local-task coordination in another).

1.2   Programming at the Multi-agent Level

Even in a relatively limited domain, it is often surprising that more complete, or almost-complete, agents are not available for quickly prototyping larger systems. This idea can probably be traced in the most detail back to Michael Huhns, who has talked about agents "volunteering" themselves to be a part of your application for over 10 years[4]. At the limit, systems might be put together from pre-existing agents that are active and declarative (knowing "what" they do, not just "how"); that hold beliefs about the world, themselves, and others; and that may represent or stand in for real-world objects.

To a lesser extent, this also includes being able to construct systems "out of the box" with agents that are completely or almost completely useful in an application without any programming at all. Such agents are available in better toolkits in at least two kinds: "middle agents" [5] and domain-specific "agent shells". The most ubiquitous (probably because they are a very common organizational feature and have been standardized [6]) are directory service agents (agent name servers, or "white pages") and matchmakers or "yellow pages" services.

In the best of all worlds, well-understood MAS applications might be constructed with little or no programming, and only proper configuration of instantiations of such reusable agents. This may already be possible in application types such as information gathering systems, as we will see in section 2.7.

1.3   Value-Added Architectures

It is important that the toolkit provides extensive, obvious value to the application programmer commensurate with the often considerable difficulty of learning the toolkit/programming environment. A parallel can be drawn to the rise and fall of blackboard architectures for DAI in the 80's [7]: The concept is fairly easy to grasp and not too hard to prototype, especially if some of the underlying APIs are available. However, the resulting systems built quickly are *slow, inefficient,* and will not *scale* to industrial applications. Thus the technology got a bad name from failed industrial adoptions that failed to use mature, carefully architected and optimized implementations [8, 9] rather than simplistic in-house demo code. The same fate can (perhaps in some circles, has) befallen MAS development ("Agents – that's just distributed objects, right? We gave up on CORBA...or was it Web Services? Grid Computing?")

Thus agent toolkits must provide significant value-added over "coding it up from scratch". This can include both bookkeeping details such as automatic linkages between high-level design and implementation [10, 11], standard behaviors, ontology support, directory service registration/deregistration, etc. It also includes the less-quantifiable "efficiency" issues that may make-or-break an actual application where the agent code is in support of the larger, wider, and more important application goals.

1.4   The "Little Engine That Could": Supporting Agenthood

Preferably, agent development tools should support the basic nature of agenthood [12] – that of flexible, robust, autonomous, structured persistent action. In an interview with Jean-Pierre Briot for *IEEE Concurrency,* Les Gasser [13] said:

[GASSER]: Yes. Here I think the critical insight about agents – the next step in the progression of adding structure to programming technology – is the idea of direct support for 'structured persistent action.' People talk about this as autonomy, they talk about this as goal-directed behavior, or whatever. But for me it's the concept of structured persistent action. In effect, ideally what the idea of agents gives, is a new programming tool, along the lines of objects, and along the lines of concurrent objects, but now a bit farther along in terms of the control capabilities built into the tool or framework itself. With agents, persistent action becomes part of the toolkit–part of the framework that the programmer doesn't have to build explicitly from scratch.

[BRIOT]: What about the other aspects that are typically included in the idea of 'agenthood' – world models, the ability to communicate, deliberative, conditional, or reactive action, and so on?

[GASSER]: I may get into a religious war here, but most of these don't seem to me to be critical or fundamental advances in programming methodology. Some of them, like communication or deliberation, are already clearly the capability of objects or even subroutines. Adding the overlay of talking about them as attributes of 'agents' doesn't do much to make 'agent' a unique concept. What's the value added, especially from a tangible system-building perspective?

[BRIOT]: So you think that 'structured persistent action' is a programming technology that both differentiates agents and is also an added value.

[GASSER]: Yes. You can now have a program that will persistently try to accomplish something, somewhat irrespective of what you do to program it. It comes with a little kind of persistence engine. My young son Liam has a book called "The Little Engine That Could." This book is about a little steam engine, a train, that took up the goal of pulling a load of toys over a hill, and that continuously tried to get there, and never gave up, never failed – it's a kid's lesson in self-reliance and perseverance. OK. Rather than the programmer controlling the failure and success of a module or component through the semantics of the program, with the structured persistent action concept you get to build a little capsule that continuously strives for success without accounting at the outset for all the possible conditions it will face or in what order. What you provide is a goal or a description of what success is, and maybe some collection of alternative methods or building blocks for getting there, and in the most advanced case, maybe even a way to learn or remember new methods when you need them. But the agent's orientation is to provide continuous seeking for that success, continuous persistence, with its own internal control regime.

Arguably, this is the most important desirable feature and often the one lacking. Few toolkits support the idea of structured persistent action. Thus we argue for four things: a focus on programming over architecture; on programming at the agent level; on what is the added value; and on support for structured persistent action. Next we will discuss DECAF as a concrete example, and how it relates to these points. Finally we will also return to the issue of developer training/education.

2   DECAF

DECAF (Distributed, Environment-Centered Agent Framework) is a Java-based toolkit for creating multi-agent systems [14]. DECAF provides the necessary architectural services of a large-grained intelligent agent [15, 16]: communication, planning, scheduling, execution monitoring, coordination, and eventually learning and self-diagnosis [17]. Functionally, DECAF is a hybrid (deliberative and reactive) architecture based on RETSINA [16, 18, 15, 19, 20] and TÆMS [21, 22]. TÆMS provides a framework useful for agent coordination by defining how agent actions and tasks relate to each other. RETSINA provides the idea of adaptability by allowing multiple outcomes, and data flow constructs.

2.1   Focus on Programming vs. Architecture

DECAF is essentially the internal "operating system" of a software agent, to which application programmers have strictly limited access. Figure 1 represents the high level structure of the DECAF architecture. Structures inside the heavy black line are internal to the architecture and the items outside the line are user-written or provided from some other outside source (such as incoming KQML/FIPA-ACL messages).

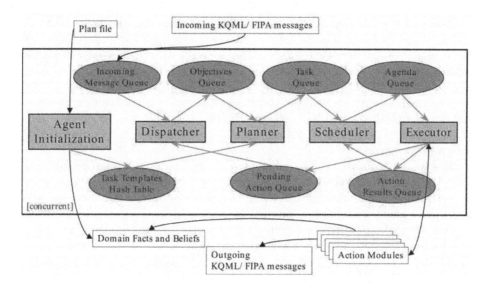

Fig. 1. DECAF Architecture Overview

As shown in Figure 1, there are five internal execution modules (rectangles) in the current DECAF implementation, and seven associated data structure queues (ovals).

2.2   Agent Initialization

The execution modules control the flow of a task through its life time. After initialization, each module runs continuously and concurrently in its own Java thread. When an agent is started, the agent initialization module will run. The *Agent Initialization* module will read the plan file as described above. Each task reduction specified in the plan file will be added to the *Task Templates Hash table* (plan library) along with the tree structure that is used to specify actions that accomplish that goal.

Note that the initializer must be concerned with several features of the Plan File. First, there may be directives, similar to C preprocessor directives, that indicate external files must be read (Similar to the *import* directive in Java). These files will be read and incorporated into the plan templates.

Next the plan may make use of a *Startup* module. The Startup task of an agent might, for example, build any domain or beliefs data/knowledgebase needed for future execution of the agent. Any subsequent changes to initial data must come from the agent actions during the completion of goals. Startup tasks may assert certain continuous maintenance goals or initial achievement goals for the agent. Actions are normally initiated as a result of an incoming message requesting that action. The Startup task is special since no message will be received to begin its execution. If such a Startup module is part of the plan file, the initialization module will add it to the *Task Queue* for immediate execution.

The use of a Startup action may not be immediately clear. If an agent is run and used in a stand alone fashion then any initialization may be done in the constructor for the agent. However, some agent actions may be written as extensions of other actions. For example, a *GetStockPrice* action may be written as a subclass of the *InformationGatherer* action. The Information gatherer may have created a database that the GetStockPrice action needs. In this case the Information Gatherer will have created the database that resides now as part of the Agent framework. It becomes a simple matter now for the GetStockPrice action to gain access.

Lastly, the plan file may be incomplete in the sense that some portions of the plan will not be known until the results of previous actions are complete (interleaved planning and execution). In this case the initialization module will build place holders in order to complete the action tree.

Specific task structures are read from the plan file, are listed in the plan library, and are not currently changed during the agent lifetime (but see the discussion of the DECAF planner). The final activity of the Agent Initialization Module does is register with the ANS and set up all socket and network communication.

2.3   Dispatcher

Agent initialization is done once and then control is passed to the *Dispatcher* which waits for incoming KQML messages which are be placed on the *Incoming Message Queue*.

An incoming message contains a KQML *performative* and its associated information become an objective indicatng which capability within the agent is to be accomplished. An incoming message can result in one of three actions by the dispatcher.

- The message is attempting to communicate as part of an ongoing conversation. The Dispatcher makes this distinction mostly by recognizing the KQML :in-reply-to field designator, which indicates the message is part of an existing conversation. In this case the dispatcher will find the corresponding action in the *Pending Action Queue* and set up the tasks to continue the agent action.
- The message indicates that it is part of a new conversation. This will be the case whenever the message does not use the :in-reply-to field. If so a new *objective* is created (equivalent to the BDI "desires" concept[23]) and placed on the *Objectives Queue* for the Planner. The dispatcher assigns a unique identifier to this message which is used to distinguish all messages that are part of the new conversation.

– The dispatcher is responsible for is the handling of error messages. If an incoming message is improperly formatted or if another internal module needs to sends an error message the Dispatcher is responsible for formatting and sending the message.

2.4   Planner

The Objectives Queue at any given moment will contain the instantiated plans / task structures (including all actions and subgoals) that should be completed in response to all incoming requests. The initial, top-level objectives are roughly equivalent to the BDI "desires" concept[23], while the expansion into plans is only part of the traditional notion of BDI "intentions", which for DECAF is divided into two reasoning levels, planning and scheduling. The *Plan scheduler* sleeps until the Objectives Queue is non-empty and will go back to sleep when the queue is empty. The purpose of the Plan Scheduler is to determine which actions can be executed now, which *should* be executed now, and in what order. This determination is currently based on whether all of the provisions for a particular task are available. Some provisions come from the incoming message and some provisions come as a result of other actions being completed. This means the objectives queue is checked any time a provision becomes available to see which actions can be executed now.

The Planner monitors the Objectives Queue and matches new goals to an existing task template as stored in the Plan Library. A copy of the instantiated plan, in the form of an HTN corresponding to that goal is placed in the *Task Queue* area, along with a unique identifier and any provisions that were passed to the agent via the incoming message. If a subsequent message comes in requesting the same goal be accomplished, then another instantiation of the same plan template will be placed in the task queue with a new unique identifier. The Task Queue at any given moment will contain the instantiated plans/task structures (including all actions and subgoals) that should be completed in response to an incoming request.

2.5   Scheduler

The *Scheduler* waits until the Task Queue is non-empty. The scheduling functions are divided into two separate modules; the *Scheduler* and the *Agenda Manager*.

The purpose of the Scheduler module is to evaluate the HTN task structure to determine a set of actions which will "best" suit the users goals. The input is a task HTN with all possible actions, and the output is a task HTN pruned to reflect the desired set of actions.

Once the set of actions have been determined, the Agenda Manager (AM module) is responsible for setting the actions into execution. This determination is based on whether all of the provisions for a particular module are available. Some provisions come from the incoming message and some provisions come as a result of other actions being completed. This means that the Task Queue structures are checked any time a provision becomes available to see which actions can be executed now.

The other responsibility of the AM is to reschedule actions when a new task is requested. Every task has a window of time that is used for execution. If subsequent tasks can be completed while currently scheduled tasks are running then a commitment is made to running the task on time. Otherwise the AM will respond with an error message to the requester that the task cannot be completed in the desired time frame.

2.6   Executor

The *Executor* is set into operation when the Agenda Queue is non-empty. Once an action is placed on the queue the Executor immediately places the task into execution. One of two things can occur at this point: The action can complete normally. (Note that "normal" completion may be returning an error or any other outcome) and the result is placed on the *Action Result Queue*. The framework waits for results and then distributes the result to downstream actions that may be waiting in the Task Queue. Once this is accomplished the Executor examines the Agenda queue to see if there is further work to be done.

The other case is when the action partially completes and returns with an indication that further actions will take place later. This is a typical result when an action sends a message to another agent requesting information, but could also happen for other blocking reasons (i.e. user or Internet I/O). The remainder of the task will be completed when the resulting KQML message is returned. To indicate that this task will complete later it is placed on the *Pending Action Queue*. Actions on this queue are keyed with a *reply-to* field in the outgoing KQML message. When an incoming message arrives, the Dispatcher will check to see if an *in-reply-to* field exists. If so, the Dispatcher will check the Pending action queue for a corresponding message. If one exists, that action will be returned to the Agenda queue for completion. If no such action exists on the Pending action queue, an error message is returned to the sender.

2.7   Programming at the Multi-agent Level

DECAF at the individual agent level is fairly general. It does not, however, support hard real-time constraints, and is fairly resource-intensive so that about 5-8 agents can be deployed on a single processor. To program at the multi-agent level, one needs to provide agents that are useful for a wide class of applications. Most of the existing DECAF agents and agent shells are oriented toward fast prototyping of *information gathering* applications. We view information gathering as a catch-all phrase indicating information retrieval, filtering, integration, analysis, and display. In particular, information gathering is done in domains where information (unique, redundant, or partially redundant) is available at many different locations and is constantly being changed or updated, with even new information sources appearing over time. Centralized access is not available from the information sources because they are being produced by different organizational entities, usually for different purposes than those of the information gathering user. Examples of information gathering domains are financial information (evaluating, tracking, and managing a stock portfolio)[18, 15], military strategic information (integration of friendly troop movements, enemy observations, weather, satellite data, civilian communications)[24], and annotation of gene sequences [25].

Solutions to the information gathering problem tend to draw on two lines of technologies: research on heterogeneous databases and research on multi-agent systems. Work on heterogeneous databases in both the database and AI communities brings to bear the concepts of ontologies, wrappers, mediators, materialization, and query planning. Work on multi-agent systems brings to the table a way to actually embody wrappers and mediators; ways to do query planning in real-time domains; ways to deal with the dynamic nature of the data and the data sources; ways to handle issues of efficient distributed computation and robustness; ways to deal with the organizational issues involved in distributed information problems.

DECAF supports the use of the RETSINA multi-agent organization[1] for building information gathering systems. The RETSINA approach consists of three general classes of agents[16, 15]:

– Information Extraction Agents, which interact directly with external data sources, i.e. wrapping sensors, databases, web pages.
– Task Agents, which interact only with other agents to handle the bulk of the information processing tasks. These include both domain-dependent agents that take care of filtering, integration, and analysis; also domain-independent "middle agents" that take care of matchmaking, service brokering, and complex query planning.
– Interface Agents, that interact directly with the end user.

A large number of these agents are all or mostly reusable [18], which contributes to faster and faster prototyping of information gathering systems. DECAF provides an implementation of these middle agents, reusable agent classes, and other tools for building multi-agent information gathering systems. Agent name servers, matchmakers, brokers, and other middle-agents support the creation of open systems where elements may come and go over time. Dynamic information change is supported by reusable Information Extraction Agent behaviors that include the ability to push data values to the user, or to set up persistant queries that pull data from providers only when the answer changes significantly.

Agent Name Server. The current DECAF Agent Name Server handles the registration of agents and "white-pages" services: mapping agent names to TCP addresses and port numbers. It is based on protocols in use at CMU's RETSINA project.

---

[1] We will usually use the word *organization* to indicate the structure of a collection of agents, and *architecture* to indicate the structure of the internals of a single agent.

Matchmaker and Broker Agents. The Matchmaker agent serves as a "yellow pages" tool to assist agents in finding other agents in the community that may provide a useful service An agent will *advertise* its capabilities with the Matchmaker and if those capabilities change or are no longer available, the agent will *unadvertise*. The Matchmaker stores the capabilities in a local database. A requester wishing to ask a query will formulate the query to the Matchmaker and *ask* for a set of matching advertisements. The requester can then and make request directly to the provider. A requester can also *subscribe* to the Matchmaker and be informed when new services or interest are added or removed.

A *Broker* agent advertises summary capabilities built from all of the providers that have registered with one Broker. The Broker in turn advertises with the Matchmaker. For example, one Broker may have all the capabilities to build a house (plumber, electrician, framer, roofer, ...). The broker can now provide a larger service than any single provider can, and often manage a large group of agents more effectively [5].

Proxy Agent. DECAF agent can communicate with any object that uses the KQML or FIPA message construct. However, web browser applets cannot (due to security concerns) communicate directly with any machine except the applet's server. The solution is a *Proxy* agent. The Proxy agent is constructed as a DECAF agent and uses fixed addresses and socket communication to talk to Java applets or any application. Through the Proxy agent, applications outside the DECAF or KQML community have access to MAS Services.

Agent Management Agent. The Agent Management Agent (AMA) creates a graphical representation of agents which are currently registered with the ANS, as well as the communication between those agents. This allows the user to have a concept of the community in which an agent is operating as well as the capabilities of the agents and the interaction between agents. The AMA frequently queries the ANS to determine which agents are currently registered. These agents are then represented in a GUI. The AMA also queries the Matchmaker to retrieve a profile provided by each agent. This profile contains information about the services provided by an agent. This profile is accessible to the AMA user by double-clicking on the agent's icon. In the future, the AMA will also have the capability of monitoring and displaying communications between these agents. Each agent will send a message to the AMA whenever it communicates with another agent, so that the user may then monitor all activity between agents.

Information Extraction Agent Shell. The main functions of an information extraction agent (IEA) are [18]: Fulfilling requests from external sources in response to a *one shot query* (e.g. "What is the price of IBM?"). Monitoring external sources for *periodic* information (e.g. "Give me the price of IBM every 30 minutes."). Monitoring sources for patterns, called *information monitoring* requests (e.g. "Notify me if the price of IBM goes below $50.")." These functions can be written in a general way so that the code can be shared for agents in any domain.

Since our IEA operates on the Web, the information gathered is from external information sources. The agent uses a set of *wrappers* and the wrapper induction algorithm STALKER [26], to extract relevant information from the web pages after being shown several marked-up examples. When the information is gathered it is stored in the local IEA "infobase" using Java wrappers on a PARKA [27] knowledgebase. This makes new IEA's fairly easy to create, and forces the difficult parts of this problem back on to KB ontology creation, rather than the production of tools to wrap web pages and dynamically answer queries. Current proposals for XML-based page annotations, when finally adopted by more sites, will make site wrapping easier syntactically, but do not in themselves solve the ontology problem – but see projects such as OWL [28]. As these technologies mature, they will lead to new reusable agent classes.

2.8 Value-Added Features

DECAF, like most toolkits, has its own set of "value-added" features beside the ones mentioned elsewhere. Mostly these fall into two categories: taking care of details for the application programmer, and the efficient use of computational resources.

Many small details are taken care of automatically for the application programmer. These include registration and deregistration from the ANS/directory service, Standard behaviors such as those required by FIPA error handling and the Agent Management Agent, and message dispatching on ontology and conversational threads.

One fairly recent and unique feature is support for automated inter-agent coordination using the GPGP (Generalized Partial Global Planning) [29, 30] approach. The idea is that each agent is capable of reasoning locally about the scheduling of its own activities, and that schedule coordination is about resolving the uncertainty of when to schedule local actions that have dependencies on non-local actions. Coordination mechanisms of many different styles can be thought of as different ways to provide information to a local scheduler in order for it to construct better schedules. Programmers indicate the presence of non-local tasks in the agent's task structures (see the next section), and these trigger automated coordination reasoning in the agent. Each possible coordination mechansim has two components: a set of mechanism-dependent protoccols, and a pattern-directed rewriting of the original task structure itself. For any single dependency, such as "task A at agent A enables task B at Agent B" many different mechanisms can be used (avoid the problem by choosing an alternative (with or without sacrifice), reservation schemes, simple predecessor side commitments (to do a task sometime, by a deadline, after an earliest start time), successor side commitments, polling approaches, shifting task dependencies by moving code, and so on.

DECAF is efficient in its use of computational resources (in the class of heavyweight process-level agents). DECAF is highly threaded – all of the main processing steps (Dispatching, Planning, Scheduling, Execution) run *concurrently*, not serially in Java threads. All domain actions that are runnable also run in their own threads. This contributes to complexity, but also responsiveness and efficiency (see the experimental results presented in [14]). It is also memory efficent – agents can run for weeks (the earliest versions of RETISINA suffered from memory leaks which prevented long-term deployment).

2.9   Support for Structured Persistent Action

Gasser continues with some ideas about how structured persistent action can be enacted:

[GASSER]: Achieving it has some requirements. I think it first takes a locus of control, a continuous operating engine. Happily, we already have this with the concepts of distributed objects and actors. But it also takes the idea of choice and the idea of options. So, rather than there being only one way of accomplishing something, that is to say an algorithm which follows a strict and predefined path, the proper concept of an agent implicitly includes both a repertoire of options or possible next steps, and the ability to choose among them at the time of action, in the actual context of action, not at the time of programming. So the idea of choice at the time of action, rather than choice at the time of programming, is a key notion. That means three aspects of an agent are critical: number one, it has to have 'knowledge' of what is possible. That is to say, it has to have the domain over which to choose, it has to have a range of options. Number two, it has to have some interaction with the world around it, which is going to give it feedback about its choice, whether it is successful or not. And number three, it has to have a control structure that is primarily iterative–that can repeat conditionally. Abstractly, it's 'repeat-until' at some level.

DECAF enacts this idea using ideas from both RETISINA (data-flow oriented control with multiple outcomes) and TÆMS (HTN plan structures indicating how action execution effects characteristics that themselves impact overall utility). DECAF encourages the programming of tasks for robust and persistent goal achievement, supporting programers in detecting problematic outcomes, and allowing multiple ways to carry out tasks to be chosen dynamically at runtime. For example, each action can also have attached to it a performance profile (description of action duration, cost, and quality) which is then used and updated internally by DECAF to provide real-time local scheduling services. The reuse of common agent behaviors is thus increased because the execution of these behaviors does not depend only on the specific construction of the task network but also on the dynamic environment in which the agent is operating. For example, a particular agent is allowed to search until a result is achieved in one application instance, while the same agent – executing the same behavior – will use whatever result is available after a certain time in another application instance. This construction also allows for a certain level of non-determinism in the use of the agent action building blocks. This part of DECAF is based on TÆMS and the design-to-time/design-to-criteria scheduling work at UMASS [31, 22].

The control or programming of DECAF agents is provided via a GUI called the *Plan-Editor*. In the Plan-Editor, executable actions are treated as basic building blocks which can be chained together to achieve a larger more complex goal in the style of an HTN (hierarchical task network). This provides a software component-style programming interface with desirable properties such as component reuse (eventually, automated via the planner) and some design-time error-checking. The chaining of activities can involve traditional looping and if-then-else constructs. This part of DECAF is an extension of the RETSINA framework [19, 21].

The plan file is the output of the Plan Editor and represents the programming of the agent. One agent consists of a set of capabilities and a collection of actions that may be scheduled and executed to achieve various objectives. These capabilities can correspond to classical AI black-and-white goals or "worth-oriented" objective functions over states [32, 20]. Currently, each capability is represented as a complete task reduction tree (HTN [33]), similar to that in RETSINA [20], with annotations drawn from the TÆMS task structure description language [21, 22]. The leaves of the tree represent basic agent actions (HTN primitive tasks). One agent can have dozens or even hundreds of actions. The basic actions must be programmed in a precise way just as any program written in C or Java must be. However, the expression of a plan for providing a complete capability is achieved via program building blocks that are not simple declarative programming language statements but are a sequence of actions connected in a manner that will achieve the goal[2]. Actions are reusable in any sequence for the achievement of many goals. Each of these capabilities and the programming to achieve the associated goal is specified in a *Plan file*.

In the Plan-Editor, a capability is developed using a Hierarchical Task Network-like tree structure in which the root node expresses the entry point of this capability "program" and the goal to be achieved. Non-leaf nodes (other than the root) represent intermediate goals or compound tasks that must be achieved before the overall goal is complete. Leaf nodes of the tree represent actions. Each task node (root, non-root and leaves) has a set of zero or more inputs called *provisions* , and a set of zero or more *outcomes* [19]. The provisions to a node may come from different actions, so no action will start until all of its provisions have been supplied by an outcome being forwarded from another node (this may of course be an external node, e.g. a KQML or FIPA ACL message). Provision arcs between nodes represent the most common type of inter-task constraint (they are a subclass of the TÆMS *enablement* relationship) on the plan specification.

A node, N_i, may have multiple outcomes but the node is considered complete as soon as one outcome has been provided. The *outcomes* represent a complete *classification* or partition of the possible results. For example, the outcome of

---

[2] This should come to no surprise to people familiar with HTN planning, but is a small conceptual hurdle for non-AI-trained agent programmers.

node N_i may be any outcome in the set of outcomes $O_1, O_2, \ldots, O_n$. If the result of the action is classified as outcome O_k then control will pass to node N_k, if the result is classified as outcome O_l control will pass to node N_l. In either case, as soon as an outcome is provided that node has completed processing. In this way conventional looping or conditional selection can be created by specifying correct control. The Plan-Editor allows such control to be specified simply by drawing boxes and connecting the outcomes to other boxes. When the picture is drawn, saving the file will create an ASCII plan file that is used to program the actions of the agent.

3   Training and Education

Even providing a toolkit with these types of advanced features is not necessarily enough to create sophisticated multi-agent applications. In particular, certain types of training are absolutely necessary in order to make much use of such toolkits. We have made some observations on this over the course of the past five years with students using DECAF for graduate courses in multi-agent systems and information gathering, and with students using DECAF for research projects. Training problems tend to fall into three classes: student mis-preparation, agent programming misconceptions, and DECAF-induced headaches.

With respect to student preparation, one of the common problems is students who have a programming background, but not an AI background. Thus, they have little conception of automated planning technology and also difficulty with the ideas of explicit goals or objectives in the AI sense, and of reflective/deliberative programs and thus flexible autonomy itself. Besides this, the average programmer will have little experience in concurrent or distributed programming. Debugging in such situations is especially troublesome. They may also have limited experience in working with or designing communication protocols. Finally, generally poor software engineering skills don't help either.

Even given good preparation, misconceptions about agents in general can hurt application programmers in our experience. Mostly this focusses on the idea of structured persistent action. Many programmers have difficulty managing a wide range of reactive behaviors (with no preconceived notions of the order of invocation of these reactions). Contingency handling and error recovery are crucial, and well supported at the language level in DECAF, yet still most programmers ignore these features because they do not entirely understand them. Of course most programmers do not consider these things in traditional programming either. Finally, plan-based behavior in general can be perplexing to programmers, even if they have an academic understanding of planning in the abstract from an "Introduction to AI" course.

DECAF itself introduces other headaches that we hope to address in newer versions. The following DECAF features seem to cause the most problems, questions, and errors:

- Multiple *outcomes* vs. different *results* [contingency planning]
- Graphical outcomes in the plan-editor vs. how the Java code reports this info to the agent
- Multiple action/thread instantiations (of the same action schema)
- Necessary naming conventions ($< ontology > \_ < taskname >$)
- Non-local task details
- Multiple messages, timeouts for responses
- Multithreaded replies, errors during replies including timeouts on responses
- Characteristic accumulation functions

4   Conclusion

In order for interesting agent applications to become commonplace, agent researchers will have to work towards much more sophisticated support for agent application programmers. We argue that such support should include at least the following four features. First, better support for actually programming fielded agents as opposed to support for research on agent architectures (which in itself is also quite important, but for the research community, not the applications community in the short term). Secondly, the ability for applications programmers to field significant portions of an application without any programming, but simply by instantiating, and then tasking or configuring, existing complete agents or agent templates. Third, that any toolkit can make a strong case for the value it brings the programmer over putting together something from scratch or from an API-based platform. Fourth, and perhaps most importantly, that we support what makes an agent an agent and not just a concurrent object: flexible autonomy in the form of structured persistent action.

We believe that DECAF is one of several toolkits that meet at least some of these objectives. Although we have experimented with architectural features with DECAF, it can be used as an agent operating system to which application programmers have strictly limited access. In the area of information gathering we have created a set of pre-existing middle agents and an information extraction shell that can be used to quickly prototype many aspects of this type of system, athough much greater support will be possible as information moves toward a more semantic web style of supply. DECAF provides value in terms of pre-existing agent behaviors, and in a high level of internal architectural efficiency. Finally, it supports the idea of structured persistent action via the use of TÆMS task structures and RETSINA data flow which allow programmers to explicitly indicate alternatives to achieve goals, and the characteristics that impact utility associated with each alternative. It also allows specification of contingencies (in the contingency planning style) that help create more robust plan networks. Our experience with DECAF has led us to make observations about the kinds of programming skills that are useful in agent application programmers, and also the common misconceptions held by people so trained.

References

1. Wooldridge, M., Jennings, N.R., eds.: Intelligent Agents - Theories, Architectures, and Languages. Lecture Notes in AI Volume 890. Springer-Verlag (1995)
2. J.-J. Meyer, M.T., ed.: Intelligent Agents VIII. LNCS Volume 2333. Springer-Verlag (2002)
3. Luck, M., et al., eds.: Agent-Based Software Development. Artech House (2004)
4. Woelk, D., Huhns, M., Tomlinson, C.: Infosleuth agents: The next generation of active objects. Technical Report INSL-054-95 (1995)
5. Decker, K.S., Sycara, K., Williamson, M.: Middle-agents for the internet. In: Proceedings of the Fifteenth International Joint Conference on Artificial Intelligence, Nagoya, Japan (1997) 578–583
6. Foundation for Intelligent Physical Agents (FIPA): Fipa '97 specification part 2: Agent communication language. (http://drogo.cselt.stet.it/fipa/)
7. Engelmore, R., Morgan, T., eds.: Blackboard Systems. Addison Wesley, Wokingham, England (1988)
8. Hayes-Roth, B.: A blackboard architecture for control. Artificial Intelligence **26** (1985) 251–321
9. Corkill, D.D., Gallagher, K.Q., Murray, K.E.: GBB: A generic blackboard development system. In: Proceedings of the Fifth National Conference on Artificial Intelligence, Philadelphia, PA. (1986) 1008–1014
10. Brazier, F., Keplicz, B., Jennings, N., Treur, J.: Formal specification of multi-agent systems: a real-world case. In: Proceedings of the 1st Intl. Conf. on Autonomous Agents, Marina del Rey (1997) 25–32
11. Nwana, H.S., Ndumu, D.T., Lee, L.C., Collis, J.C.: ZEUS: a toolkit and approach for building distributed multi-agent systems. In Etzioni, O., Müller, J.P., Bradshaw, J.M., eds.: Proceedings of the Third International Conference on Autonomous Agents (Agents'99), Seattle, WA, USA, ACM Press (1999) 360–361
12. Wooldridge, M., Jennings, N.: Intelligent agents: Theory and practice. The Knowledge Engineering Review **10** (1995) 115–152
13. Gasser, L.: Agents and concurrent objects. IEEE Concurrency (1998) An interview by Jean-Pierre Briot.
14. Graham, J., Decker, K.: Towards a distributed, environment-centered agent framework. In Jennings, N., Lesperance, Y., eds.: Intelligent Agents VI. LNAI-1757. Springer Verlag (2000) 290–304
15. Decker, K.S., Sycara, K.: Intelligent adaptive information agents. Journal of Intelligent Information Systems **9** (1997) 239–260
16. Sycara, K., Decker, K.S., Pannu, A., Williamson, M., Zeng, D.: Distributed intelligent agents. IEEE Expert **11** (1996) 36–46
17. Horling, B., Lesser, V., Vincent, R., Bazzan, A., Xuan, P.: Diagnosis as an integral part of multi-agent adaptability. Tech Report CS-TR-99-03, UMass (1999)
18. Decker, K.S., Pannu, A., Sycara, K., Williamson, M.: Designing behaviors for information agents. In: Proceedings of the 1st Intl. Conf. on Autonomous Agents, Marina del Rey (1997) 404–413
19. Williamson, M., Decker, K.S., Sycara, K.: Unified information and control flow in hierarchical task networks. In: Proceedings of the AAAI-96 workshop on Theories of Planning, Action, and Control. (1996)
20. Williamson, M., Decker, K.S., Sycara, K.: Executing decision-theoretic plans in multi-agent environments. In: AAAI Fall Symposium on Plan Execution. (1996) AAAI Report FS-96-01.

21. Decker, K.S., Lesser, V.R.: Quantitative modeling of complex computational task environments. In: Proceedings of the Eleventh National Conference on Artificial Intelligence, Washington (1993) 217–224

22. Wagner, T., Garvey, A., Lesser, V.: Complex goal criteria and its application in design-to-criteria scheduling. In: Proceedings of the Fourteenth National Conference on Artificial Intelligence, Providence (1997)

23. Rao, A., Georgeff, M.: BDI agents: From theory to practice. In: Proceedings of the First International Conference on Multi-Agent Systems, San Francisco, AAAI Press (1995) 312–319

24. Harvey, T., Decker, K., Rambow, O.: Integrating the communicative plans of multiple, independent agents. In: Workshop on Communicative Agents: The use of natural language in embodied systems. (1999) Autonomous Agents 99.

25. Decker, K., Khan, S., Schmidt, C., Situ, G., Makkena, R., Michaud, D.: Biomas: A multi-agent system for genomic annotation. International Journal of Cooperative Information Systems **11** (2002)

26. Muslea, I., Minton, S., Knobloch, C.: Stalker: Learning expectation rules for simistructured web-based information sources. In: Papers from the 1998 Workshop on AI and Information Gathering. (1998) also Technical Report ws-98-14, University of Southern California.

27. Hendler, J., Kilian Stoffel, M.T.: Advances in high performance knowledge representation. Technical Report CS-TR-3672, University of Maryland Institute for Advanced Computer Studies (1996) Also cross-referenced as UMIACS-TR-96-56.

28. Dean, M., Connolly, D., van Harmelen, F., Hendler, J., Horrocks, I., McGuinness, D.L., Patel-Schneider, P.F., Stein, L.A.: Web ontology language (OWL) reference version 1.0. W3C working draft 12 november.
    `http://www.w3.org/TR/2002/WD-owl-ref-20021112/` (2002)

29. Chen, W., Decker, K.: Coordination mechanisms for dependency relationships among multiple agents (poster). In: Proceedings of the 1st Intl. Joint Conf. on Autonomous Agents and Mult-Agent Systems, Bologna (2002)

30. Decker, K., Li, J.: Coordinating mutually exclusive resources using gpgp. Autonomous Agents and Multi-Agent Systems **3** (2000) 133–157

31. Garvey, A., Humphrey, M., Lesser, V.: Task interdependencies in design-to-time real-time scheduling. In: Proceedings of the Eleventh National Conference on Artificial Intelligence, Washington (1993) 580–585

32. Rosenschein, J.S., Zlotkin, G.: Rules of Encounter: Designing Conventions for Automated Negotiation among Computers. MIT Press, Cambridge, Mass. (1994)

33. Erol, K., Nau, D., Hendler, J.: Semantics for hierarchical task-network planning. Technical report CS-TR-3239, UMIACS-TR-94-31, Computer Science Dept., University of Maryland (1994)

Implementing Industrial Multi-agent Systems Using JACK™

Rick Evertsz[1], Martyn Fletcher[1], Richard Jones[1], Jacquie Jarvis[1],
James Brusey[2], and Sandy Dance[3]

[1] Agent Oriented Software Pty. Ltd. (AOS),
156 Pelham Street, Carlton, Melbourne, Victoria 3053, Australia
{rick.evertsz,martyn.fletcher,richard.jones,jacquie.jarvis}
@agent-software.com
[2] Institute for Manufacturing, University of Cambridge,
Mill Lane, Cambridge CB2 1RX, United Kingdom
jpb54@eng.cam.ac.uk
[3] Bureau of Meteorology Research Centre,
150 Lonsdale Street, Melbourne, Victoria 3000, Australia
s.dance@bom.gov.au

Abstract. JACK™ is an implementation of the Belief/Desire/Intention model of rational agency with extensions to support the design and execution of agent systems where team structures, real-time control, repeatability and linkage with legacy code are critical. This chapter presents the JACK™ multi-agent systems platform. The chapter begins with a discussion of agent programming concepts as they relate to JACK™, and then presents experiences from the development of two industrial applications that made use of JACK™ (a meteorological alerting environment and a responsive manufacturing set-up).

1 Introduction

Over the past decade, there has been an increased industry interest in the application of multi-agent systems. With the advent of distributed software applications, traditional approaches to programming the interaction between sub-systems has proven to be time consuming and error prone. Typically, distributed systems are embedded in, and must interact with, a changing environment. The interaction with the environment is particularly problematic where there are many external *entities* that must be controlled, serviced or modelled. In the past, implementing such systems has entailed explicit programming of the interaction with each external entity. If this is more than a simple client/server interaction, then the application can become hard to manage, that is, difficult to implement, maintain or change. Furthermore, the application may not have the required flexibility or responsiveness to its environment.

Agent-based approaches have proven to be well suited where complex interaction with an ever-changing environment is required. Arguably, the most significant attribute of agent-based systems is that each agent is an *autonomous* computational entity. Autonomy, coupled with an ability to perceive the environment, act upon it and communicate with other agents, provides system builders with a very powerful form of encapsulation. A given agent can be defined in terms of its goals, knowledge and social

M. Dastani, J. Dix, A. El Fallah-Seghrouchni (Eds.): PROMAS 2003, LNAI 3067, pp. 18–48, 2004.

capability, and then left to perform its function autonomously within the environment it was designed to function in. This is a very effective way of building distributed systems – each agent in the system is responsible for pursuing its own goals, reacting to events and communicating with other agents in the system. There is no need to explicitly program the interactions of the whole system; rather, the interactions *emerge* as a by-product of the individual goals and capabilities of the constituent agents. In the next section, we will further expand our discussion of the motivation for adopting agent-oriented design and programming in industry.

This chapter provides an overview of the Belief/Desire/Intention (BDI) paradigm and the JACK™ intelligent agents platform, and presents in some depth two industrial applications of JACK™. The BDI paradigm underlies JACK™ and has been extensively studied in academia [1–3] and has been applied to a number of problems in industry [4–7].

2   Agent Programming Concepts

In the software industry, the term software agent has been used to denote a wide range of programming approaches. Nevertheless, within the computer science research community, the consensus on the core attributes of software agents seems to be as follows (and we shall adopt this view of agency throughout this chapter):

Autonomous. An agent operates without continuous external supervision.
Proactive/Reactive. An agent exhibits both goal-directed and reactive behaviours.
Situated. An agent perceives a relevant subset of its environment, and reacts to changes
    in a timely, quasi real-time fashion.
Social. An agent can interact with other agents to achieve joint goals.

In this section on agent programming concepts we discuss why these core attributes of agents are critical for developing industrial-strength autonomous and multi-agent systems. We highlight the motivation for building industrial applications using the agent paradigm and describe how the Belief/Desire/Intention (BDI) model of rational agency provides a solid foundation for engineering such commercial systems.

2.1   The Motivation for Agent-Oriented Programming in Industry

Increasingly, software applications need to be more reactive and distributed in nature. Examples include the telecommunications industry where dynamic interactions between mobile entities can require complex coordination protocols. Techniques developed to implement single-threaded control in relatively static environments do not scale well to dynamic, distributed domains that require multiple threads of interaction. The pressing practical need for more event-driven, decentralised and multi-threaded software has led to an interest in the application of agent-oriented techniques within industry.

To illustrate this point, consider an air traffic management application where the goal is to optimise the flow of aircraft landing at a major airport. At any given moment, there will be a collection of aircraft approaching from various directions, altitudes, speeds and distances. In an ideal world, they would all arrive at the runway perfectly spaced to avoid conflicts, and would optimise the utilisation of the precious runway resource. Naturally, in the real world this does not happen without continuous and expert human intervention by an air traffic flow manager. The flow manager must monitor the progress of the aircraft, estimate when they will arrive at the airport, generate a landing sequence that ensures that they do not compete for the same piece of runway time, and then issue speed instructions to ensure that the aircraft arrive at the airport as sequenced. This is a very dynamic and complex domain; for example,

- an aircraft can drift from its assigned landing time due to factors such as unanticipated headwinds, or
- a pilot, with extensive local knowledge of the airport, may cut corners on the flight path in an attempt to "jump the queue".

Thus, the flow manager must constantly monitor the progress of the (upwards of fifty) aircraft and adjust their speeds and trajectories to bring them back into line with the sequence. This is such a complex task, that human flow managers use "rules of thumb" to short-circuit the computation required to produce a truly optimal schedule. As a result, the schedule is sub-optimal in terms of ideal utilisation of the runway resource, but is workable and avoids runway collisions among aircraft.

Implementing the flow management function using a conventional software approach is non-trivial. It requires a number of functions that must be applied in a constantly changing environment. These functions include applying the performance profile for each type of aircraft, estimating the effects of wind, optimising the sequence of arriving aircraft, generating flow instructions that satisfy the sequence, and predicting the behaviour of pilots based on their familiarity with the airspace. These functions need to be run periodically, but must also be triggered in response to unanticipated events (e.g. radar position data showing that an aircraft has diverged from its expected flight plan).

Because of the inherent complexity of interactions between the entities and the environment, traditional software approaches lead to a monolithic code-base that is error-prone and difficult to alter without breaking the carefully coded handling of the dynamic aspects of the problem. These approaches involve constructs such as a process scheduler that loops through each of the aircraft, checking their progress and updating the landing schedule in a rigid and therefore potentially maladaptive fashion.

If the environment changes during the execution of the loop, what is the process scheduler to do? Should it interrupt the loop and start again with the first aircraft, or should it continue to the end in the hope that its computations will still be applicable? These considerations make it very difficult to build software that can survive in a highly dynamic environment, and provide strong motivation for the adoption of agent-oriented programming within industries where unpredictable events, resource failure, and the unplanned introduction of heterogeneous entities are commonplace.

Agent-oriented programming is well suited to such dynamic problems. For instance, an Aircraft Agent can *autonomously* monitor the state of each physical aircraft. The agent is equipped with the appropriate performance profile for the aircraft type, and can take input from a Wind Agent that models the winds aloft. The Sequencer Agent is responsible for computing the optimal landing sequence, requesting an Estimated

Time of Arrival from each Aircraft Agent, and then assigning a new landing time that respects the sequence. The Aircraft Agent then uses its performance profile and the Wind Agent's input to compute the speed alteration required to arrive at the airport as sequenced.

The aircraft flow management problem is greatly simplified by adopting this agent-based approach, because each real world entity is mirrored by an autonomous entity within the software itself. Indeed an agent-based flow management system was successfully operationally tested at Sydney Airport (Australia) in 1995, and was based on an architecture very similar to the one just described [7].

2.2 The Belief/Desire/Intention (BDI) Paradigm

Due to space limitations, this overview of the BDI paradigm will not attempt to provide a comprehensive review. Rather, our goal is to lay the foundation for subsequent sections by outlining BDI as it pertains to the JACK™ intelligent agent platform. For a more comprehensive review, please refer to [3].

JACK™ is based on the Belief/Desire/Intention (BDI) model; a paradigm that explicates rational decision making about actions. Based on work by Bratman [8] on situated rational agents, and developed further at SRI International (Menlo Park, California), this approach has been applied to a wide range of problems, from its early focus on fault diagnosis for Space Shuttle missions [9], through simulation of intelligent entities such as combat pilots [10], to teamed unmanned air vehicle control [11].

The BDI paradigm was developed in response to a perceived problem with existing Artificial Intelligence (AI) approaches to the planning problem. The planning problem can be stated informally as: "Given a goal, generate a sequence of actions that will achieve that goal". Research on this problem was successful in developing general-purpose techniques, mostly based on some variant of means-ends reasoning (e.g. the work of Fikes and Nilsson [12]). However, these approaches only addressed the offline planning problem – how to achieve the goal given infinite time and resources. They did not address the temporal pressures that apply when trying to achieve the goal within the context of a fluctuating environment that presents a multitude of interacting, conflicting and changing opportunities.

Yet, this is the rule rather than the exception in modern industrial situations; it is rare that an agent situated in the real world can take as long as it likes to solve a problem. The world is constantly changing, and with it comes demands on the agent requiring that it reconsider its priorities. When you sat down to read this chapter, your goal may have been to learn about the practical applications of agent programming, and you might have set aside a couple of hours for this endeavour. However, if you unexpectedly received a phone call from a friend asking to be picked up from the airport in thirty minutes time, you might decide to read this article less thoroughly, perhaps returning to it tomorrow. If you were then informed that a burst pipe was flooding your home, you would very likely drop everything and scramble to deal with the unexpected crisis. Though inconvenient, we must deal with an environment that is in constant flux, and this reality applies equally well to software systems that are situated in the real world (such as the air traffic management system referred to earlier).

This then was the motivation for the development of the BDI paradigm. Agents are typically situated in a dynamic environment and must constantly review their goals and activities, and should also be aware of the resource-bounded nature of their reasoning. Bratman *et al.* [13] presents the case for this resource-bounded view of rational agency.

Georgeff and Lansky [14] developed an early implementation of the BDI approach to agents – the Procedural Reasoning System (PRS). PRS was the forebear of a lineage of commercial BDI implementations that includes dMARS [1] and has culminated in JACK^{TM} [15]. PRS was developed at SRI International and has been applied to fault diagnosis of the Space Shuttle, telecommunications network management and air traffic management.

To better address the requirements of commercial software environments, in the early 1990s, PRS was re-implemented in C (C-PRS [16]) and also re-designed and implemented in C++ as (dMARS [1]). Though re-designed from the ground up, this second generation BDI implementation, dMARS, was largely backwards compatible with PRS and enabled the operational testing of the PRS-based OASIS air traffic management system at Sydney airport [7]. dMARS was also used to implement SWARMM, an air combat modelling system, with agents taking on the role of synthetic pilots for the purposes of evaluating air combat tactics [10].

After eight years of use by the Royal Australian Air Force (as of 2003), a successor to SWARMM is being implemented in JACK^{TM}. JACK^{TM} is implemented in Java^{TM} and includes significant extensions to the BDI paradigm (in particular, its support for team coordinated activity). JACK^{TM} was specifically designed for commercial application and will be described fully in section 3, but first we will describe the key features of BDI agent systems.

2.3 The PRS Family and the BDI Paradigm

Although the members of the PRS family of BDI agent systems differ from one another in terms of implementation detail and range of ancillary features, they are based on a similar interpretation of BDI. This is due in part to the fact that there is considerable overlap between the members of the teams that designed PRS, C-PRS, dMARS and JACK^{TM}. Although it is not the purpose of this chapter to provide a comparative review of these systems, it is beneficial to outline the common features of these BDI implementations. This provides an insight into the aspects of the BDI paradigm that have a proven track record of practical application within industry. As the latest incarnation of commercial BDI implementations that stem directly from PRS, JACK^{TM} has dispensed with some of the more esoteric PRS attributes, concentrating instead on providing a compact and efficient set of core features. In addition to these core features, JACK^{TM} has extended the BDI paradigm to deal with inter-agent coordination, and includes new constructs and tools that support the software engineering process. These extensions will be covered in section 3. The key programming constructs of a BDI design are as follows:

Events. Deliberation is triggered by events. Events can be received from the environment but are also internally generated. Such internally generated events function as *goals*. This is a key aspect of PRS-based BDI.

Plans. The procedural knowledge of the agent (what Bratman *et al.* [13] refer to as "plans-as-recipes"). Plans define how the agent should behave in response to events. Non-deterministic choice allows the agent to try alternative plans to achieve the same goal, and to fill out the lower-level details of the plan (what Bratman *et al.* [13] call "partial plans").

Beliefs. An agent's knowledge of its environment, but not including plans (plans are procedural knowledge about what action sequences can satisfy a given goal). Plans are represented separately from declarative beliefs.

Agents. Autonomous computational entities with their own external identity and private internal state.

Intentions. The currently active plan instantiations, i.e. the plan *instances* that the agent is committed to. Plans are abstract entities that describe *potential* patterns of behaviour. A plan becomes an intention when the agent instantiates it with symbolic references to concrete entities in the environment, and commits to its execution.

Meta-level reasoning. If more than one plan is applicable for a particular event, infrastructure is provided that enables *meta-plans* to be invoked. A *meta-plan* is a user-provided plan that encapsulates the reasoning required by an agent type to choose between the agent's applicable plans. Note that different agent types may have different meta-plans. Where no meta-plan is provided by the user, the default behaviour is to use the first declared plan that is applicable. The meta-plan facility allows the agent to reflect upon its choices and consider the resource-bounded aspects of pursuing a course of action.

Pattern-directed inference. Plans become *relevant* in response to events. Plans also match and are constrained by contexts; i.e. even if a plan matches an event, it may not become *applicable* because its Context Condition is not satisfied by the internal state of the agent.

Message passing. Agents communicate with one another by transmitting and receiving messages.

2.4   Reasons for the Commercial Success of BDI

Despite the relative novelty of agent-oriented programming, especially in industry, there have been a few landmark commercial projects employing BDI-based agent technology. Notable examples include fault diagnosis for the Space Shuttle [9] and the Human Variability in Computer Generated Forces project [4]. This uptake is partly due to the availability of robust, commercially supported BDI implementations. However, there are other more fundamental reasons for the success of the BDI approach:

– The BDI paradigm has strong appeal because it maps well to the way that people *believe* that they think. BDI is not intended to be a theory of human cognition but it seems to provide a good fit to people's intuitions about their reasoning processes. As such, it greatly facilitates the encoding of software entities that need to mimic the relevant domain-specific aspects of human expertise.

– One of the key features of BDI is its support for deliberation. However, this feature alone does not differentiate it from earlier AI approaches to modelling reasoning. Because BDI agents generate behaviour in the context of a changing environment,

they can exhibit more flexible / reactive behaviour than traditional AI approaches. BDI-based autonomous software entities can pursue a goal, or even multiple and conflicting concurrent goals, without losing the ability to switch attention when the external environment requires immediate action.
– The BDI paradigm has a strong theoretical grounding. This has led to its continued investigation in academic circles, and has given industry confidence in the technology (cf. Rao and Georgeff, 1995 [2]; d'Inverno and Luck, 1997 [1]; and Wooldridge, 2000 [3]).

The next section will present the JACK™ implementation of the BDI model in some detail, and will describe the industry-driven extensions that have been added.

3   An Overview of JACK™

This section presents an overview of JACK™ in terms of:

– the major features of the JACK™ Agent Language (a mature implementation of the BDI paradigm written as an extension to Java™), and
– the JACK™ Development Environment (JDE) that provides graphical tools to support the design, implementation and execution tracing of BDI agents.

These features have been central to JACK's popularity in various industrial sectors.

3.1   History of the JACK™ Agent Language

Like many AI systems, PRS was implemented in Lisp because Lisp is well suited to the implementation of new representation languages. However, this flexibility comes at the expense of efficiency; the very language features that make Lisp good for rapid prototyping, make it less well suited to deployment in industrial domains.

The development of dMARS was undertaken so that the agent-oriented strengths of PRS could be exploited in an industrial context. Implemented in C++, dMARS was successful in this respect, but the use of C++ meant that the implementation was effectively fixed. Adding new features to dMARS, or making fundamental changes to the architecture, was very time consuming, and error-prone. This was a major drawback because dMARS was not the last word in BDI implementations. There is still a need to investigate new agent-oriented approaches within the BDI paradigm.

To this end, work began on JACK™ in 1997. Java™ was chosen as the host language because it freed the designers from the concerns of memory management. This allowed the exploration of new agent-oriented concepts while providing a lightweight, efficient and cross-platform BDI foundation. As a result, JACK™ is in widespread use in both industry and academia, and significant new functionality has been added since those early days (e.g. JACK Teams).

3.2   Implementation Approach to the JACK™ Agent Language

The JACK™ Agent Language extends Java™ to provide agent-oriented programming support. These extensions are both syntactic and semantic. Syntactic extensions include keywords (e.g. *Agent, Plan, Event*) and attributes that define relationships such as which plans can be triggered by a given event signature. Semantic extensions support the specification of reasoning methods that conform to the BDI paradigm, rather than Java's imperative model: each step is interleaved within the BDI execution model, allowing a plan to be interrupted in response to new events.

The JACK™ Agent Compiler maps JACK™ Agent Language constructs onto pure Java™ classes and statements that can be used by other Java™ code. The JACK™ Agent Kernel is a set of classes that, amongst other things, manages task concurrency and provides a high-performance communications infrastructure for inter-agent messaging. This kernel also supports multiple agents within a single process, allowing agents that share much of their code to be grouped together.

Significantly, from a research perspective, JACK™ supports the incorporation of new functionality through a plug-in architecture that enables new agent-oriented models to be investigated while still using the other JACK™ components. This involves overriding default methods or supplying new classes for runtime support. The JACK FIPA plug-in is a good example of a third-party plug-in. This extension enables JACK™ to interoperate with FIPA-compliant agents[1].

3.3 JACK™ Agent Language Components

This section provides a brief overview of the JACK™ Agent Language. Full details can be found in the JACK™ Manual[2].

A minimal JACK™ application is defined in terms of one or more *agents/teams*, *plans*, *events*, and either *beliefsets* or *views*. Optionally, the application can also include *capabilities*. Agents and teams are used to represent the autonomous computational entities of an application. The Team class is used to encapsulate the coordinated aspects of (multiple) agent behaviour. Teams include much of the functionality of agents; for convenience, we refer to such functionality as being a property of *agent/teams*. Programming constructs in the JACK™ Agent Language include:

Event. Events are the central motivating factor in agents/teams. Without events, the agent/team would be in a state of torpor, unmotivated to think or act. Events can be generated in response to external stimuli or as a result of internal computation. The internal processing of an agent/team generates events that trigger further computation. JACK™ has two main categories of event: *Normal Events* and *BDI Events*. Normal Events are used to represent ephemeral phenomena such as environmental percepts; if the agent/team does not successfully handle the event with its first attempt, the event is discarded because the world will have changed in the interim. In contrast, BDI Events are used to represent *goals* rather than transitory stimuli. When an agent/team services a BDI Event, it commits to successfully handling the event; this can involve trying a number of alternative solution paths until the goal is satisfied.

---

[1] See http://www.fipa.org and http://www.agentcities.org
[2] Available on-line from http://www.agent-software.com

Plan. Plans are *procedures* that define how to respond to events. When an event is generated, JACK™ computes the set of plans that are *relevant* to the event (i.e. those plans that *match* the event). Each relevant plan is further filtered by its *context condition*, i.e. a statement that defines the conditions under which the plan is applicable. The set of relevant plans whose context condition is satisfied by the current situation then becomes subject to a process of *deliberation*, where the agent selects the plan that will form its next *intention*. Plans have a *body* that defines the steps to be executed in response to the event. A plan step is either a JACK reasoning statement or a Java statement. Support is provided for the functional decomposition of the plan body through the use of *reasoning methods*. The JACK runtime infrastructure guarantees that plan step execution (including reasoning method execution) is atomic.

Beliefset. Beliefsets are used to represent the agent's declarative beliefs in a first order, tuple-based relational form. The value fields of a beliefset relation can be of any type, including primitive Java types and user-defined classes. A beliefset can be either *open world* or *closed world*, and the JACK™ kernel ensures its logical consistency. Beliefsets provide a number of useful functions over and above standard information retrieval, for example, an event can be automatically generated on beliefset update, leading the agent to consider whether it should change its activities as a result.

View. A *view* is a data abstraction mechanism that allows agents to use heterogeneous data sources without being concerned with their interface. In essence, they make the interface to an external data source the same as a beliefset.

Agent. Because JACK™ is based on the BDI paradigm, a JACK™ agent has beliefs, desires and intentions. These are part of the internal state of the agent and are not directly accessible by other agents in the system. Beliefs, as described by Bratman *et al.* [13] are represented by the agent's plans, beliefsets and views. These define the *knowledge* that the agent has – *procedural* knowledge in the case of plans, and *facts* in the case of beliefsets and views. The agent's procedural knowledge defines the action sequences that can achieve its desires. Although JACK™ does not have an explicit representation of desires, at any given moment in time a JACK™ agent's desires are embodied in the set of plans that are *applicable* to the current internal state of the agent. Each applicable plan loosely corresponds to a desire, i.e. an activity the agent would embark upon if other desires were not also competing for the same computational resources. When an applicable plan is selected it becomes an *intention*, i.e. the agent commits to satisfying the desire using the selected plan. The JACK™ execution model is described in more detail below.

Team. Teams are an extension of the BDI paradigm that facilitate the modelling of social structures and coordinated behaviour. JACK™ introduces the notion of teams as separate reasoning entities (separate from team members). The behaviour of a team, and in particular the coordinated activity of the team members, is defined directly for the team entity. Thus, in the software model, each team exists as an entity with separate beliefs from those of its members. This generic team-based capability provides a flexible basis upon which a wide variety of teaming algorithms can be designed, developed, and tested. JACK™ supports the programming of team-oriented solutions, with appropriate constructs for expressing social relationships between team members, as well as for expressing coordinated activity. JACK™ includes the communication facilities needed for executing coordinated activity in an application.

Capability. Capabilities are used to organise the functional components of an agent (events, plans, beliefsets and other capabilities) so that the components can be reused across agents. Since capabilities can contain sub-capabilities, an agent's competence can be defined as a hierarchy of capabilities. Capabilities were added to JACK™ in response to a pressing software engineering requirement to support the development of libraries of agent-oriented functionality that can be re-used across applications.

3.4 Agent Execution Model

The previous section provided a glimpse of JACK's execution model. As might be expected from its commercial focus, JACK™ does not currently have a formal execution model (other than the software implementation itself). This section presents an informal, and necessarily brief, overview of JACK's execution model. Although this overview leaves out detail that a JACK™ programmer would consider essential, it will provide the reader with a good understanding of the execution model underlying the applications described in subsequent sections. A JACK™ application is made up of one or more autonomous agents/teams. Therefore, it will suffice to describe the execution model from the perspective of an agent/team. We will first outline the agent execution model and will follow this with a description of how it is augmented in teams.

The execution proceeds as follows:

- Add any newly generated events to the event queue.
- Compute the set of plans that match the event at the head of the event queue.
- Select one of these plans for execution (i.e. create an intention).
- If the selected plan matched a BDI Goal Event, then add the intention to the intention stack that generated the BDI Goal Event. Otherwise, create a new intention stack for the intention.
- Select an intention stack to execute. Select the intention from the top of the stack and execute the next step in that intention. This step may involve the generation of a new event.
- Repeat the cycle.

In the case of a BDI Goal Event, the selection of the plan that will form the new intention (part of the *deliberation* process) can be quite complex. Meta-level plans can be used to make an intricate choice from the set of applicable plans. On plan failure, the agent can also reconsider alternative plan choices in an effort to satisfy the goal. Alternatively, it can re-compute the applicable plan set (in the new context) and exclude the failed plan.

3.5 Team Execution Model

In contrast to agents, the team execution model consists of two phases, an initial team formation phase and a loop that corresponds to the agent execution model (but includes extra team-specific operations). The team execution model is relatively complex and cannot be fully described within the confines of this chapter. Therefore the following account will only describe the major features of the team execution model. For a full description, refer to the JACK Teams Manual[3].

In the initial phase the team is formed by selecting the team members. A team definition includes a number of *roles*, i.e. definitions of the events that entities must handle if they are to fill the *tendered* role. Each prospective team member has a corresponding definition of the events a team *tenderer* (i.e. the *containing* team) must handle if it is to take on the entity as a role *filler*. At runtime, team formation is triggered by the posting of a TEAMFORMATIONEVENT by the JACK Teams infrastructure. This event is handled by a plan that selects the actual instances that will fill the tendered roles. If the user does not provide a plan to handle the TEAMFORMATIONEVENT, a system provided default plan is used. This initialisation process is triggered automatically as part of the team instance construction. Furthermore, role fillers (also referred to as *sub-teams*) can be detached and attached at runtime, thereby supporting dynamic team formation and re-formation.

Once the team formation phase is complete, the team execution model repeats a cycle that is very similar to that for agents. However, team execution includes a belief propagation step that handles dissemination of information up and down the team hierarchy. A team can have access to a *synthesized* beliefset that is derived from the beliefs of its sub-teams. JACK[TM] supports the definition of *filters* that determine if and when the propagation should occur, and what subset of beliefs should be propagated to the containing team. Similarly, sub-teams can inherit a synthesized subset of the beliefs of the containing team. Belief propagation is triggered by changes to a team or team member's beliefset.

3.6   JACK Development Environment

JACK[TM] has been applied to a number of domains that require agents to take on functions that, because of their complexity, have only been handled by humans. These include decision support applications (such meteorological alerting, described in this chapter). JACK[TM] has also been extensively applied to the modelling of human behaviour; for example, military commanders and air combat pilots. Such applications involve a knowledge engineering phase, and in the case of military simulation, a lengthy and comprehensive model validation phase. Producing an accurate implementation of the Subject Matter Expert's (SME's) domain-specific knowledge requires skilful analysis and experience of JACK[TM] programming. In the past, the process has worked most efficiently when the analyst has JACK[TM] programming skills, particularly in the case where an agent needs to be modified as a result of SME feedback. Even though the BDI paradigm maps naturally to the way that SMEs think about their problem solving activities, the difficulty involved in translating their expertise into JACK[TM] code via a programmer has, in the past, limited acceptance of JACK.

With this in mind, JACK[TM] was augmented with a set of graphical tools that support the design, implementation and tracing of agent applications. The JACK[TM] Development Environment (JDE) provides a set of graphical tools for building agent-oriented applications. In this graphical interface, agents, team structures, and their components

---

[3] Available on-line from http://www.agent-software.com

are represented by icons connected by lines that show their relationship to one another. This diagrammatic representation uses natural language to describe the goals, contexts, reasoning steps, and actions of agents/teams. The graphical and natural language descriptions can then be fleshed-out by programmers to produce executable behaviour models whose computational structure maps closely to the SME/analyst specifications. This facilitates the process of knowledge encoding/editing and ensures that SMEs and analysts can follow the application's runtime behaviour and so determine if and how it should be adjusted. In decision support and human behaviour modelling domains, JACK's graphical toolset is vital in providing the SME/analyst with control over the iterative process of encoding/evaluating/modifying agent/team behaviour.

Examples of JDE design diagrams are shown in figures 3, 4, 5, and 6.

3.7   JACK Sim Simulation Tool

Discrete event simulation is concerned with the modelling of behaviour in terms of entities that undergo discrete state transitions over time. Entity behaviours can be partitioned into various *simulation worldviews*. Traditionally, three major simulation world views have been distinguished, namely *activity*, *event* and *process* [17]. JACK™ provides a new simulation worldview – the *BDI worldview*. In the BDI worldview, entity behaviours are encapsulated within agents and the BDI execution model is used to drive the simulation. The BDI worldview provides a much richer and intuitive interaction model than is afforded by traditional simulation worldviews and has proved to be especially useful for the simulation of distributed systems.

JACK™ provides concepts, programming constructs and run-time support to directly support the BDI world view, thereby making simulation model development using the BDI world view significantly easier. JACK™ also has constructs that facilitate the interfacing of agents with existing applications. JACK™ is neutral with respect to time management – three types of clock (*real-time*, *dilated* and *simulation*) are supported. Every agent has a timer that is by default set to the real time clock. Clocks can be shared between agents on either a machine (real-time) or process (dilated, simulation) basis. Inter-machine sharing of real-time clocks and inter-machine/inter-process sharing of dilated and simulation clocks is the responsibility of the application developer. Using JACK™ for simulation model development offers the following advantages:

- support for a BDI world view,
- support for an extensible time management infrastructure,
- ability to code in Java™ where appropriate,
- support for the interfacing to and encapsulation of existing applications in an agent-friendly manner.

JACK™ has been used to develop simulations in areas such as:

- manufacturing control,
- virtual enterprise management,
- mission management for teamed Uninhabited Aerial Vehicles (UAVs),
- military command and control.

In addition JACK™ has been used to augment the behaviour of Computer Generated Forces (CGF) in existing simulation environments, such as CAEN, OTB and STAGE.

These applications are used to assess the feasibility of particular strategies and tactics, but performance and sensitivity analyses were not conducted. If such analyses are required then the simulation runs must be *repeatable*, that is, given the same inputs, they should produce the same outputs. This is not an issue with conventional simulation languages, as the simulation executes within a single thread of control within a single process. However, when the simulation executes over multiple threads or multiple processes, then repeatability needs to be explicitly addressed. JACK^{TM} was designed so that within a single JACK^{TM} process, agent execution is repeatable so long as there is no inter-agent communication. In practice this means that repeatability is constrained to applications consisting of a single agent. JACK Sim was developed to remove this constraint; with JACK Sim, repeatability is guaranteed for multi-agent applications, regardless of whether the agents reside in multiple processes or on multiple machines. JACK Sim also provides support for model management and visualization.

The JACK Sim Time Control framework includes a network of agents that manage the simulation entity execution across multiple processes, and a distinct Time Source agent who is responsible for advancing the simulation clock. The Time Control Framework makes sure that all agents complete their reasoning before the simulation time can advance to the next time step. The execution control mechanism ensures that only one agent at a time is active, and that the currently active agent performs its reasoning exhaustively before the next agent is allowed to progress.

JACK Sim recognizes and supports time stepped models as well as event driven models. Time stepped models are agents that interact explicitly with the Time Control framework via a handshaking protocol. The Time Dispatcher agent of the Time Control framework notifies the time stepped model agent about how time is advanced, and the latter replies after having performed its reasoning for the time step at hand.

In addition to the Time Control framework, JACK Sim provides simulation facilities at infrastructure level. This includes, firstly, support for separating simulation models from scenarios. In essence, the collection of models constitutes a domain of possible simulations, which requires a scenario definition to be instantiated for any particular simulation. Secondly, JACK Sim includes a versatile visualisation framework to represent models and model state through figures, shapes, texts and colours.

4   An Embedded System Example: Agent-Based Manufacturing

Agent-based Manufacturing Systems (AMS) offer a novel paradigm to address some critical problems faced by manufacturing businesses as they come to grips with the 21st Century market. This is particularly so when there is demand for mass customisation. AMS has not received much attention in the general-purpose manufacturing community, but it needs addressing if businesses are to buy into the vision of agent-based manufacturing, deploy this technology in their factories and so reap the many benefits associated with agent technology.

4.1   Rationale for Agent-Based Manufacturing

Traditional manufacturing control systems are hierarchical and are geared to mass production of low-variety goods. Often a schedule of the manufacturing operations on a given day is developed well in advance. As the schedule is executed, unexpected events, typical of many production, warehousing and supply chain environments, tend to invalidate the schedule and change how operations are managed. These events include the introduction of rush orders, machine failures or handling of returned goods. Furthermore, in today's markets consumer want goods that are customised to their specific needs and they are not prepared to wait long times for delivery. For example, consumers want to specify how to mix and match constituent elements of a desired product, possibly via a web page, and have it arrive on their doorstep the next day.

In other words, manufacturing businesses are being pushed by market forces to provide mass customisation of their product families and to react more quickly to consumer demands. Meanwhile, these companies do not wish to throw away their existing factories or the investment they have made in both hardware and product marketing. Hence a new technological approach is needed to make, handle and transport products in a flexible fashion to cope with these "one of a kind" demands. After investigating several international manufacturing companies, we have come to the conclusion that one of the major processes in the manufacturing chain where flexibility is high, and therefore where there are good opportunities for mass customisation, is automated packaging. In this section we describe a component-based approach to providing such flexibility in the "pick and place" packing of Gillette gift boxes. Our model separates out resource dependencies (e.g. robot manoeuvres) from product requirements (e.g. a definition of desired grooming items to be placed in the gift box). These items are razors, shaving foam, shaving gel and deodorant.

4.2 Features of an Agent-Based Manufacturing System

The Agent-based Manufacturing System (AMS) is a distributed paradigm that is receiving increased popularity [17]. It provides elegant mechanisms to handle disturbances in the manufacturing process, manage fluctuations in demand, and cope with the demands of mass customisation. An Agent-based Manufacturing System covers a range of decision-making processes within both the manufacturing and business worlds. This decision-making aims to provide re-configurable "plug-and-play" manufacturing business systems. The entities making such decisions are frequently called *holons* [18], and are commonly implemented using agent technologies. The layers at which these agents take decisions are: supply chain management, planning and scheduling of production operations, and real-time control of intelligent machines.

As defined by Mařík *et al.* [19],

> "[Agent-based] Holons are autonomous cooperative units which can be considered as elementary building blocks of manufacturing systems with decentralised control. Each holon usually contains:
> A hardware/equipment part able to physically influence the real world (e.g. a device, tool or other manufacturing unit, a transporter, or storage facility etc).
> A control part responsible for both the hardware/equipment part control and communications with the rest of the holonic community."

We note that the community may also include people to aid manufacturing decision-making. Interested readers are referred to Jarvis *et al.* [6] for an overview of the classic agent-based and holonic principles and the current state of the art in applying these principles to a range of manufacturing environments. As a consequence of trying to use this body of research to develop an agent-based manufacturing system demonstration, two critical technologies needed for making smart decisions have been identified: Automatic Identification (Auto ID) systems [20], and platforms for implementing autonomous agent and multi-agent systems [21].

Automatic identification (Auto ID) systems are used to read/write information to tags via high frequency radio waves. These electronic tags can replace barcodes and uniquely identify goods, thereby enabling decisions to be made by the agents on an item-specific level and removing the line-of-sight requirement when reading. Within the scope of this agent system, major aims of our ongoing research are:

- To demonstrate that agent-based control can be integrated with the Auto ID infrastructure into manufacturing systems so the user has the ability to dynamically change how orders are made and managed [22].
- To show that flexible and robust operations can be achieved even when raw materials supply is random and varying, and order attributes regularly change.
- To illustrate interactive order adjustment and dynamic modification of manufacturing operations in the case of errors and failure to satisfy quality control tests.
- To fully exploit the potential agility and reliability of the physical system [23].

Answers to these questions will help companies to be more cost effective, to respond more quickly, and to form closer collaborative networks with both customers and suppliers, i.e. creating a virtual enterprise that spans several organisations for the manufacture of customised goods. Yet the consequence of this strategy is that business models need updating and manufacturing processes must be re-engineered to cope with the added complexity that agility demands. We define agility in this context as "the capability of the system, both in part and as a whole, to conduct business as usual in an environment where change is frequent and unpredictable". Agents are a key technology to provide this agility.

4.3   An AMS Demonstrator at Cambridge University

Agent Oriented Software Ltd. is working closely with the Centre for Distributed Automation and Control within the Institute for Manufacturing at Cambridge University to investigate how to best develop and deploy agent-based manufacturing solutions into industry. One strand of this investigation is to construct an agent-based manufacturing system demonstrator. Therefore the goal is to design, develop and integrate an agent-based packing cell to demonstrate how an agent-based manufacturing system offers more agility. The layout is shown in Figure 1 and the system is characterised by:

Business Problems.   There are three business questions to be addressed. First, how can consumable goods be packed together in a flexible way to meet specific and variable customer/retail needs? Second, what is the best way to use intelligent warehouse, production and packing resources in order to maximise efficiency in a factory where uncertainty, failures and changes are commonplace? Third, what is the best way for a product to decide how best to make, manage and deliver itself so that it is cost effective and satisfies the buyer's requirements?

Fig. 1. The Cambridge Agent-based packing cell

Solution. Agents are introduced onto the shop-floor to model both *resources* (e.g. conveyor shuttles, a robot, storage units) and *products* (gift boxes and items like razor blades). Every agent uses its own intelligence and interaction with others to determine how best to use facilities and get the orders packed effectively. The system enables the customer to select any three of four types of grooming product, pack them into one of two box styles, and change how their order should be packed on the fly. This solution is now more robust to changes in order requirements than conventional packing lines.

Benefits. The demand from customers for unique combinations of products to be packaged together has led to an examination of new control system technologies that will revolutionise the retail and production industries. Intelligent agents better utilise factory resources, make products more efficiently and so increase the reactivity of manufacturing businesses to changing market needs. Rush orders can buy packing services to get themselves made quicker, partially-packed orders can be broken down so that urgent orders can be made, resources can use market economies to ensure they are getting used optimally.

This cell comprises a storage unit to hold items, a Fanuc M6i robot to move items throughout the cell, a Montrack™ shuttle conveyor to transport batches of raw materials (items) and the boxes into which items are to be placed around the cell. The plan view of the AMS system is given in Figure 2. The cell has three conveyor loops and

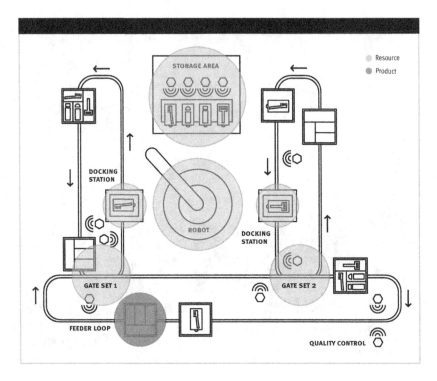

Fig. 2. Layout of the cell

independently controlled gates that guide shuttle navigation around the track. There are also two docking stations where shuttles are held so that the robot can pick and place items into the boxes that they carry. The system demonstrates many of the processes associated with agile manufacturing.

Some agile/intelligent manufacturing scenarios that the cell demonstrates are:

– Introduction of batch orders whereby individual products (i.e. boxes) manage their own resource allocation. This allocation includes acquiring a suitable tray, shuttle and items to accomplish the goal of packing that box. The system also negotiates with the docking stations to reserve a processing slot.
– Docking stations cooperating to evenly distribute workload at runtime.
– Handling of rush orders that must be packed earliest and how this influences the schedules of the docking stations and the other boxes to be packed.
– The interaction between shuttles and gates to ensure routing of shuttles around the track is both shortest time and gives highest priority to urgent shuttles.
– Failure of a docking station and how this resource change affects how and where shuttles are processed, fault tolerance and reconfiguration.
– Organising a storage unit when the robot is no longer busy so that items of the correct types or most frequently used are located at the head of each chute.
– Unpacking completed boxes so that urgent orders can be satisfied quickly.

4.4   Implementation of an AMS Using JACK™

The implementation is a realisation of the above design ideas, constrained by:

- The facilities offered by a specific agent development and execution environment.
- The peculiarities of the physical hardware.
- The lack of robust operations from its low-level support software that the agents rely upon. For instance, the inability to guarantee electronic product code (EPC) readings using radio-frequency (RF) tags with automatic identification (Auto ID) systems.
- The inefficiency of the blackboard system [24] that interfaces to the Programmable Logic Controller (PLC) and robot.
- The agent types that have been implemented in the control system (with the number of instances) are: Order Agent (an instance is spawned for each box ordered), Production Manager Agent (1 instance), Gate Agent (2 instances), Reader Agent (7 instances), Docking Station Agent (2 instances), Robot Agent (1 instance), Storage Agent (1 instance), Box Manager Agent (1 instance), and Track Agent (1 instance).

Each of these agent types has been encoded as an agent using JACK™. We focus now on the features of the robot agent because it is one of the more complex resource agents, and its processing typifies the interactions an autonomous agent has within itself and with the external world. The robot agent supports the material handling functional objective via:

- Scheduling jobs based on reward.
- Performing various pick and place operations in order to pack boxes, unpacking boxes, sorting the storage area and unloading items into storage.
- Interacting with the physical robot.

Each of these is modelled as a JACK™ capability (containing appropriate events, plans and beliefsets) within the robot. The JDE Design Diagram in Figure 3 shows the components that make up a robot agent. The components are denoted as follows: (i) Agent – stick man in rectangle, (ii) capability – rectangle, (iii) plan – rounded rectangle, (iv) beliefset – cylinder, (v) event – envelope (shown in Figure 4).

Consider an internal operation of the robot – the decision as to which pick and place action to perform. The SCHEDULEROBOT plan (Figure 4) posts a ROBOTJOBARRIVED event to itself, indicating that the robot should now execute a job (i.e. the one with the highest reward).

Four plans in the PERFORMING capability can handle this event. The choice as to which one will handle the event initially is determined at runtime using the context condition of these plans. The context condition filters on the basis of the number of items and boxes on a shuttle.

Figure 4 illustrates this event/plan relationship. The remaining events handled and sent by the ROBOTAGENT have been removed from the figure for clarity. The interaction that an agent has with other agents is orchestrated through the exchange of messages. Again the JDE can be used to define these interactions. Figure 5 shows an example of such interaction between the robot and order agents.

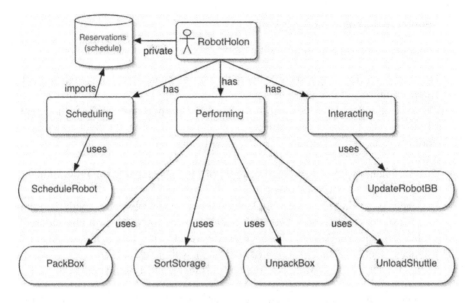

Fig. 3. JACK Design of Robot Agent

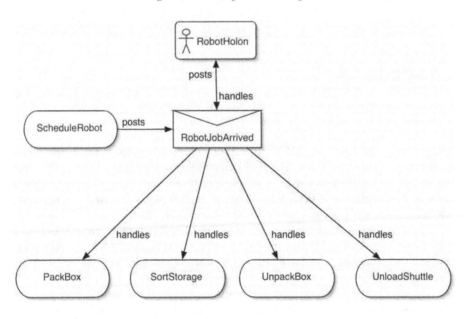

Fig. 4. Robot Agent's Performance Interactions

Explanation of the architectures and interfaces for the other agent types has been omitted for economy.

The various agents interact with each other through the exchange of messages. These messages are either the offering of a service or requesting a service. An indi-

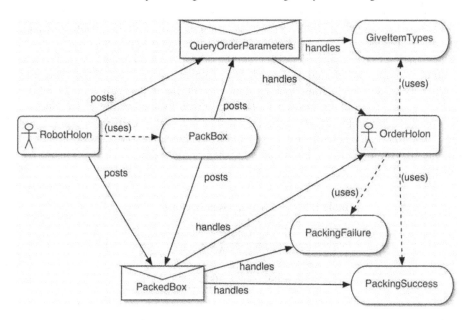

Fig. 5. Robot-to-Order Agent Interactions

vidual agent decides on what work to perform based on the value of the service less the cost of performing the work. In other words, agents prioritise work according to their estimated profit. This mechanism, while not necessarily producing optimal behaviour, allows many of the intricacies of the physical system, such as poorly performing robots or slow conveyors, to be modelled and dealt with efficiently. In addition, it allows external pressures, such as the need to handle rush orders, to influence each agent's decision making.

To coordinate the actions and decisions of agents, events are sent either synchronously or asynchronously. No agent is forced to process or reply to a message because each agent is autonomous but, generally speaking, good cooperation is encouraged by the agents responding to information requests with truthful data, and by executing appropriate plans to achieve the goals associated with incoming events.

Negotiation between the order agent and resource agents, as well as between resource agents (for fault tolerance), is managed solely in terms of price. The customer sets the price per box, when the batch order is placed via an e-manufacturing web page, and this price is used throughout the manufacturing process for sequencing the spawning of order agents, 'buying' empty boxes/items, using a shuttle, reserving a slot in the docking station's schedule, utilising the robot's time and so forth.

Hence demand and supply is matched in the course of the negotiation through a simple protocol: order agents in need of a particular service distribute requests to predefined instances of the resource agent class. The resource agents in turn evaluate the request in terms of their schedule and their status, and issue replies (bids) back to the order agent with the cost of the job. These costs are used by the order agent to select resources that are the cheapest.

In classic agent design, this is viewed as awarding a contract. For example, having already secured the services of a shuttle holding the correct type of empty box, consider the negotiation between an order agent and the docking station agents to agree where that order's empty box should be packed. The protocol proceeds as follows. The order agent announces to the loading docking station agent that it wants a job done and that the reward for undertaking this job is the price given by the customer. The docking station considers the job, by determining whether it can physically handle the shuttle and box. If the station is faulty, it returns a bid of infinite value. If not, it determines the slot into which the job would be placed. For instance, the existing schedule is shown in Table 1.

Table 1. Initial Reservations in Docking Station

Slot	Shuttle EPC	Reward
1	B00000000C000200A00D1704	$20
2	B00000000C000200A00D2645	$12
3	B00000000C000200A00D3199	$7

If a job worth $15 is requested, then the station could make an offer of Slot 2. Upon receiving this response, the order agent issues the same request to the unloading docking station agent, which will give a similar 'best slot' reply. The order agent then evaluates both bids and selects the one with the earliest slot. The order agent informs the chosen station that it needs to book the named slot for its shuttle at the given price. The docking station inserts the tuple into its private reservation beliefset and so demotes other jobs whose rewards were lower.

The order agents associated with these demotions are not informed of the sequence change; only the order agent of the newly inserted tuple is informed to confirm the deal. The order agent then informs the track agent to set the destination of the available shuttle to the selected docking station. Beyond responsiveness and the ability to cope with failed stations, this protocol has the merit that workload becomes evenly distributed across stations over time. This is an example of interaction between order and resource agents. Now consider another example, resource to resource interaction. When a shuttle approaches a switch gate, it first passes a RF tag reader. The EPC of the tag attached to the shuttle is gained and processed by the Auto ID software system called the Savant and EPC Information System Server. A reader agent is regularly polling the server for the EPC of the last shuttle to enter the reader's range.

Upon arrival, the reader agent informs the appropriate gate agent of the shuttle's presence. Each gate has two inputs and two outputs, and so the gate can decide which of two waiting shuttles to let through. This decision is currently made on a FIFO basis. The gate agent interacts with the track agent to determine the destination of the inbound shuttle and to determine if there is available space into which the shuttle can move. The track agent maintains a model of which shuttle is in what zone using a set of queues. The queue is added to when a shuttle enters a zone and popped when it departs. The track agent also keeps a model of the maximum number of shuttles that can be present in each zone (this is fixed at start-up and is tightly coupled with the track's configuration).

Hence the track agent is able to decide if another shuttle can enter a given zone based on the shuttle's intended destination. If space is available then the gate agent is informed and so it can interact with the blackboard to set the hardware's input/output choice and thus let the shuttle through. These are some of the typical agent interactions within the AMS.

4.5 Lessons from Attempting to Use JACK™ for Agent-Based Manufacturing

Using JACK™ agent system to control industrial automation equipment and to develop an automated manufacturing system taught us some valuable lessons about developing agent systems. These ranged from the importance of having a "yellow pages" directory for finding agents, to the value of logging mechanisms to help with understanding the dynamic aspects of a system.

It is useful to have a standard yellow pages mechanism, such as that defined by FIPA, to provide a list of agents that provide a particular service. This is an important facility as it changes the way the agent classes are coded. For example, it makes it straightforward to add agent instances to cope with added hardware, effectively plugging in extra holons based on demand. Instead, in the current version, there was a tendency to name specific agent instances within the code for a generic agent class, thus limiting the generality of the class.

Well-designed, and preferably standard, protocols are important for ensuring that inter-agent messages that need replies are replied to. Such protocols also help to avoid sending spurious replies that are not listened to. Although JACK™ catches these errors at runtime, the source of the problem can be difficult to track down. In addition, it is important to help the programmer think in high-level terms by providing abstract communication protocol support. For example, when one agent relies on another for a particular service, one way to communicate this requirement is the contract net protocol. We believe that the agent programming language and associated libraries should support this so that the programmer can simply say "get service X from any supplier of class C using the contract net protocol." JACK™ does not directly support this feature at the time of writing.

It is critical that synchronisation and mutual exclusion issues are handled correctly. JACK™ provides a powerful mechanism to help with these issues since most processing for an agent is performed in a single thread, with the sequence of steps in a plan actually being implemented as a finite state machine (FSM). This ensures that each step in a plan is processed atomically. In addition, since JACK™ restricts the use of global data and encourages message passing between agents instead, there would seem to be less likelihood of encountering synchronisation issues. In fact, we found several instances of race conditions while debugging the system. Most of these were traced to updating Java™ data structures over several plan steps, where JACK™ could interrupt processing between steps to give processing time to other plans. A key lesson was to move any data structure update statements to their own Java™ method to ensure that JACK™ treated them atomically.

Another area that led to synchronisation problems was in the integration of legacy code. The code dealt with the task of communicating with a Programmable Logic Controller (PLC) by reflecting register memory inside the PLC and providing a mechanism to update it. This PLC communication system made use of an interaction protocol that was not robust to delays, and it was possible under some circumstances to miss the receipt of messages. Unfortunately, missing messages about the state of the registers could be catastrophic (as they were not stateless) and would eventually halt the operation of the control system.

Simulation and emulation are key tools when developing physically instantiated control systems. Agent programming can be quite complicated. The overall behaviour of the system may not be what was expected and it is important to be able to (a) reproduce particular situations in a controlled environment in order to isolate and debug problems, and (b) rapidly test the system under a variety of conditions to prove robustness. We found that building an emulation of our physical environment that linked in with the JACK™ control system was worth the extra effort that it required and resulted in significant time savings.

New approaches are required to simplify the process of debugging a multi-agent system. Although JACK™ is essentially Java-based, it can be cumbersome to try to debug JACK™ code using traditional Java™ debugging environments. Instead, we found that logging tools, such as Apache's Log4J, were useful in helping to isolate problems in particular areas of code. Log4J has the advantage that logging for individual Java™ classes can be turned on or off without recompilation. We expect that recent additions to JACK™, such as the agent message trace facility, will help with debugging agent systems in the future.

As with object-oriented programming, it is important to clearly delineate the responsibilities of each entity [25]. For example, the idea of "containment" might be implemented by having the container knowing about all objects inside it, or alternatively, by having each contained object have a reference to the container (or possibly by a combination of both). Similarly, in part-oriented control [26], an agent representing the part is responsible for moving the part through the system and getting it machined or processed. An alternative is for resource agents to control the movements of parts. In an environment, such as ours, where several software engineers develop the system collaboratively, it is important that individual decisions about which tasks an agent should be responsible for make sense in terms of a larger picture. This approach is clearly well aligned with the BDI paradigm in that to clearly understand and communicate how an agent should behave, it is useful to ascribe to it beliefs, intentions and desires.

Real world events tend to be more noise-filled and more difficult to interpret than those occurring in idealised simulations. However filtering the noise from real world event data can be error prone. Incorrect filters may cause some events to be missed or additional events to be implied. Bugs in the event filtering may appear externally to be bugs in the reaction of agents. To avoid this, it is useful to keep an internal representation of the state of the world. This representation can then be used to debug the event filters independently of the agent's reaction, by comparing the internal representation with the actual state of the world. Even though an agent might access this internal representation directly, it is still useful to provide event triggers to the agents, rather than have them poll for changes in the state of the world. We found that event triggers based on an internal world state representation could be more uniform than those produced by real world sensors, and this reduced the number of different plans required to handle them.

For example, when a single part has just been packed into a gift box, this is similar to the arrival of a gift box with a single part that was packed previously. Both events require the next part to be packed, even though what has changed in the world is slightly different.

The AMS has been successfully demonstrated to many visitors to the Cambridge automation laboratory, including a live demonstration via video link-up to a conference in Atlanta [27]. In the next section, we examine a quite different agent system, also created using JACK™.

5   A Decision Support System Example: Meteorological Forecasting

The Australian Bureau of Meteorology (BoM) is involved in an ongoing review of its information distribution systems. As part of that review the BoM is reassessing its forecasting and alerting capabilities. The BoM's information environment is particularly complex, being both distributed and dynamic in nature [5]. These properties and previous experience led the BoM to choose a distributed multi-agent solution based on JACK™ [5].

The initial deployed system, known as "Intelligent Alerts" focused on a subset of aviation weather forecasting (air pressure forecasts), producing alerts to be displayed on forecasters' desktops [28]. The system demonstrated a variety of desirable features such as extensibility, robustness in a changing environment and a reduction in the cognitive load on forecasters [28]. Extensions to the current system are underway including more comprehensive filtering of locations and alerts [29].

5.1   Problem Definition and System Requirements

The driving force for the Intelligent Alerts system was the umbrella project known as the Forecast Streamlining and Enhancement Project (FSEP). FSEP aims to improve quality, quantity, consistency and timeliness of weather products and services to both the general community and major BoM clients such as the aviation industry, fire fighters and emergency services [5]. BoM customers require real-time alerting of major weather events. The aviation industry in particular requires rapid amendment of forecasts where current data suggests they may be inaccurate. Comparing weather conditions to forecast values can achieve this, however, due to the volume of data involved, the analysis must be automated.

When the BoM sought a solution for their alerting needs, their environment had several factors that indicated a multi-agent system would provide an appropriate solution. The BoM is an information rich organisation dealing with a complex, evolving and distributed environment [5, 28]. These factors are seen as the hallmark of domains in which multi-agent systems offer advantages over traditional solutions [29]. The BoM's specific requirements included a system that is able to:

- Evolve over time. The system was required to interoperate with existing systems in the short term, yet allow easy integration of future components.

- Behave in a distributed, open and platform agnostic manner. The BoM operates in a heterogeneous network environment with forecasters using a diverse range of hardware and software. The BoM has offices across Australia and different groups within the BoM need to be able to deploy components of the system with minimal inter-group interaction. New components need to be located by other entities on the network and used appropriately [29].
- Handle large volumes of data produced by both agents and existing systems within the BoM. As mentioned above, the BoM is an information rich environment. For a system to operate effectively in such an environment, the solution had to scale gracefully as data volume increases.
- Deal with a range of goals, some of which may at times conflict. The system had to be able to pursue multiple goals concurrently. Ideally resolution of contention between conflicting goals should be an automatic process.
- Resolve inconsistencies in data where reports from different sources may conflict. The BoM has multiple sources of data describing similar phenomena. For example, multiple weather models are used within the BoM, all producing different predictions given the same set of initial values. The system had to deal with these types of inconsistencies and ambiguities.
- Provide appropriate level of detail to users of the system. *Alert pollution* occurs when a user is inundated with such large amounts of information they begin to ignore all incoming alerts. In order to reduce the problem, the system had to make intelligent decisions before sending alerts to users. Users themselves would also be able to specify user-level alert filters based on their current information requirements.

In addition to the close fit between multi-agent systems and the problem domain, the BoM had previous favourable experiences with agent systems used in the context of forecasting. Previous work by the BoM [30] used an agent-based system for detecting *microbursts* (regions of high-shear and strong down-drafts associated with thunderstorms that are considered hazardous to aircraft). The system's results compared favourably with those of more complex solutions and indicated the usefulness of agents for solving problems within the BoM.

As mentioned above, the initial system targeted aviation forecasting and was restricted to the analysis of atmospheric pressure readings from automatic weather stations (AWS). This data was compared to Terminal Aerodrome Forecasts (TAFs), a forecast produced by the BoM related to conditions close to an airport. Inconsistencies between AWS data and TAF predictions may lead to an alert being sent to the forecaster. The TAF generation process allows for forecasters to issue forecast amendments. Hence alerts concerning inconsistencies are of particular interest to forecasters generating TAFs [5].

5.2 Architecture

The deployed system architecture is comprised of information routing agents, alerting agents, external data sources and alert viewing user interfaces. Figure 6 shows a

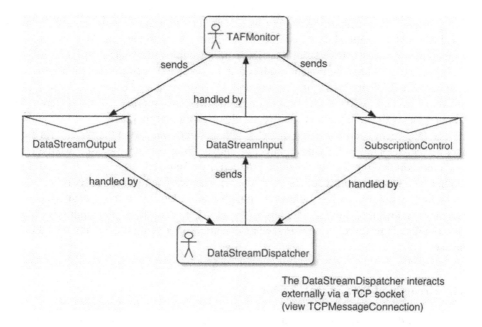

Fig. 6. Overview of the BoM Application Design

JACK™ Design Tool diagram with an overview of the application showing a single alerting agent (the TAFMonitor).

A TAFMonitor agent monitors terminal area forecasts comparing them to AWS readings of currently observed values. A DataStreamDispatcher agent is responsible for message routing and subscription control within the system. Entities subscribe to data feeds provided through the DataStreamDispatcher using SubscriptionControl events. Producers send data to the DataStreamDispatcher (via DataStreamOutput events), which then routes that data to Subscribers via DataStreamInput events. The TAFMonitor agent acts as both a subscriber (to the AWS and TAF data streams) and a producer of data in the form of TAF alert messages.

In addition to the event delivery paths shown in Figure 6, the DataStreamDispatcher agent is also able to route messages sent across standard TCP streams, allowing integration with non-agent legacy systems. The AWS data stream is delivered into the system via this pathway. The Alert GUI, which subscribes to the Alerts generated by the TAFMonitor agent, is not depicted in this figure.

This architecture, with its relatively small number of components (many of which contain only several lines of code), exemplifies the tendency for agent-based solutions to produce relatively concise solutions to complex problems.

5.3 Implementation

JACK™ was chosen as the agent platform for the Intelligent Alerts system. JACK's embodiment of BDI concepts was seen as central to its suitability for this project. The ability to deal with a rapidly changing world, the fact that the system can affect the world (through the amendment of forecasts) and the ability to have reactive and goal-directed behaviour, all proved useful attributes in the deployed system [28].

Initially the TAFMonitor agent produced alerts when a 2 hectopascals (hPa) difference between TAF predicted air pressure and AWS observations occurred. As part of an overall strategy to avoid alert pollution, an alert is only produced if the difference becomes larger than the previous difference plus a given margin [28].

The Intelligent Alerts user interface (UI) was an important part of the system. As the interface between the underlying architecture and the forecaster or forecast consumer, it was important that the UI improved the productivity of the end-user rather than adding another task to their workload. As such, the UI was designed to require as little user interaction as possible, whilst allowing enough configurability to tailor data feeds to those most relevant to the individual user. The ability to drill down into summary data for more details when required was seen as essential in reducing the cognitive load on the user.

5.4   Strengths of the Current System

The initially deployed system provides an end to end demonstration of all the functional requirements of the system, that is, subscriptions, data routing, data source communication, self-describing data, service description and location mechanisms.

In addition to the systemic advantages provided by the BDI, multi-agent approach previously mentioned, the deployed system exhibited the following specific advantages, as highlighted in [5, 28]:

- Post-Hoc feedback to the forecaster, after the period of validity for the forecast has expired, allows the forecaster to see how close to actual conditions their forecast came.
- The automation of delivering alerts to external consumers of meteorological data means forecasters are able to concentrate on analysis during extreme weather conditions rather than the dissemination of information to interested parties.
- Easy extensibility with volcanic ash alerts. As a test for system flexibility, a new alert type was added incorporating Volcanic Ash warnings from the Volcanic Ash Advisory Centre (VAAC). BoM developers subscribed to a VAAC email list for volcanic ash alerts and fed the alerts into a Java^{TM} process that delivers them in XML format to an Ash Alerts agent. Subscribers to the Ash Alert agent were able to view the content of the email in their alert GUI. This addition took less than 2 person days of development – an indication of the ease with which the current system could be extended.
- The use of a publish/subscribe paradigm allowed agents to be added and removed easily from the system. After the replacement of a subscriber, the new entity automatically re-subscribes to its relevant data feeds. Similarly, when a data publisher is replaced or restarted, any subscribers automatically re-subscribe to the publisher. This type of self-healing is important in a distributed system where manual intervention is neither desirable nor practical.

- JACK™ provided a flexible implementation platform allowing for the rapid development of new plans to deal with new situations. Using JACK™ *capabilities* allowed the re-use of related clusters of behaviour between agent types. The rapid development (2 days) of the Volcanic Ash agent indicates the level of flexibility provided by the JACK™ platform.
- The use of code-independent data structures such as XML allows data structure extension without recompilation.

5.5 Future Directions

Whilst the system in its current form performed well in the environment it was designed for, as the system evolves to embrace a larger subset of the BoM's information flow, it will require various extensions. Most obvious is the inclusion of a wider variety of data sources leading to an increase in the types of alerts available on the system. As the number and diversity of alerting agents grows, the need to design new agents, and understand and use the new services they provide, will increase. Work is currently underway on both these fronts in a new collaboration between the RMIT Agents Group, the BoM and Agent Oriented Software [29]. A powerful alert filter definition language will also prove more important. As the number of alerts in the system increases, users will require a system with a sufficiently expressive mechanism for defining the alerts they deem to be salient.

6 Discussion

We believe that JACK™ is an important and novel contribution to the field of agent-oriented software engineering. Rather than invent a new language, an existing popular language (Java™) has been augmented with constructs for agent communication, knowledge representation, and for both deliberative (goal-based) and reactive (event-based) programming. This has been achieved in a way that allows the programmer to mix familiar Java™ statements with agent programming constructs. Although JACK™ is strongly oriented toward the BDI paradigm, its component-based architecture supports a wide variety of agent programming styles.

The JACK™ language is supported by an integrated development environment (IDE) that allows the programmer to layout the structure of an agent application using a graphical interface, and this has been important in involving Subject Matter Experts in the development process. Experience with developing systems involving multi-agent coordination led to the addition of JACK Teams, which provides a general framework for team-based agent coordination. Together with JACK Sim, these tools provide a rich environment for agent-oriented software development.

A simple way to demonstrate the suitability of JACK™ (and possibly of agent programming in general), is to examine cases where JACK™ has been used in industry. In this chapter we have examined two industrial applications of JACK™ – an Agent-based Manufacturing System (AMS) and a meteorological alerting decision support system.

The AMS was a sizeable development effort and involved integration with complex physical systems and interfacing with legacy code. Not surprisingly, there were a number of general lessons learnt about how to construct such agent systems, and some more specific lessons about how to make best use of JACK^{TM}. The general lessons related to the importance of standard protocols and services, such as those proposed by FIPA, the usefulness of simulation or emulation, particularly when dealing with robotic systems, and the importance of clearly defining roles and responsibilities when designing each agent and their interaction with other agents. In terms of specific lessons about JACK^{TM}, we found that understanding how JACK^{TM} converts plan steps into a finite state machine helped with debugging some problems involving synchronisation – particularly where Java^{TM} native data structures were used. Also, we found that logging and message traces were useful tools when diagnosing problems with dynamic aspects of the system.

The AMS system was developed with a Holonic framework [17, 19] in mind, rather than a BDI one. An advantage of JACK^{TM} is that it is sufficiently flexible to allow this. In addition, the ability to be proactive, alongside an event driven, reactive structure, was an important feature, and allowed the behaviour of the system to be more sophisticated than if it had been purely reactive. However, from the work on this system so far, it is not clear whether a BDI approach would be more suitable.

The Intelligent Alerts meteorological forecasting system provides real-time alerts of *significant* changes in weather data, allowing the forecaster to provide the aviation industry with timely warnings of impending shifts in climate. The ability to integrate with legacy forecasting systems was a key prerequisite. JACK's implementation as an extension of Java^{TM} allows it to leverage all of the capability of that language and greatly facilitates integration with legacy software systems. This factor cannot be over-emphasised – if they are to be adopted by industry, multi-agent systems must be no more difficult to integrate than conventional software.

The agent-oriented BDI architecture of the Intelligent Alerts system provided benefits that are characteristic of the approach. Perhaps most important was the ability to mix reactive and proactive modes of behaviour and deal with multiple concurrent goals. At times, the weather is in a state of high flux, thus it is vital that the Intelligent Alerts system can react to these changes in the context of its long-term *desires*, such as to not flood the user with alerts.

The two applications of JACK^{TM} described in this chapter would have been difficult to implement outside of the multi-agent paradigm. Decomposing each application into a collection of autonomous agents, each motivated to fulfil its role in the system, greatly reduced the complexity of the undertaking. Although functional decomposition is not new, the encapsulation of functionality within *autonomous computational entities* is a relatively novel approach in industry. In addition, the BDI paradigm is a useful abstraction when thinking and communicating about how such autonomous entities should behave. Based on our experience of the successful commercial application of JACK^{TM} in dynamic, distributed domains, it is our belief that multi-agent systems have come of age and will be more widely adopted by industry in the near-term.

Acknowledgements

The Meteorological Forecasting Decision Support System was a collaborative project between Agent Oriented Software Ltd., the Australian Bureau of Meteorology and the

RMIT Agents Group in Melbourne, Australia. The work was supported by an Australian Research Council Linkage Grant (grant LP0347025, "Open agent architectures for intelligent distributed decision making").

We thank Jeff Schultz and Ralph Rönnquist for their valuable comments on earlier drafts of this chapter. We would also like to thank the anonymous reviewers for their insightful suggestions and comments.

References

1. d'Inverno, M., Kinny, D., Luck, M., Wooldridge, M.: A formal specification of dmars. In Singh, M., Rao, A., Wooldridge, M., eds.: Intelligent Agents IV: Proceedings of the Fourth International Workshop on Agent Theories, Architectures, and Languages. Volume LNAI 1365., Springer-Verlag (1998) 155–176

2. Rao, A.S., Georgeff, M.P.: BDI agents: From theory to practice. In: Proceedings of the First International Conference on Multi-Agent Systems (ICMAS-95), Menlo Park, California, AAAI Press (1995) 312–319

3. Wooldridge, M.: Reasoning about Rational Agents. MIT Press (2000)

4. Agent Oriented Software: Human variability in computer generated forces (HV-CGF). http://www.agent-software.com/shared/solutions/hvcgf.html (2003)

5. Dance, S., Gorman, M.: Intelligent agents in the Australian Bureau of Meteorology. In: Challenges in Open Agent Systems Workshop, in Autonomous Agents and MultiAgents Systems (AAMAS02), Bologna, Italy (2002)

6. Jarvis, D., Jarvis, J., Lucas, A., Rönnquist, R., McFarlane, D.C.: Implementing a multi-agent system approach to collaborative autonomous manufacturing operations. In: Proceedings of IEEE International Conference on Systems Man and Cybernetics. (2001)

7. Ljungberg, M., Lucas, A.: The OASIS air-traffic management system. In: Proceedings of the Second Pacific Rim International Conference on Artificial Intelligence, PRICAI '92, Seoul, Korea (1992)

8. Bratman, M.E.: Intention, Plans, and Practical Reasoning. Harvard University Press, Cambridge, MA (USA) (1987)

9. Georgeff, M.P., Ingrand, F.F.: Monitoring and control of spacecraft systems using procedural reasoning. In: Proceedings of the Space Operations Automation and Robotics Workshop, Melbourne, Australia (1989)

10. Murray, G., Steuart, S., Appla, D., McIlroy, D., Heinze, C., Cross, M., Chandran, A., Raszka, R., Rao, A.S., Pegler, A., Morley, D., Busetta, P.: The challenge of whole air mission modelling. In: Proceedings of Australian Joint Conference on Artificial Intelligence AI '95, Melbourne, Australia (1995)

11. Lucas, A., Rönnquist, R., Ljungberg, M., Howden, N., Corke, P., Sikka, P.: Teamed UAVs – a new approach with intelligent agents. In: 2nd AIAA "Unmanned Unlimited" Systems, Technologies, and Operations – Aerospace, Land, and Sea Conference. (2003)

12. Fikes, R., Nilsson, N.: Strips: A new approach to the application of theorem proving to problem solving. Artificial Intelligence **2** (1971) 189–208

13. Bratman, M.E., Isreal, D.J., Pollack, M.E.: Plans and resource-bounded practical reasoning. Computational Intelligence **4** (1988)

14. Georgeff, M.P., Lansky, A.L.: Procedural knowledge. In: Proceedings of the IEEE Special Issue on Knowledge Representation 74. (1986) 1383–1398

15. Agent Oriented Software: Jack™ manual. http://www.agent-software.com/shared/demosNdocs/JACK_Manual.pdf (2003)

16. Ingrand, F.F.: C-PRS Development Environment (Version 1.4.0). ACS Technologies, Labege Cedex, France. (1994)
17. Bussmann, S., Sieverding, J.: Holonic control of an engine assembly plant – an industrial evaluation. In: Proceedings of the IEEE International Conference on Systems, Man, and Cybernetics, Berlin, Springer-Verlag (2001) 169–174
18. Koestler, A.: The Ghost in the Machine. Arkana (1967)
19. Mařík, V., Fletcher, M., Pěchouček, M.: Holons and agents: Recent developments and mutual impacts. In: Multi-Agent Systems and Applications II. Number 2322 in LNAI, Heidelberg, Springer-Verlag (2002)
20. Sarma, S., Brock, D.L., Ashton, K.: The networked physical world – proposals for engineering the next generation of computing, commerce and automatic identification. Technical Report MIT-AUTOID-WH-001, MIT Auto-ID Center (2000)
21. Suda, H.: Future factory system in Japan. Journal of Advanced Automation Technology **1** (1989)
22. Brussel, H.V., Bongaerts, L., Wyns, J., Valckenaers, P., Ginderachter, T.A.V.: Conceptual framework for holonic manufacturing: Identification of manufacturing holons. Journal of Manufacturing Systems **18** (1999)
23. Vrba, P., Hrdonka, V.: Material handling problem: FIPA compliant agent implementation. In: Proceedings of the Twelfth International Workshop on Distributed and Expert Systems Applications DEXA. (2001) 635–639
24. Chirn, J.L., McFarlane, D.C.: Building holonic systems in today's factories: A migration strategy. Journal of Applied System Studies **2** (2000) special issue on Holonic and Multi-Agent Systems.
25. Beck, K., Cunningham, W.: A laboratory for teaching object-oriented thinking. SIGPLAN Notices **24** (1989)
26. Kärkkäinen, M., Holmström, J., Främling, K., Artto, K.: Intelligent products – a step towards a more effective project delivery chain. Computers In Industry **50** (2003) 141–151
27. Brusey, J., Fletcher, M., Harrison, M., Thorne, A., Hodges, S., McFarlane, D.: Auto-id based control demonstration phase 2: Pick and place packing with holonic control. Technical Report CAM-AUTOID-WH-011, Auto-ID Center (2003) http://www.autoidlabs.org/researcharchive.
28. Dance, S., Gorman, M., Padgham, L., Winikoff, M.: A deployed multi agent system for meteorological alerts. In: Deployed Applications of Autonomous Agents and Multiagent Systems Workshop, AAMAS03, Melbourne, Australia (2003) 19–26
29. Mathieson, I., Dance, S., Padgham, L., Gorman, M., Winikoff, M.: An open meteorological alerting system: issues and solutions. In Estivill-Castro, V., ed.: Proceedings of the 27th Australasian Computer Science Conference. Volume 26 of Conferences in Research and Practice in Information Technology., The University of Otago, Dunedin, New Zealand (2004) (to appear).
30. Dance, S., Potts, R.: Microburst detection using agent networks. Journal of Atmospheric and Oceanic Technology **19** (2002) 646–653

Programming Software Agents as Designing Executable Business Processes: A Model-Driven Perspective

Jörg P. Müller[1], Bernhard Bauer[2], and Thomas Friese[3]

[1] Siemens AG Corporate Technology
Intelligent Autonomous Systems
Otto-Hahn-Ring 6, D-81739 München, Germany
joerg.p.mueller@siemens.com
[2] Programming of Distributed Systems,
Institute of Computer Science, University of Augsburg
D-86135 Augsburg
bernhard.bauer@informatik.uni-augsburg.de
[3] Dept. of Mathematics and Computer Science
University of Marburg
D-35032 Marburg, Germany
friese@informatik.uni-marburg.de

Abstract. The contribution of this paper is fourfold. First, we sketch an architecture of agent-enabled business process management that cleanly separates between agent capabilities, business process modeling, and the modeling of services that are employed to actually implement processes. Second, we demonstrate how the Model-Driven Architecture (MDA) paradigm can be beneficially employed at all three layers of the agent-enabled business process architecture. Third, we describe an instance of a platform independent model based on the new UML2 standard, and sketch a mapping to a platform dependent model based on the Business Process Execution Language for Web Services (BPEL4WS). Fourth, we point out the relationship between the programming of multiagent systems, and the design of agent-enabled business processes. Our key thesis is that designing business processes based on an agent-enabled business processes modeling and enactment framework is a useful way of programming agents – a way that may help agent technology to gain much wider acceptance in industry.

1 Introduction

Over the past few years, enterprises have undergone a thorough transformation in reaction to challenges such as globalization, unstable demand, and mass customization. A key to maintaining competitiveness is the ability of an enterprise to describe, standardize, and adapt the way it reacts to certain types of business events, and how it interacts with suppliers, partners, competitors, and customers. Today, virtually all larger enterprises describe these procedures and interactions in terms of *business processes,* and invest huge efforts to describe and standardize these processes.

M. Dastani, J. Dix, A. El Fallah-Seghrouchni (Eds.): PROMAS 2003, LNAI 3067, pp. 49–71, 2004.

The trend to process-centered modeling and operation of enterprises brings new opportunities for software technologies that support the monitoring, management, and optimization of processes. On the other hand it requires software technologies to relate to business processes, to understand them and to hook into them where required.

Software agents are computer systems capable of flexible autonomous action in a dynamic, unpredictable and open environment [16]. These characteristics give agent technology a high potential to support process-centered modeling and operation of businesses. Consequently, there have been various research efforts of using agent technology in business process management, one of the earliest examples being ADEPT [15]. Recently, agent technology has also started to attract business analysts in the context of adaptive supply network management [20].

However, the focus of ADEPT was essentially focused on communication and collaboration in business process management. Its outcome was a research prototype, not a usable business process support platform. Migrating agent technology successfully to business applications requires the provision of end-to-end solutions that integrate with standards, that preserve companies' investment in hardware, software platforms, tools, and people, that enables the incremental introduction of new technologies (see also [18]), and that can deal gracefully with moving to new technology platforms.

One main objective of this paper is to sketch an architecture of agent-enabled business process management that cleanly separates between agent capabilities, business process modeling, and the modeling of services that are employed to actually implement processes. We regard software agents as software components primarily responsible for

- the intelligent evaluation, selection and customization of business processes and activities matching service requests;
- and for the robust and flexible enactment of these processes or activities, including monitoring, exception and failure handling, and decision support.

Enactment of business processes relies on an underlying service layer, an information and communication runtime infrastructure providing the possibility of registering and discovering services and of communicating service requests and responses.

A second objective is to demonstrate how the Model-Driven Architecture (MDA) [17] paradigm can be beneficially employed at all three layers of the agent-enabled business process architecture, in order to allow system designers to focus on the functionality and behavior of a distributed application or system, independent of the technology or technologies in which it will be implemented.

Based on this model-driven approach, our third objective is to demonstrate an instance of a platform independent model based on the new UML2 standard [22], extending the scope of the Unified Modeling Language to the design of processes, and sketch a mapping to a platform dependent model based on the Business Process Execution Language for Web Services (BPEL4WS) [13]. We discuss design-time and run-time aspects of a methodology for agent-enabled business process modeling.

Finally, the fourth objective of this paper is to point out a relationship between the programming of multiagent systems, which is the key topic of the volume at hand, and the design of agent-enabled business processes. Our key thesis here is that designing business processes based on an agent-enabled business processes modeling and enactment framework can be regarded as one way of programming agents – one way that may help agent technology to gain much wider acceptance in industry.

This paper is not a primarily a technical paper although it does contain technical elements. Our primary intention is to bring forward a position sketching the need and requirements for, and key aspects of, an architecture and development framework for programming agents for industrial applications, which in our opinion is not sufficiently reflected in most existing research on agent-oriented software engineering and agent programming. Many of the details remain to be fleshed out in future research, but we feel it is worth pointing them out. We hope that the reader agrees with this.

The structure of the paper is as follows: In Section 2, we provide a conceptual architecture for agent-enabled business processes and set the technological background. Section 3 provides an application example that will serve as a demonstration vehicle throughout the paper. In Section 4, a model-driven design methodology for agent-enabled business processes is provided including examples for platform-independent and platform-specific models. Section 5 then outlines a runtime architecture for enactment of agent-enabled business processes. We conclude in Section 6 with some discussion of future research opportunities.

2 Background

In this section, we describe a conceptual architecture defining the relationship between web services, business processes, and software agents.

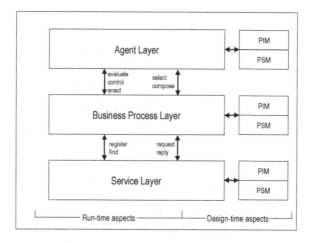

Fig. 1. Conceptual architecture for agent-enabled business processes

2.1 Conceptual Architecture

Figure 1 illustrates the essence of our conception in an abstract three-tier architecture. We regard software agents as software components primarily responsible for the intelligent evaluation, selection and customization of business processes and activities matching service requests and for the robust and flexible enactment of these processes or activities, including monitoring, exception and failure handling, and decision support. Enactment of business processes relies on an underlying service layer, an information and communication runtime infrastructure providing the possibility of registering with and discovering services and of communicating service requests and responses. For grounding this conceptual architecture in a real IT environment, we propose the Model-Driven Architecture (MDA) approach (see [17] and [25]) in order to achieve a separation of business and application logic from underlying platform technologies. The core idea of the MDA is to first describe a software artifact by a platform independent model (PIM), and then provide mappings to a number of platform-specific models (PSM). Our claim is that MDA can be applied beneficially at all three layers of our conceptual architecture. At the agent layer, it can be used to specify the behavior of agents, there strategies and objective functions in an abstract manner. At the business process layer, it can be used to accommodate the use of different business process representations (such as SCOR, event-driven process chains, or activity diagrams of UML 2.0). Finally, at the service level, it can be used to ground the architecture on different service-oriented platforms, such as web services/.NET, Java RMI, Peer-to-Peer Platforms, or agent communication platforms available as part of FIPA-compliant agent infrastructure (e.g., Jade/Leap).

In the following, we provide a short overview of the major technological aspects at the different conceptual layers.

2.2 Model-Driven Architecture

The Model Driven Architecture (MDA) (for details see [25]; this section is also based on this reference) is a framework for software development driven by the Object Management Group (OMG). Key to MDA is the importance of models in the software development process. Within MDA the software development process is driven by the activity of modeling the software system. The MDA development process does not look very different from a traditional lifecycle, containing the same phases (requirements, analysis, low-level design, coding, testing, and deployment). One of the major differences lies in the nature of the artifacts that are created during the development process. The artifacts are formal models, i.e. models that can be understood by computers. The following three models are at the core of the MDA:

- **Platform Independent Model (PIM):** This model is defined at a high level of abstraction; it is independent of any implementation technology. It describes a software system that supports some business. Within a PIM, the system is modeled from the viewpoint of how it best supports the business. Whether a system will be implemented on a mainframe with a relational database, on an agent platform or on an EJB application server plays no role in a PIM.
- **Platform Specific Model (PSM):** In the next step, the PIM is transformed into one or more PSMs. It is tailored to specify a system in terms of the implementation constructs available in one specific implementation technology. E,g. an agent

PSM is a model of the system in terms of an agent platform. A PIM is transformed into one or more PSMs. For each specific technology platform a separate PSM is generated. Most of the systems today span several technologies; therefore it is common to have many PSMs with one PIM.

- **Code:** The final step in the development is the transformation of each PSM to code. Because a PSM fits its technology rather closely, this transformation is relatively straightforward.

2.3 Service Layer: Web Services

Describing software architecture in a service-oriented fashion, while being increasingly popular, is not a new idea; it is what CORBA has been about more than a decade ago. Recently, the concept of web services has given new momentum to service-oriented architecture. Web services are self-contained, self-describing, modular applications that can be published, located, and invoked across the Web using existing web protocols and infrastructure. The core web service standards are the Web Service Definition Language (WSDL), Simple Object Access Protocol (SOAP), and Universal Description, Discovery and Integration (UDDI). The combination of relative simplicity, platform independence, and leveraging of HTTP positions web services to become an important architecture for wide-scale distributed computing [8].

2.3.1 Web Service Definition

WSDL is an XML based specification for describing what a program module does (interface description), what the result of the module's activity is, and how to communicate with it. A WSDL document resides at a URL location, e.g. at a UDDI, and is linked to the module, which itself may reside at any location. Web Services exchange information through SOAP messages. SOAP is a protocol for Remote Procedure Call / Remote Method Invocation over HTTP. SOAP uses XML to define the message format and how variables and parameters required by the program are sent to it to invoke its methods. The program in turn, sends the results of its process back to the request originator in another SOAP message. Because HTTP is one of the transport mechanisms used by SOAP, a Web Service method call can be made to and from any Web enabled computer anywhere in the world.

2.3.2 Web Service Choreography

According to [23], web service choreography describes the specification of the interaction (i.e., ordering of messages) among a collection of services from the perspective of one service or a collection thereof. Web service choreography allows applications to combine existing web services in order to obtain more elaborated value-added web services. Note that choreography deals with the definition of these interactions, not with their execution. Several standards are currently under development for the definition of languages for Web Service composition or Web Service Choreography: For instance, IBM and Microsoft have developed process languages, the Web Services Flow Language (WSFL) and XLANG, respectively. These have been merged into the Business Process Execution Language for Web Service BPEL4WS, see Section 2.4.

2.4 Business Process Layer

The notion of service choreography logically leads to the notion of business processes. A business process is a group of business activities undertaken by an organization in pursuit of a common goal. The process-driven approach has become the predominant means of describing and structuring corporate IT and information systems. Hence, we argue that the notion of business processes is a mostly adequate basis for specifying agents and multiagent systems.

Driven by the availability of web services platforms (see Section 2.3), a number of architectures, presentations, and platforms for web-based business processes have been proposed, starting with the already mentioned BPEL4WS, but also including the Business Process Modeling Language (BPML) defined by the Business Process Management Initiative BPMI [4]. Another example is the ebXML *Business Process Specification Schema* [5], providing a standard framework by which business systems may be configured to support execution of business collaborations. We use BPEL4WS in the examples used throughout this paper; however, the adherence to MDA ensures transferability to other process models and infrastructure.

2.5 Agent Layer

From a sufficiently abstract perspective, a business process is essentially a computer program; composing a business process is very similar to program synthesis, and enacting a business process is program execution. Automated business process composition is not too different from artificial intelligence planning, which implies that AI planning techniques are applicable but that at the same time we should not hope for efficient general solutions of the business process composition problem, as they most probably do not exist. However, business processes are more than plans or programs: they incorporate knowledge about organizations, and they contain tasks that can only be solved by or in collaboration with humans. This is where we believe agents come into play. We claim that the role of agents in the context of business processes is threefold:

- Agents can be used to support the evaluation of existing business processes at request time, leading to recommendation regarding the assignment of a business process to an incoming service request.
- Agents can combine planning methods with knowledge about structure, authorities, and competencies of organizational units to modify existing business processes, or to create new instances of business processes from scratch.
- Agents can monitor, manage, and execute business processes in a robust and intelligent fashion, involving content- and capability-based routing of tasks, autonomous initiation and monitoring of process execution, situated recognition of and reaction to failures or other critical events, and longer-term self-optimization.

The agent layer in our conceptual architecture needs to provide methods and tools to model process-aware agents and to support (semi-)automated evaluation, selection, composition, adaptation, and robust execution of business processes.

Our perspective extends Huhns's [12] view on the relationship of agents and Web Services in the following way: While Huhns describes agents as intelligent web services, we claim that agents should be regarded primarily as driven by and responsible for business processes. While executing or monitoring business processes, they may interact or negotiate with (web) services that may again trigger agents responsible for the business process initiated by the service request. We believe that by decoupling the notion of process from the notion of service and by using the model-driven approach, we can achieve more modular, more re-usable and technology-independent specifications of multi-agent systems.

In this paper, we shall not provide a full specification of the agent layer of our architecture. This is beyond the scope of this overview paper and is a topic for future research. However, in Section 5 we sketch an agent-based process execution layer.

In the remainder of this section, we note a few requirements for an agent-enabled business process architecture.

- *Semantic process definitions*: Evaluating, composing and adapting processes and monitoring process execution require a machine-understandable description of the behavior of processes and their activities. The use of semantic markup languages, like DAML-OIL or OWL for the definition of ontologies and DAML-S for semantic service descriptions, is one obvious approach to add information on top of pure syntactical Web Services descriptions.

- *Self-organization, self-description and self-configuration:* The ability of organizations to adapt the design and execution of collaborative processes based on semantic information of the agents/organizations, the environment and the services available in its surroundings are other key functions that distinguish agents. In this context, we advocate a two-level approach where peer-to-peer concepts for resilience, de-central coordination, and self-organization are applied to achieve a short-term, reactive flexibility, and where multiagent coordination concepts such as multiagent planning are used for longer-term adaptation and self-organization (see Section 5).

- *Flexible interaction:* The availability of an open interaction model enables interaction among previously unknown parties and the tailoring of interactions to the partners capabilities and preferences by using automated negotiation. The big challenge in this context is how economically motivated agents can be equipped with domain-specific valuation models enabling them to efficiently engage in negotiations from the perspective of the business process or the organization(s) they represent.

- *Individualization*: The availability of domain-specific and extensible representations of context, profiles, and preferences is also a prerequisite for customization of e.g. services and goods to the needs or context of a person. Individualization takes the specific context or situation of a user into account and can be applied at different levels: User context, service level, interface level and infrastructure level (see e.g., [10]).

3   Application Example

To illustrate our approach, we introduce an application example taken from the UML 2.0 Superstructure specification (see Figure 2); a similar example is given in [11]. The original example describes a Supply Chain scenario with different types of activities attributed to different organizational units. In this paper, agents represent the individual units.

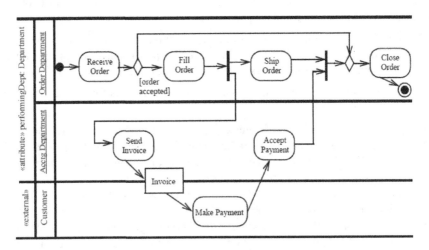

Fig. 2. UML activity diagram for the order processing example

Round-cornered rectangles denote actions, diamonds denote alternatives, rectangles denote comments, texts in brackets denote constraints. The order processing activity diagram is partitioned into "swim lanes." The three swim lanes denote the responsibilities for the different portions of the process.

The order agent initiates the process by receiving an order using *Receive Order*. This order can contain information about e.g. price and delivery date for the item corresponding to the Customer's constraints. The order agent checks the order and either rejects the order with the effect of closing the order (*Close Order*) or accepts it. In the latter case an order is filled (*Fill Order*) and two sub-processes are triggered, namely the order is shipped (*Ship Order*) and the accounting department produces the invoice and sends the invoice to the external customer (*Send Invoice*) who makes the payment (*Make Payment*). Payment is then accepted (*Accept Payment*) by the accounting department. If both sub-processes succeed the order is closed (*Close Order*).

4   Modeling Agent-Enabled Business Processes

In the remainder of this paper, we describe an instance of the conceptual architecture for agent-enabled business processes in Section 2.1. As indicated in, instantiating this architecture entails dealing with both design-time and run-time issues. In this Section, we focus on design-time aspects, i.e., at the modeling of agent-enabled business processes. In Section 5, we sketch a corresponding run-time model.

4.1 Overview

A straightforward method of implementing the conceptual architecture described in Section 2.1 would be to independently define three models corresponding to the three layers of the conceptual architecture: an agent model, a business process model, and a service model. We believe that this could be done by extending most existing methodologies, such as GAIA [24] or Tropos [9] by the business process layer, connecting agent model and service model. While doing this seems a worthwhile exercise, our approach in this paper is different. Instead of starting from the green field and describing a completely new unified framework to design the three models and their interrelationship, we set out from existing representation standards, platforms, and tools, and develop a pragmatic and simplified structure.

In this simplification, the original three-layer hierarchy is mapped into a two-stage procedure as illustrated in Figure 3. In particular, the agent layer is not explicitly represented in our development process. Rather, our idea is to enhance the service- and process-related elements with appropriate metadata and functionality. An instantiation of our model that fully complies with the three-tier architecture is left for future work.

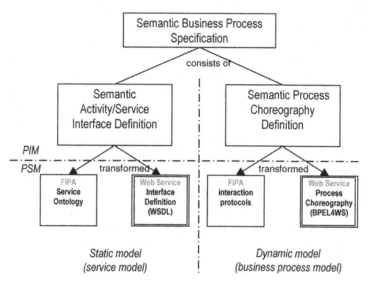

Fig. 3. Overview of model-driven development methodology for agent-enabled business processses

Figure 3 illustrates the top-down development process starting with a semantic business process specification using and extending UML 2.0 activity diagrams (similar to the one depicted in for our example). This specification consists of two models:

- a static model, which is essentially the service model in our conceptual architecture, even though enhanced with metadata, such as the description of pre- and post-conditions for service invocation, and with exception definitions;
- a dynamic model, which is essentially the business process layer in the conceptual architecture, even though enhanced with planning methods and exception handling capabilities based on the semantic service descriptions.

Each of these two models is described by one platform-independent model and one or more platform-specific models. We propose the usage of UML 2.0 for the Platform-Independent Model both for service definition and process choreography definition. In addition, we provide exemplary mappings to Platform Specific Models, using WSDL to specify the services/activities and using BPEL4WS for the process choreography. In the following, the different models and mappings are investigated in more detail. However because of lack of space we will mainly focus on WSDL and BPEL4WS.

This view is similar to that of DAML-S, however from a service specification perspective. The relevant key elements of DAML-S are:

- **Service Profiles** provide a means to describe the services offered by the providers, and the services needed by the requesters. Some properties of the profile provide human-readable information like service name, a textual description or contact information (phone, fax,…). Moreover the functionality is defined by inputs of the service, outputs of the service, preconditions of the service; and effects of the service. This is comparable with the Service Interface Definition in Figure 3.
- **Service Model** describes the processes and their composition with the related properties parameter, input, (conditional) output, participant, precondition, and (conditional) effect as well as the binding. This is comparable with the Semantic Process Choreography Definition in Figure 3.

Service Grounding specifies the details of how to access the service - details having mainly to do with protocol and message formats, serialization, transport, and addressing. A grounding can be thought of as a mapping from an abstract to a concrete specification of those service description elements that are required for interacting with the service.

For the platform independent model we propose to use Activity Diagrams (as shown in) provided in UML 2.0 to model business processes. An activity diagram depicts behavior using a control and data-flow model. In particular it describes activities and flows in different details. They are applied e.g. for business process modeling, description of use cases and in particular defining implementation relations (i.e., refinements) of operations.

4.2 Semantic Activity/Service Interface Definition

In this section we shall present a platform-independent model and an example of a platform-specific instantiation of the semantic activity/service interface definition.

4.2.1 Platform-Independent Model

Activity diagrams allow the specification of activities, as depicted in Figure 4, as a specification of a parameterized behavior that is expressed as a flow of execution by sequencing of subordinate units (whose primitive elements are individual actions).

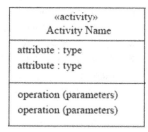

Fig. 4. Notation for activities in UML 2.0

We add the required semantic metadata information to the platform-independent model by using stereotypes in the activities, namely <<pre-conditions>>, <<post-condition>>, <<effects>> for defining the pre-conditions, post-conditions, and conditional affects of an activity. The underlying notation could be e.g. OCL from the UML specification or some Semantic Web language. This is illustrated in Figure 5.

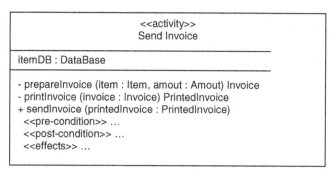

Fig. 5. Semantically enhanced activity definition

4.2.2 A Platform Specific Model Based on WSDL

4.2.2.1 Modeling Web Services Interfaces
The static description of a Web Service in WSDL is mainly concerned with defining its interfaces. A WSDL definition consists of the following parts: *Ports* define the concrete Internet address of a Web Service, i.e., its URL and communication port; *Services* cover several ports and define the physical address of an end point; *Messages* are the format for a specific information exchange, where `request` and `response` are two dedicated messages; *PortTypes* group messages to logical operations; *Bindings* bind PortTypes to their implementation, usually SOAP, and define the concrete interface of a Web Service. In [1] UML is applied for modeling WSDL descriptions.

We follow this approach for modeling WSDL descriptions. Since BPEL4WS does not require us to deal with concrete addresses and physical addresses, we will not cover *Ports* and *Services*.

One class is defined for an overall *WSDL description*. This class is stereotyped with <<wsdl description>> to mark it as a WSDL description. Each *element* of a non-complex type is modeled by stereotyped (<<element>>) attribute. *Complex types* of elements are modeled as separate classes with stereotype <<element>>.

Messages are depicted by <<wsdl message>> stereotyped operations in class diagrams; parameters denote the *part name:type* information of a message.

For each *PortType* a class is defined stereotyped with <<wsdl portType>>. This *PortType* is attached to a <<wsdl description>> class using aggregation; for each operation an operation of the class is used.

Again, for each *Binding* a class is defined stereotyped with <<wsdl binding>> and attached to a service by aggregation with <<port>> stereotype and for each operation an operation is applied.

Figure 6 illustrates an excerpt of our example specification in UML. The WSDL description has one element, i.e., *OrderDepartmentDescription*. It accepts different messages, including *receiveOrder()* and *sendInvoice()*. The parameters and their types are omitted in the figure, but can be found in the following WSDL description. The *portType sendInvoice* supports one operation, named *sendInvoiceToCustomer()*. This WSDL specification can be derived from the platform-independent model, giving additional information describing e.g. the interfaces and dependencies in detail. This example gives an idea of how the transformation can be performed.

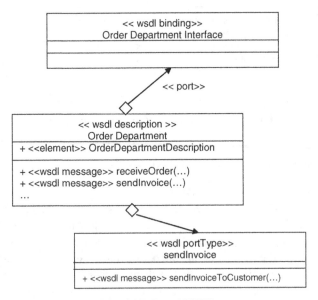

Fig. 6. UML and WSDL

4.2.2.2 Mapping UML Specifications to WSDL

The following listing shows an excerpt of the WSDL description obtained from the UML specification :

```
<definitions targetNamespace="…"
        xmlns:…
        […]
        <message name="receiveOrder">
                <part name="item" type="Item"/>
                <part name="amount" type="Amount"/>
        </message>

        <!-- portTypes supported by the Order Department -->
        <portType name="sendInvoice">
                <operation name="sendInvoiceToCustomer">
                        <input message="receiveOrder"/>
                        <output message="sendInvoice"/>
                </operation>
        </portType>
        […]
    </definitions>
```

4.3 Semantic Process Choreography Definition

Based on the service interface definitions described in the previous subsection, this section deals with dynamic aspects of semantic process choreography, i.e. with how processes are composed from activities. We start with the platform-independent modeling of semantic process choreography, and give an exemplary mapping of a PIM to a PSM based on BPEL4WS.

4.3.1 Platform Independent Model

UML 2.0 activity diagrams allow the definition of complex activities (sub-processes) defining the parameters, pre-conditions and post-conditions as shown in Figure 7.

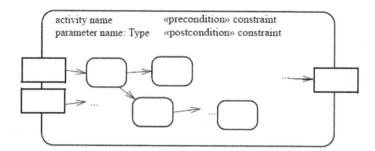

Fig. 7. Activities with parameters and pre- and post-conditions

Moreover, UML2 supports the representation of events that can be used to obtain a basic model of exceptions and exception handling behaviors. An example using the UML Accept Event Action construct is given in Figure 8.

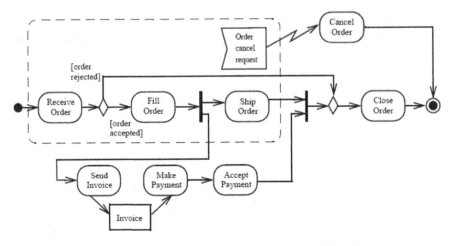

Fig. 8. Representation of events/exceptions in UML2.0

The example describes an event (denoted by the Accept Event Action *Order cancel request*) that can occur during the execution of a part of the process denoted by the dotted rectangle with rounded corners. In this case it comprises the activities *Receive Order*, *Fill Order*, and *Ship Order*. This results in cancellation of the order.

For a semantic grounding of complex activities and to describe meta-data we can add stereotypes <<effects>> and <<exceptions>> to the complex activity descriptions.

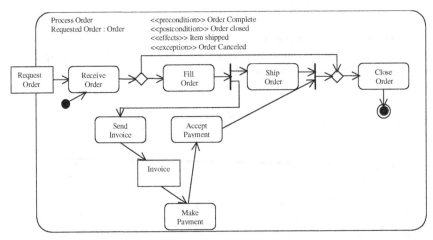

Fig. 9. The example (Figure 2) as a UML2.0 Activity Diagram; swim lanes omitted for simplicity

Figure 9 shows the UML2 activity diagram representation for the original example. The diagram contains the semantic metadata information required for use by the agent layer. It should be noted here that most of this information can actually be encoded by using existing UML2 language features. The only feature used in Figure 9 which is currently not available in UML2 are the <<effects>> and <<exceptions>> stereotype which we added for compatibility with DAML.

4.3.2 A Platform Specific Model: Mapping UML to BPEL4WS

In this section we show an exemplary instantiation of the PIM developed in Section 4.3.1 as a PSM. The basic idea is to implement the PSM by first performing a mapping from the UML activity diagrams into sequence diagrams defining the real message exchanges between the agents, and then to derive BPEL4WS process definitions from the sequence diagrams, which can be done in a relatively straightforward manner. Note, that for a fully automated transformation (code generation) additional information are necessary, which is beyond the scope of this paper. Figure 10 shows the corresponding sequence diagram (we omit the case where the order is rejected).

BPEL4WS (Business Process Execution Language for Web Services; [11]) defines a notation for specifying business process behavior based on Web Services. Processes in BPEL4WS export and import functionality via Web Service interfaces exclusively.

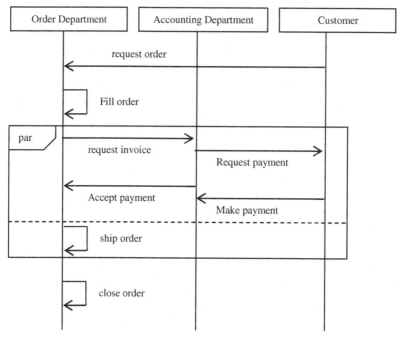

Fig. 10. PSM for Semantic Process Choreography Definition

The process specified in Figure 9 (including its representation as a sequence diagram shown in Figure 10) defines a re-usable process template. E.g., for the order department, it can be written in pseudo-code as follows:

```
while (ordering) do
    receive request order
    invoke fill order
    parallel
        seq
            receive accept-payment
            invoke payment-accepted
        invoke ship-order
    close order
od
```

```
<process name="Process Order"
    targetNamespace=[...]
    xmlns=[...]
    <partners>
        <partner name="AccountingDepartment"
            serviceLinkType="Accounting"
            partnerRole="accounting"
            myRole="order department"/>
    </partners>
    <assign> order-continue-yes=true </assign>
    <while condition="order-continue-yes"
        <sequence>
            <receive partner="Customer"
                portType="OrderInformation"
                operation="orderItem"
                inputContainer="item">
            </receive>
            <invoke partner="OrderDepartment"
                portType="OrderItem"
                operation="order">
            </invoke>
            <flow>
              <sequence>
                <receive partner="AccountingDepartment"
                    portType="SendInvoice"
                    operation="sendInvoiceToCustomer"
                    inputContainer="receivedOrder">
                </receive>
                <invoke partner="OrderingDepartment"
                    portType="PaymentAcception"
                    operation="acceptPayment">
                </invoke>

              </sequence>
                <invoke partner="OrderingDepartment"
                    portType="ShipingOrders"
                    operation="shipOrder">
                </invoke>
            </flow>
            <invoke partner="OrderingDepartment"
                portType="ShipOrdering"
                operation="shipOrder">
            </invoke>
        </sequence>
    </while>
</process>
```

Fig. 11. BPEL4WS Representation of the example process

Figure 11 illustrates the BPEL4WS definition of this example process. The business processes use the following components of BPEL4WS (following [13]):

- *Service Linking, Partners and Service References*: The relationship of a business process with a partner is typically peer-to-peer, requiring a two-way dependency at the service level. The notion of service links is used to directly model peer-to-peer partner relationships. Service links define the relationship with a partner by the message and port types used in the interactions in both directions. However, the actual partner service may be dynamically determined within the process.

- *Messages Properties*: The data in a message consists conceptually of two parts: application data and protocol-relevant data, where the protocols can be business protocols or infrastructure protocols providing higher quality of service, like security and transaction. The business protocol data is usually found embedded in the application-visible message parts, whereas the infrastructure protocols almost always add implicit extra parts to the message types to represent protocol headers that are separate from application data. Business processes might need to gain access to and manipulate both kinds of protocol-relevant data. The notion of message properties is defined as a general way of naming and representing distinguished data elements within a message, whether in application-visible data or in message context. Message properties are defined in a sufficiently general way to cover message context consisting of implicit parts, but the use focuses on properties embedded in application-visible data that is used in the definition of business protocols and abstract business processes. A property definition creates a globally unique name and associates it with an XML Schema type. The intent is to create a name that has greater significance than the type itself.

- *Data Handling:* Business processes model stateful interactions. The state involved consists of messages received and sent as well as other relevant data such as timeout values. The maintenance of the state of a business process requires the use of state variables, which are called containers. Furthermore, the data from the state needs to be extracted and combined in interesting ways to control the behavior of the process, which requires data expressions. Finally, state update requires the notion of assignment. BPEL4WS provides these features for XML data types and WSDL message types. In BPEL4WS, Data handling is performed by using the following features:

  - *Expressions*: BPEL4WS uses several types of expressions: Boolean-valued expressions used for transition conditions, join conditions, while conditions, and switch cases; deadline-valued expressions used with the "until" attribute of onAlarm and wait; duration-valued expressions used for "for" attribute of onAlarm and wait; general expressions based on XPath 1.0 used in assignments. Moreover, BPEL4WS provides an extensible mechanism for the language used in these expressions. The language is specified by the *expressionLanguage* attribute of the process element.

  - *Containers:* Containers provide the means for holding messages that constitute the state of a business process. Containers can hold messages, either received or temporary defined, that act as "temporary variables" for computation and are never exchanged with partners. Containers can be specified as input or output containers for invoke, receive, and reply activities. At the beginning of a process all containers are not initialized. Containers can be initialized by a variety of means including assignment and receiving a message. Containers can be partially initialized with property assignment or when some but not all parts in the message type of the container are assigned values.

- *Assignments:* Copying data from one container to another is a common task within a business process. The *assign* activity can be used to copy data from one container to another, as well as to construct and insert new data using expressions.

- *Activities*: BPEL4WS distinguishes between two types of activities: basic and structured activities.

  - *basic activities*: The `receive` construct allows the business process to do a blocking wait for a matching message to arrive. The `reply` construct allows the business process to send a message in reply to a message that was received through a `receive`. The combination of a `receive` and a `reply` forms a request-response operation on the WSDL portType for the process. The `invoke` construct allows the business process to invoke a one-way or request-response operation on a portType offered by a partner. The `assign` construct can be used to update the values of containers with new data. An `assign` construct can contain any number of elementary assignments. The `throw` construct generates a fault from inside the business process. The `terminate` construct allows to immediately terminate a business process. The `wait` construct allows to wait for a given time period or until a certain time has passed. Exactly one of the expiration criteria must be specified. The `empty` construct enables insertion of "no-op" instructions into business processes. This is useful for synchronization of parallel activities, for instance.

  - *structured activities*: The `sequence` construct allows one to define a collection of activities to be performed sequentially. The `switch` construct allows selecting exactly one branch of execution from a set of choices. The `while` construct allows one to indicate that an activity is to be repeated until a certain success criteria has been met. The `pick` construct allows blocking and waiting for exactly a suitable message to arrive or for a time-out alarm to go off. When one of these triggers occurs, the associated activity is executed and the pick completes. The `flow` construct allows specifying one or more activities to be executed in parallel. Links can be used within parallel activities to define arbitrary control structures. The `scope` construct allows defining a nested activity with its own associated fault and compensation handlers. The `compensate` construct is used to invoke compensation on an inner scope that has already completed its execution normally. This construct can be invoked only from within a fault handler or another compensation handler.

5 Agent-Enabled Business Process Enactment

In this section, we sketch an infrastructure for agent-enabled business process enactment. This infrastructure is an instance of the model-driven architecture framework described in Section 4. Figure 12 shows the architecture of the run-time system.

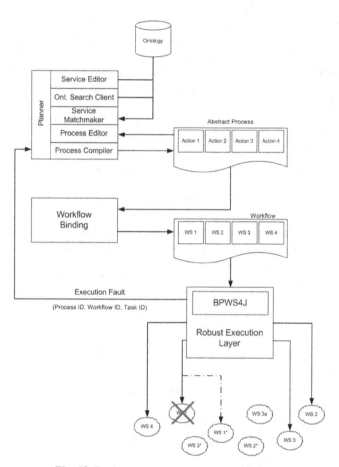

Fig. 12. Business process enactment architecture

The system is arranged in a two-tier hybrid architecture [19]. The upper tier provides a planning mechanism based on a library of process descriptions, the process repository. In the ideal case the planner starts from the platform independent description of the process descriptions, performs the planning and transforms this platform independent processes or workflows into platform specific processes and workflows, like BPEL4WS. Currently, the planner selects plans from the plan library based on a goal description and a precondition (both of which are first order formulae matched against plan metadata). The planning tier provides a number of additional tools such as a service editor, a service matchmaker used to find suitable service instances, and a process editor and compiler which are able to create abstract process descriptions to populate the process repository. When an entry in the process repository matching a pair `<goal, precondition>` has been found, a BPEL4WS workflow instance is generated by a workflow-binding module. This module instantiates variables in the abstract process by constants obtained by the matching with `<goal, precondition>`. Thus, each abstract action in the process description is instantiated by a task corresponding to a web service invocation. The corresponding workflow is then passed on to the business process execution engine. In our current implementation, we use IBMs BPWS4J business process execution engine to enact BPEL4WS business process descriptions which have been generated from UML2 representations. Existing fields of BPEL4WS process descriptions are used to transfer identifying information of processes, workflows, and tasks from the planning to the execution layer and back.

The business process execution engine now executes the workflow step-by-step. However, instead of directly calling individual web services, the calls from the execution engine go to the lower tier, the so-called Robust Execution Layer (REL), which acts as a proxy for the execution engine. The intention of the REL is to provide a higher level of execution reliability. This is achieved by means of an underlying peer-to-peer network maintained by the REL. In our implementation, we use the Resource Management Framework (RMF) developed at Siemens [7]. Individual web services are registered as resources in the peer-to-peer system. Services can be replicated using the RMF's replication mechanism. If a selected service fails, the Robust Execution Layer tries to transparently re-route the request to a replicated service and carries out compensation activities if necessary to prevent or resolve inconsistent transactional states. E.g., if the task represented by web service WS1 fails (see Figure 12), the RMF can transparently re-route the request to the replicated web service WS1*.

A simple rollback concept is provided to compensate in case of failure. For this, the BPEL4WS task descriptions contain links to compensation actions. If a task fails (e.g., WS3) and the REF is not able to find an alternative (replicated) service, the REL will call an appropriate fault handler in the execution engine. Then, the execution engine tries to compensate the previously executed tasks, starting with the most recent ones. If a task does not have a compensation routine, or compensation fails, the rollback stops and the process execution engine reports an execution fault to the planner (see Figure 12). For instance, assume that WS3 and WS1 can be compensated, but WS2 cannot. In this case, a failure would be reported indicating the identifier of the abstract process, of the workflow instance and of the failed task (in this case WS3).

The planner will then try and elaborate alternatives either by trying to locally amend the plan (e.g., suggesting an alternative task WS3a), or by looking up an alternative process in the business process repository, taking the effects of the performed tasks that could not be compensated into account. The amended process description is again instantiated and the corresponding BPEL4WS workflow is sent to the Robust Execution Layer.

6 Conclusions and Outlook

The foremost goal of this paper was to point out a relationship between the programming of multiagent systems, which is the key topic of the volume at hand, and the design of agent-enabled business processes. Our key thesis here is that designing business processes based on an agent-enabled business processes modeling and enactment framework should be regarded as a very practicable way of programming specific types of agents, i.e., agents that assist humans and organizations in monitoring, managing, and optimizing business processes.

The technical contributions of this paper were the (i) definition of a conceptual architecture of agent-enabled business process management that cleanly separates between agent capabilities, business process modeling, and the modeling of services that are employed to actually implement processes; (ii) a sketch of implementing the conceptual architecture based on using the Model-Driven Architecture (MDA) paradigm at all three layers of the agent-enabled business process architecture, in order to allow system designers to focus on the functionality and behavior of a distributed application or system, independent of the technology or technologies in which it will be implemented; and (iii) to outline an instance of a platform independent model based on the new UML2 standard, extending the scope of the Unified Modeling Language to the design of processes, and sketch a mapping to a platform dependent model based on the Business Process Execution Language for Web Services (BPEL4WS). We discuss design-time and run-time aspects of a methodology for agent-enabled business process modeling.

As noted in the introduction, the current paper deliberately leaves a number of questions and technical issues open. Firstly, this includes most of the agent layer of the conceptual architecture. Currently we have shown how semantic process and service information can be modeled in a technology-neutral way using industrial modeling standards. Obviously, it will also be necessary to model the agents that actually make use of this information. We believe that current agent design methodologies can be used at this point; however, certain extensions may be required to make these methodologies cope with the notion of business processes and to leverage the concept of a Model-Driven Architecture to the agent layer. Achieving this requires further research.

A second open issue is the extension of our model to enable code generation. In order to be able to generate executable code from platform-specific models, transformation rules will need to be designed and additional platform-specific information needs to be encoded. We believe that these transformation rules can be defined directly on the UML meta model. However, the verification of this hypothesis is open.

In summary, there is still some way to go to achieve the vision of business-process aware agents that can understand semantically enhanced business process definitions, that can help in the design of business processes, that can select appropriate business processes for execution, monitor distributed business process execution, recognize and fix problems in a collaborative manner. We hope that with this paper, we succeeded in setting a starting point and defining an overall approach that will help researchers and practitioners to ultimately build such technology based on existing standards for service-oriented computing, business process management, and software architecture.

References

1. Armstrong, Ch. (2002) 'Modelling Web Services with UML', Talk given at the OMG Web Services Workshop 2002.
2. Barbuceanu, M., Fox M.S. (1997) 'Coordinating Multiple Agents in the Supply Chain'. Proceedings of WET-ICE 97, Boston, pp. 134-141.
3. B. Bauer, J. P. Müller, J. Odell: Agent UML: A Formalism for Specifying Multiagent Software Systems. International Journal of Software Engineering and Knowledge Engineering (IJSEKE) 11(3): 207-230, 2001.
4. BPMI (2003), 10 June, http://www.bpmi.org/
5. ebXML (2003) 'ebXML Business Process Specification Schema', June 2003, http://www.ebxml.org/specs/ebBPSS.pdf
6. FIPA (2003), FIPA specifications, http://www.fipa.org/specs/fipa00030/
7. Friese T., Freisleben B., Rusitschka S., Southall A. A Framework for Resource Management in Peer-to-Peer Networks. In Proceedings of NetObjectDays 2002, Volume 2591 of Lecture Notes in Computer Science, pp. 4—21, Springer-Verlag.
8. Fuchs, I. (2002) 'Web Services and Business Process Management Platforms – Understanding Their Relationship and Defining an Implementation Approach', http://www.ebpml.org/ihf.doc
9. Giunchiglia F., Mylopoulos J, and Perini A. The Tropos Software Development Methodology: Processes, Models, and Diagrams. In Agent-oriented Software Engineering III. Lecture Notes in Computer Science, volume 2585, pp. 162—173. Springer-Verlag, 2003.
10. Guo Y., J. P. Müller, C. Weinhardt. Learning User Preferences for Multi-attribute Negotiation: An Evolutionary Approach. In Proceedings of the 3rd International Central and Eastern European Conference on Multi-Agent Systems, volume 2691 of Lecture Notes in Artificial Intelligence, pages 303-310, Prague, Czech Republic. Springer-Verlag, 2003.
11. Huget M.-P. "An Application of Agent UML to Supply Chain Management". In Proceedings of Agent Oriented Information System (AOIS-02), Paolo Giorgini and Yves Lespérance and Gerd Wagner and Eric Yu (eds.), Bologna, Italie, July 2002. (Short presentation of the technical report ULCS-02-015)
12. Huhns, M.N. (2002) 'Agents as Web Services', IEEE Internet Computing, July/August 2002, pp. 93-95.
13. IBM (2003) BPEL4WS: Business Process Execution Language for Web Services, http://www-106.ibm.com/developerworks/webservices/library/ws-bpel/
14. IBM Business Process Execution Language for Web Services Java Run Time. http://www.alphaworks.ibm.com/tech/bpws4j
15. Jennings N.R., P. Faratin, T. J. Norman, P. O'Brien and B. Odgers (2000) "Autonomous Agents for Business Process Management" Int. Journal of Applied Artificial Intelligence 14 (2) 145-189.
16. Jennings N.R., K. Sycara, and M. Wooldridge. A Roadmap of Agent Research and Development. Autonomous Agents and Multi-Agent Systems, 1(1):7--38, 1998.
17. Model Driven Architecture homepage. The Object Management Group (OMG). http://www.omg.org/mda/

18. Müller, J.P., Bauer, B. (2002) 'Agent-oriented Software Technologies: Flaws and Reme-dies', *Proceedings of Workshop on Agent Oriented Software Engineering (AOSE 2002)*, Bologna, pp. 210-227.

19. Müller, J.P. The Design of Autonomous Agents – A Layered Approach, volume 1177 of Lecture Notes in Artificial Intelligence. Springer-Verlag, 1996.

20. Radjou, N., Orlov, L. M., und Nakashima, T.: Adaptive Agents Boost Supply Network Flexibility. 2002. March 2002 Tech Strategy Brief. Forrester Research.

21. Thöne, S., Depke R., Engels G. (2002) 'Process-Oriented, Flexible Composition of Web Services with UML', Proc. of Joint Workshop on Conceptual Modeling Approaches for e-Business (eCOMO 2002); Tampere; (to appear)

22. UML Homepage. The Object Management Group. http://www.omg.org/uml/

23. W3C Web Services glossary. http://www.w3.org/TR/ws-gloss/

24. Wooldridge M., Jennings J.R., and Kinny D. The Gaia Methodology for Agent-Oriented Analysis and Design. Journal of Autonomous Agents and Multiagent Systems, volume 3, number 3, 2000, pp. 285—312.

25. Kleppe M., Warmer J., Bast W. MDA Explained – The Model Driven Architecture: Prac-tice and Promise, Addison Wesley, 2003

Verifiable Multi-agent Programs

Rafael H. Bordini[1], Michael Fisher[1], Willem Visser[2], and Michael Wooldridge[1]

[1] Department of Computer Science
University of Liverpool
Liverpool L69 3BX, UK
{R.Bordini,M.Fisher,M.J.Wooldridge}@csc.liv.ac.uk
[2] RIACS/NASA Ames Research Center
Moffett Field, CA 94035, USA
wvisser@email.arc.nasa.gov

Abstract. AgentSpeak is a reactive planning language for programming autonomous agents. It has recently been shown that model checking techniques can be applied to the verification of AgentSpeak systems, through a translation to PROMELA, the model specification language for the SPIN LTL model-checking system. In this paper, we introduce an alternative verification approach for AgentSpeak, by translating AgentSpeak to Java and then applying JPF2, a general purpose Java model checker. The primary advantage of this approach is that Java is the language of choice for most agent implementations, and the approach is thus much closer to the current practice of agent development than the PROMELA-based approach. Also, models of AgentSpeak agents represented in Java are both clearer and more natural than those given in PROMELA. We examine both alternatives by means of a practical application, provide a qualitative comparison between them, and identify some key issues for future research.

1 Introduction

In order to provide generic development tools for rational agents, a number of rational agent programming languages are now being developed, for example by extending conventional programming languages with capabilities from the BDI (Belief-Desire-Intention) theory of agency [23, 28]. Such languages provide high-level abstractions that aid the construction of dynamic, autonomous components, together with the deliberation that goes on within them. AgentSpeak(L) is an influential example of such a language [21]. AgentSpeak(L) is essentially a logic programming language with abstractions provided for key aspects of rational agency, such as beliefs, goals and plans.

As agent-based systems are increasingly deployed, the *verification* of such systems – showing that a system is correct with respect to its specification – is a correspondingly important issue, especially as agent systems are applied to safety-critical applications such as autonomous spacecraft control [19]. However, there is so far a lack of verification tools specifically designed with *rational* agents in mind, and this issue is the main focus of this paper. Currently, the most

M. Dastani, J. Dix, A. El Fallah-Seghrouchni (Eds.): PROMAS 2003, LNAI 3067, pp. 72–89, 2004.

successful approach to the verification of computer systems against formally expressed requirements is that of *model checking* [6]. Model checking was originally developed for verifying that finite state concurrent systems implement specifications expressed in temporal logic. Historically, model-checking techniques have been most widely applied to the verification of hardware systems, but recently they have been increasingly used in the verification of software systems and communications protocols [14, 27].

Our aim in this paper is to consider model checking techniques for verifying systems implemented in AgentSpeak(L). In [3], preliminary model-checking techniques for AgentSpeak(L) were reported. That work was based on a translation from AgentSpeak(L) to PROMELA, the finite state model specification language for the SPIN LTL model checker [14]. In this paper, we present an alternative approach, based on the translation of AgentSpeak(L) agents into Java and verifying via a general purpose Java model checker [27]. The set of tools derived from the work on both approaches is called CASP, and was briefly described in [5]. We present an example scenario, with comparative qualitative results obtained for the two approaches. Thus, this work forms the basis for increasingly sophisticated rational agent verification techniques to be developed in the future, particularly through translation to Java.

This paper is structured as follows. The next section presents AgentSpeak(L), a BDI logic programming language inspired by reactive planning systems. Section 3 presents our approach to programming and verifying multi-agent systems. It presents the AgentSpeak(F) language, a finite state version of AgentSpeak(L), and it presents a simplified BDI logic in which properties to be verified against AgentSpeak(F) multi-agent systems can be written. Our approach allows us to take advantage of existing LTL model-checkers; in Section 4, we briefly recall our previous work on using SPIN [14], but we also mention a new alternative, which is to use JPF2 [27]. We describe a practical experience with model checking an AgentSpeak(F) system in Section 5; we use here a scenario with two garbage collecting robots. That section also briefly compares SPIN and JPF2. Finally, we discuss related work in Section 6 and discuss future work and conclusions in Section 7.

2   AgentSpeak(L)

The AgentSpeak(L) programming language was introduced in [21]. It is a natural extension of logic programming for the BDI agent architecture, and provides an elegant abstract framework for programming BDI agents. In this paper, we only give a brief introduction to AgentSpeak(L); see [21, 4] for more details.

An AgentSpeak(L) agent is created by the specification of a set of base beliefs and a set of plans. A *belief atom* is simply a first-order predicate in the usual notation, and belief atoms or their negations are *belief literals*. An *initial set of beliefs* is just a collection of ground belief atoms.

AgentSpeak(L) distinguishes two types of goals: *achievement goals* and *test goals*. Achievement goals are predicates (as for beliefs) prefixed with the '!' operator, while test goals are prefixed with the '?'operator. Achievement goals state that the agent wants to achieve a state of the world where the associated predicate is true. (In practice, these start off the execution of *subplans*.) A *test goal* states that the agent wants to test whether the associated predicate is one of its beliefs (i.e., whether it can be unified with a predicate in that agent's base beliefs).

Next, the notion of a *triggering event* is introduced. It is a very important concept in this language, as triggering events define which events may initiate the execution of plans; the idea of *event*, both internal and external, will be made clear below. There are two types of triggering events: those related to the *addition* ('+') and *deletion* ('−') of mental attitudes (beliefs or goals).

Plans refer to the *basic actions* that an agent is able to perform on its environment. Such actions are also defined as first-order predicates, but with special predicate symbols (called *action symbols*) used to distinguish them. The actual syntax of AgentSpeak(L) programs is based on the definition of plans, below. Recall that the designer of an AgentSpeak(L) agent specifies a set of beliefs and a set of plans only.

If e is a triggering event, $b_1, \ldots, b_m$ are belief literals, and $h_1, \ldots, h_n$ are goals or actions, then "$e : b_1 \wedge \ldots \wedge b_m \leftarrow h_1; \ldots; h_n.$" is a *plan*. An AgentSpeak(L) plan has a *head* (the expression to the left of the arrow), which is formed from a triggering event (denoting the purpose for that plan), and a conjunction of belief literals representing a *context* (separated from the triggering event by ':'). The conjunction of literals in the context must be satisfied if the plan is to be executed (the context must be a logical consequence of that agent's current beliefs). A plan also has a *body*, which is a sequence of basic actions or (sub)goals that the agent has to achieve (or test) when the plan is triggered.

Although the interpretation of AgentSpeak(L) programs is not explained here, some of the related notions are given next. *Intentions* are particular courses of actions to which an agent has committed in order to achieve a particular goal; each intention is a stack of *partially instantiated plans*, i.e., plans where some of the variables have been instantiated. An *event*, which may trigger the execution of a plan, can be *external*, when originating from perception of the agent's environment, or *internal*, when generated from the agent's own execution of a plan (e.g., an achievement goal within a plan body is a goal-addition event which may be a triggering event). An agent's definition also includes three selection functions: $\mathcal{S}_{\mathcal{E}}$ selects an event from the set of events; $\mathcal{S}_{\mathcal{O}}$ selects an option or an applicable plan from a set of applicable plans; and $\mathcal{S}_{\mathcal{I}}$ selects an intention from the set of intentions (the chosen intention is then executed).

3   Verifying AgentSpeak(F) Systems

Recall that our main goal in this research is to facilitate model checking of AgentSpeak(L) systems. However, model checking as a paradigm is predominantly applied to *finite state* systems. A first key step in our research was thus to restrict AgentSpeak(L) to finite state systems: the result is AgentSpeak(F), a finite state version of AgentSpeak(L). This language was first defined in [3] and is briefly presented here so that we can later give an example of our approach to programming and verifying multi-agent systems. The idea is to translate multi-agent systems defined in this language into the input language of existing model checkers, so that we can take advantage of the extensive range of tools for model checking that are available.

Further, we would like to be able to verify that systems implemented in AgentSpeak(L) satisfy (or do not satisfy) properties expressed in a BDI logic [23]. Such logics formalise all the main concepts of the BDI architecture used in reactive planning systems such as those generated by AgentSpeak(L) agents. This section also presents a simplified form of BDI logic which we are able to convert into Linear Temporal Logic (LTL) formulæ, so that we can use existing LTL model-checkers for verifying our multi-agent systems.

The purpose of this section is to introduce the features and limitations of the languages used in our approach to code the system and to produce specifications the system should satisfy. Their use will be made clear in Section 5, where we present a case study.

3.1   AgentSpeak(F)

The grammar in Figure 1 gives the concrete syntax of AgentSpeak(F). In the grammar, P stands for any predicate symbol, A for action symbols, and terms t_i are either constants or variables. As in Prolog, an uppercase initial letter is used for variables and lowercase for constants and predicate symbols (cf., Prolog atoms). Note that first order terms (cf., Prolog structures) are not allowed in the present version of AgentSpeak(F); we discuss this restriction later.

$$
\begin{array}{llll}
ag & ::= & bs \ ps & \\
bs & ::= & at_1. \ \ldots \ at_n. & (n \geq 0) \\
at & ::= & \mathsf{P}(t_1, \ldots, t_n) & (n \geq 0) \\
ps & ::= & p_1 \ \ldots \ p_n & (n \geq 1) \\
p & ::= & te : ct \ \texttt{<-} \ h \ . & \\
te & ::= & \texttt{+}at \ \mid \ \texttt{-}at \ \mid \ \texttt{+}g \ \mid \ \texttt{-}g & \\
ct & ::= & \texttt{true} \ \mid \ l_1 \ \& \ldots \& \ l_n & (n \geq 1) \\
h & ::= & \texttt{true} \ \mid \ f_1 \ ; \ \ldots \ ; \ f_n & (n \geq 1) \\
l & ::= & at \ \mid \ \texttt{not} \ (\ at \ ) & \\
f & ::= & \mathsf{A}(t_1, \ldots, t_n) \ \mid \ g \ \mid \ u & (n \geq 0) \\
g & ::= & \texttt{!}at \ \mid \ \texttt{?}at & \\
u & ::= & \texttt{+}at \ \mid \ \texttt{-}at &
\end{array}
$$

Fig. 1. The Concrete Syntax of AgentSpeak(F).

There are some special action symbols which are denoted by an initial '.' character (they are referred to as internal actions in [2]). The action '.send' is used for inter-agent communication, and is interpreted as follows. If an AgentSpeak(F) agent l_1 executes .send(l_2, ilf, at), a message will be inserted in the mailbox of agent l_2, having l_1 as sender, illocutionary force ilf, and propositional content at (an atomic AgentSpeak(F) formula). At this stage, only three illocutionary forces can be used: tell, untell, and achieve (unless others are defined by the user). They have the same informal semantics as in the well-known KQML agent communication language [17]. In particular, achieve corresponds to including *at* as a goal addition in the receiving agent's set of events; tell and untell change the belief base and the appropriate events are generated. These communicative acts only change an agent's internal data structures after user-defined trust functions are checked. There is one specific trust function for belief changes, and another for achievement goals. The latter defines a power relation (as other agents have power over an agent's goals), whereas the belief trust function simply defines the trustworthiness of information sources.

Another internal action symbol that is available is .print, which takes a string as a parameter and is used for printing out messages. Other pre-defined internal actions are, for example, used for conditional and arithmetic operations.

The main difference between AgentSpeak(F) and AgentSpeak(L) is that first order terms are disallowed. The full set of features currently disallowed in AgentSpeak(F) are as follows:

- uninstantiated variables in triggering events;
- uninstantiated variables in negated literals in a plan's context (as originally defined by Rao [21]);
- the same predicate symbol with different arities (at present, the different predicates would be treated as the same, with either random extra arguments or ignoring some of them);
- first order terms (rather than just constants and variables).

The first restriction means that an achievement goal cannot be called with an uninstantiated variable; this is the usual means for a goal to return values to be used in the plan where it was called. However, as mentioned in [16], this restriction can be overcome by storing such values in the belief base, and using test goals to retrieve them. Hence, syntactic mechanisms for dealing with this restriction can be implemented (i.e., this problem can be solved by preprocessing). On the second restriction, we point out that the interpreter presented in [2] allows for uninstantiated variables in negated literals. However, this was not allowed in Rao's original definition of AgentSpeak(L), so the second restriction is not an unreasonable one.

Finally, we remark that the multi-agent system is specified by the user as a collection of AgentSpeak(F) source files, one for each agent in the system. The user can change various predefined functions which are part of the interpretation of AgentSpeak(L) agents. Also, the user has to provide the environment where the agents will be situated; this must be done in the model language of the model checker itself rather than AgentSpeak(F).

3.2   Specifying BDI Properties

In the context of verifying multi-agent systems implemented in AgentSpeak(L), the most appropriate way of specifying the properties that the system satisfy (or do not satisfy) is by expressing those properties using BDI logics [23]. In this section, we show how simple BDI logical properties can be mapped down into Linear Temporal Logic (LTL) formulæ and associated predicates over the AgentSpeak(L) data structures in the system.

In [4], a way of interpreting the informational, motivational, and deliberative modalities of BDI logics for AgentSpeak(L) agents was given; this is based on the operational semantics of AgentSpeak(L). This framework was used to prove which of the asymmetry thesis principles [23] are enforced by AgentSpeak(L). This is relevant in assuring the rationality of agents programmed in Agent-Speak(L). In this work, we use that same framework for interpreting the BDI modalities in terms of data structures within the model of an AgentSpeak(F) agent given in the model checker input language. This way, we can translate (temporal) BDI properties into LTL formulæ. The particular logical language that is used for specifying such properties is given next.

The logical language we use here is a simplified version of $\mathcal{LORA}$ [28], which is based on modal logics of intentionality, dynamic logic, and CTL*. In the restricted version of the logic used here, we limit the underlying temporal logics to LTL rather than CTL*, given that LTL formulæ (excluding the "next" operator $\bigcirc$) can be automatically processed by our target model-checkers. Other restrictions, aimed at making the logic directly translatable into LTL formulæ, are described below.

Let pe be any valid boolean expression in the model specification language of the model checker being used, l be any agent label, x be a variable ranging over agent labels, and at and a be atomic and action formulæ defined in the AgentSpeak(F) syntax (see Section 3.1), except with no variables allowed. Then the set of well-formed formulæ (wff) of this logical language is defined inductively as follows:

1. pe is a wff;
2. at is a wff;
3. (Bel l at), (Des l at), and (Int l at) are wff;
4. $\forall x.(M\ x\ at)$ and $\exists x.(M\ x\ at)$ are wff, where $M \in \{\mathsf{Bel}, \mathsf{Des}, \mathsf{Int}\}$ and x ranges over a finite set of agent labels;
5. (Does l a) is a wff;
6. if φ and ψ are wff, so are $(\neg\varphi)$, $(\varphi \wedge \psi)$, $(\varphi \vee \psi)$, $(\varphi \Rightarrow \psi)$, $(\varphi \Leftrightarrow \psi)$, always $(\Box\varphi)$, eventually $(\Diamond\varphi)$, until $(\varphi\ \mathcal{U}\ \psi)$, and "release", the dual of until $(\varphi\ \mathcal{R}\ \psi)$;
7. nothing else is a wff.

In the syntax above, agent labels denoted by l, and over which variable x ranges, are the ones associated with each AgentSpeak(F) program during the translation process. That is, the labels given as input to the translator form the finite set of agent labels over which the quantifiers are defined. The only unusual operator in this language is (Does l a), which holds if the agent denoted by l has requested action a and that is the next action to be executed by the environment. An AgentSpeak(F) atomic formula at is used to refer to what is actually true of the environment. In practical terms, this amounts to checking whether the predicate is in the data structure where the percepts are stored by the environment. We do not give semantics (even informally) to the other operators above, as they have been extensively used in the multi-agent systems literature, and formal semantics can be found in the references given above.

The concrete syntax used in the system for writing formulæ of the language above is also dependent on the underlying model checker. Before we pass the LTL formula on to the model checker, we translate Bel, Des, and Int into predicates accessing the AgentSpeak(F) data structures modelled in the model checker's input language (according to the definitions in the previous section). The Does modality is implemented by checking the first action in the environment's data structure where agents insert the actions they want to see executed by the environment process That first item in such data structure is the action that is going to be executed next by the environment (as soon as it is scheduled for execution).

4   Using Existing Model Checkers

4.1   Previous Work on Using SPIN

In [3], we showed how to convert programs in AgentSpeak(F) into PROMELA, so that SPIN could be used in model-checking AgentSpeak(F) systems. In fact, the restrictions imposed on AgentSpeak(F) in relation to AgentSpeak(L) were aimed at facilitating the generation of PROMELA models of BDI agents. In order to ensure that AgentSpeak(F) multi-agent systems to be model checked could be converted into PROMELA, the maximum size of types, data structures, and communication channels must be specified. This means that, for a translator from AgentSpeak(L)-like programs into a model checking system to work, it requires a series of parameters stating the expected maximum number of entries in certain data structures used in an AgentSpeak(L) interpreter. The list of all parameters needed by our automatic translator is given in [3]. Having a PROMELA model of the AgentSpeak(F) multi-agent system and a LTL formula representing the original BDI specification (following the approach mentioned in Section 3.2), we can then use SPIN to formally verify our systems.

4.2   JPF2

Java PathFinder 2 (JPF2) [27] is an explicit state on-the-fly model checker that takes compiled Java programs (i.e., bytecode class-files) and analyses all paths through the program the bytecodes represent for deadlock, assertion violations and linear time temporal logic (LTL) properties. An earlier version of JPF2, called JPF1, translated Java source code to PROMELA to allow model checking with SPIN, whereas JPF2 analyses Java bytecodes directly with the aid of a special purpose Java Virtual Machine (JVM). JPF2 can therefore analyse any Java program, even one making heavy use of Java libraries – as is the case for the

AgentSpeak(F) model used here. However, because JPF2 works on the bytecode level, rather than an abstract model specification (as is the case with PROMELA), it is considerably slower than SPIN.

4.3 Java Models of AgentSpeak(F) Agents

In order to use JPF2 as the underlying model-checker, we need to translate our AgentSpeak(F) multi-agent systems into Java code rather than PROMELA. Obviously, this is a much easier task, as PROMELA is a very limited language (as it is intended for the verification of simple communication protocols). While we followed the main ideas used in generating a PROMELA model of the system [3], the Java model is *much* more elegant, as we can use instances of objects (such as plans) in representing the set of intentions (a set of partially instantiated plans). Also, in Java, we can handle such things as unification of logical terms in a much simpler way, and even manage a proper "plan library" which was not possible in PROMELA (where the resulting part of the model accounting for the plan library was very cumbersome).

The translation from AgentSpeak(F) to Java is fully automated; that is, it does not require any manual work from the users. Note, however, that this is for AgentSpeak(F) only, the restricted version of AgentSpeak(L) presented in Section 3.1. The translation to Java can be also quite useful for the development of agent-based applications: users can specify the agents' high-level reasoning in AgentSpeak and also have the advantages of Java code (e.g., portability and integration with existing agent software).

Our AgentSpeak(F) model in PROMELA was already known to be very demanding in terms of memory and processing time needed during verification by SPIN, and similar problems occurred with JPF2. In Section 7 we mention how we plan to tackle this problem in future work. Meanwhile, in order to reduce the state space generated by the model checkers, we have fixed an order in which the agents run, and each is given one AgentSpeak(L) reasoning cycle in turn (agents' execution is, of course, interspersed with the execution of the environment). This is not ideal as it slightly changes the semantics of the AgentSpeak(L) system, but note that some existing agent-based systems actually simulate multi-agent systems (e.g. [26]) in this very same way; it simply means giving a strictly fair distribution of computational resources, as one agent cannot perform more reasoning cycles than the others in a given period of time. This change was made both in the PROMELA and in the Java models of AgentSpeak(F).

5   Model Checking in Practice

To the best of our knowledge, this is the first study where two model checkers are compared in the verification of the same high-level agent description. In this section, we report a practical exercise in model-checking multi-agent systems following the approach described in the previous section where both JPF2 and SPIN have been used. The scenario used here is clearly not a fully described problem, but it shows an important aspect of multi-agent systems, which is the natural abstraction that results from separating high-level reasoning from the details of acting in an environment. The idea is to verify that the general reasoning of agents is correct, before moving to implementation.

5.1   The Mars Scenario

The scenario used here involves two robots that are collecting garbage on the planet Mars. Robot r1 searches for pieces of garbage and when one is found, the robot picks it up, takes it to the location of r2, drops the garbage there, and returns to the location where it found the garbage and continues its search from that position. Robot r2 is situated at an incinerator; whenever garbage is taken to its location by r1, r2 just puts it in the incinerator. One or two pieces of garbage are randomly scattered on the grid. Another source of non-determinism is a certain imprecision of the robot's arm that grabs the pieces of garbage. The action of picking up garbage may fail, but it is assumed that the mechanism is good enough so that it never fails more than twice; that is, in the worst case robot r1 has to attempt to pick up a piece of garbage three times, but by then r1 will definitely have grabbed it. The Mars terrain to be cleared of pieces of garbage is abstractly represented here as a finite 2D grid. The AgentSpeak(F) code for r1 is given in Figure 2. In the figure, we have annotated each plan with a label, so that we can refer to them in the text below.

The only initial beliefs this agent needs are about the position of agent r2 (i.e, its location on the "grid" into which the terrain is divided), and that, to start with, what the robot is doing is checking for the presence of garbage in all the slots of the territory grid. All the plans are explained below.

Plan p1 is used when the agent perceives that it is in a new position and it is currently checking for garbage. If there is no garbage perceived in that slot, all it has to do is a basic action next(slot) which moves the robot to the next slot in the grid, except the one where the incinerator is; garbage in that position is dealt with by robot r2. Note that this is a basic action from the point of view of the agent's reasoning: it is assumed that the robot has the mechanisms to move itself to a next position on the territory grid, automatically skipping the incinerator's position.

The environment provides percepts stating whether a piece of garbage is present in r1 or r2's position. When r1 perceives garbage in its position, a belief garbage(r1) is added to its belief base, hence plan p2 can be used (if the agent is still in its operation mode where it is checking for garbage, rather then moving them to r2 or coming back). The task of dealing with a perceived piece of garbage is accomplished in three parts. It involves achieving subgoals which: (i) make sure that the robot will stop checking for garbage in a consistent manner (e.g., remembering where it was so that the search can eventually be resumed); (ii) actually taking the garbage (garb) to r2; and (iii) resuming the task of checking the slots for garbage. Each of these goals are achieved by the following three plans respectively.

When the agent intends to achieve subgoal (i) above, plan p3 is its only option, and it is always applicable (i.e., it has an empty context). The agent retrieves from its belief base its own current position (which will be in its belief

```
                          Agent r1

Beliefs
pos(r2,2,2).
checking(slots).

Plans
+pos(r1,X1,Y1) : checking(slots) & not(garbage(r1))      (p1)
    <- next(slot).

+garbage(r1) : checking(slots)                           (p2)
    <- !stop(check);
       !take(garb,r2);
       !continue(check).

+!stop(check) : true                                     (p3)
    <- ?pos(r1,X1,Y1);
       +pos(back,X1,Y1);
       -checking(slots).

+!take(S,L) : true                                       (p4)
    <- !ensure_pick(S);
       !go(L);
       drop(S).

+!ensure_pick(S) : garbage(r1)                           (p5)
    <- pick(garb);
       !ensure_pick(S).

+!ensure_pick(S) : true <- true.                         (p6)

+!continue(check) : true                                 (p7)
    <- !go(back);
       -pos(back,X1,Y1);
       +checking(slots);
       next(slot).

+!go(L) : pos(L,X1,Y1) & pos(r1,X1,Y1)                   (p8)
    <- true.

+!go(L) : true                                           (p9)
    <- ?pos(L,X1,Y1);
       moveTowards(X1,Y1);
       !go(L).
```

Fig. 2. AgentSpeak(F) Code for Robot r1.

base from perception of the environment). It then makes a note to itself of where is the position it will need to go back to when it is to resume searching for garbage. This is done by adding a belief to its belief base: +pos(back,X1,Y1). It also removes from its belief base the information that it is presently searching for garbage, as this is no longer true (it will soon intend to take the garbage to r2 and then go back).

Subgoal (ii) is achieved by plan p4, which states that in order for the robot to take garbage to r2, it should pick it up, then achieve the subgoal of going to the position where r2 is, and when r1 is there, it can finally drop the garbage. Note that `pick(garb)` and `drop(garb)` are again basic actions, i.e., things that are assumed the robot can "physically" perform in the environment, by means of its hardware apparatus.

Plans p5 and p6 together ensure that the robot will keep trying to pick up a piece of garbage until it can no longer perceive garbage on the grid (i.e., the grabbing mechanism succeeded). Recall that the grabbing mechanism is imprecise, so the robot may need to try a few times before it succeeds.

Plan p7 is used for the agent to continue the task of checking the grid slots for garbage. The agent needs to achieve the subgoal of going back to its previous position (`!go(back)`), and once there, it can remove the note it has made of that position, remember itself that it is now again checking the slots for garbage, and then proceed to the next slot.

The last two plans are used for achieving the goal of going to a specific position on the grid where L is located. Plan p9 retrieves the belief the agent has about the location of reference L, then causes the agent to move itself towards those coordinates `moveTowards(Xl,Yl)`, and to keep going towards L (this is a recursive goal). Plan p8 provides the end of the recursion[1], saying that there is nothing else to do in order to achieve the goal of going towards L, if agent r1 is already at that position.

Agent r2 is defined by the very simple AgentSpeak(F) code in Figure 3. All it does is to burn the pieces of garbage (`burn(garb)`) when it senses that there is garbage on its location. A belief `+garbage(r2)` is added to the agent's belief base by belief revision (from the perception of the environment).

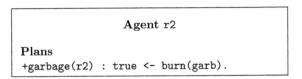

Fig. 3. AgentSpeak(F) Code for Robot r2.

The environment simulating the Mars territory to be cleaned was written both as a PROMELA process and a Java class. A matrix of size 5×5 is used for that purpose. Two pieces of garbage were scattered randomly in the territory (using non-determinism in the model). Whenever the environment changes (due to an agent performing an action), the percepts are updated with the agents'

---

[1] Note that the default applicable plan selection function uses the order in which the plans were written, so p8 must appear before p9.

positions and corresponding facts about the presence of garbage in the current position of each agent.

We now turn to the practical experience with the scenario. We comment on the corrections we had to make to arrive to the code above, and the specifications we know it now does (or does not) satisfy.

5.2   Experimental Results

Verification is particularly important for agent-oriented languages. Because we are specifying an agent's high-level reasoning only, it is difficult to ensure that such agent will behave as expected in all circumstances. In the first implemented version of this scenario, we did not skip r2's position when the basic action next(slot) was requested by r1. This created a series of inconsistent behaviours when the robot was passing by r2's position while searching for garbage to be removed. As usual, ordinary programming errors can be detected too. For example, in an earlier version of the AgentSpeak(F) code, plan p2 had an empty context, which made the agent again act inconsistently when passing by a slot with garbage on it, when on its way to deliver a piece of garbage to r1 and back (i.e., when there was garbage in one of its trajectory between another dirty slot and r2). Of course, such configuration of the Mars territory was considered by the model-checker, which showed the problem clearly. In our experience, it also happens that specifications that seem to be correct, turn out not to be, shedding light on the details of the application scenario. An example of such situation is given below. The following specifications were used in the verification of our system:

$$\Box((\text{Bel r1 garbage(r1)}) \Rightarrow \Diamond\text{garbage(r2)}) \tag{1}$$

$$\Box((\text{pos(r1,2,2)} \land (\text{Does r1 drop(garb)})) \Rightarrow \\ \Diamond(\text{Des r1 go(back)})) \tag{2}$$

$$\Diamond((\text{Int r1 take(garb,r2)}) \land \Diamond(\text{Does r1 drop(garb)})) \tag{3}$$

$$\Diamond((\text{Int r1 continue(check)}) \land (\text{Bel r1 checking(slots)})) \tag{4}$$

$$\Box((\text{Des r1 continue(check)}) \Rightarrow \Diamond(\text{Does r1 next(slot)})) \tag{5}$$

$$\Box((\text{Does r1 next(slot)}) \Rightarrow (\neg\text{pos(r1,2,2)}\land \\ (\text{Bel r1 checking(slots)}))) \tag{6}$$

Specification (1) says that it is always the case that, if r1 perceives garbage on its location, then eventually it will be true of the environment that there is garbage in r2's location. Although specification (1) appeared to us as a valid specification of the system, unforeseen situations could happen in which that property would not hold. It is possible that r2 incinerates the garbage in its position while r1 is still there. Before r1 proceeds with belief revision, it still believes there is garbage in its position (the same position as r2, where r1 itself took the piece of garbage it encountered). However, if that was the last piece of garbage in the whole Mars territory, at that point it is true that r1 believes garbage(r1), yet it is not true that eventually there will be garbage in r2's position (as that one still believed by r1 no longer exists). All other specifications were fully verified by both model-checkers and are thus valid properties of the system.

Specification (2) means that whenever r1 is at the incinerator (i.e., r2's position) and executes the action of dropping the piece of garbage it has picked up somewhere else, then eventually it will desire[2] to go back to the position where it found that piece of garbage. Next, with Specification (3) we guarantee that in all execution paths of the system, at some point in time the robot will intend to take some piece of garbage to r2 and eventually after that it will drop the piece of garbage it found. Specification (4) says that in all possible executions of the system, eventually r1 will both intend to go back to its former position on the grid and continue its task of searching garbage, and it will also believe that it is doing so. This is partly a way of stating that r1 will not stop its main task after one delivery of garbage to r2. With Specification (5), we ensure that whenever r1 desires to continue checking for garbage, it will eventually execute the next(slot) action, which is used for that purpose. Finally, Specification (6) says that whenever r1 executes such action for checking the slots for garbage, it actually believes it is doing so and it is not the case that it is positioned at the incinerator. Robot r2 is responsible for all garbage in that position of the grid, so there is no need for r1 to check for garbage there. In fact, we initially overlooked this fact in the model, which caused the robot to behave in unexpected ways.

Some statistics produced by SPIN and JPF2 when verifying Specification (4), using the current (preliminary) version of the PROMELA and Java models, are as follows. In SPIN, the state space had 333,413 states, verification used 210.51 MB of memory, and took nearly 65.78 seconds to complete. In JPF2, there were 236,946 states, verification used 366.68 MB of memory, and took 18:49:16 hours to complete. However, in another setting of the scenario, where garbage is placed at fixed positions $(1, 1)$ and $(3, 3)$, the verification took JPF2 76.63 seconds to finish, and 5.25 seconds for SPIN. It appears that JPF2 is not presently scaling as well as SPIN.

Note that we do not aim, in this paper, to compare in detail the performance of both model-checkers; figures are given just as a reference for the scale of time and space required in this scenario for an arbitrary specification. However, some of the advantages of each of these model checkers are discussed next.

5.3   Comparing SPIN and JPF2

At present, SPIN can handle larger state spaces than JPF2, and is also faster, as seen by the sample results above. However, the input language of JPF2 (stan-

---

[2] Note that an intention requires an applicable plan whereas a desire does not. In the BDI theory, intentions are desired states of affair which an agents has committed itself to achieve. In practice, this requires the execution of a plan, and in AgentSpeak in particular this means that a relevant and applicable plan for handling an event must have been found.

dard Java code) is far more interesting for our purposes than PROMELA. First, the PROMELA model of an AgentSpeak(F) agent is very large and cumbersome (because PROMELA is too impoverished a language for the sophisticated interpretation needed by AgentSpeak(L)-like languages). Second, Java is used as a basis of many agent platforms, and it is the language that has been used the most in actual implementation of multi-agent system. It is thus more likely that this latter alternative will be used in practice by developers of multi-agent systems. Finally, abstraction techniques used with JPF2 may provide a way to model-check AgentSpeak(L) programs directly, thus avoiding finiteness restrictions.

Therefore, at present, there are trade-offs involved in choosing which target notation/model checker to use: one can translate to a notation which is cumbersome but with a powerful model checker attached, or one can translate to a more suitable target notation, but with a slower model checker. This may point towards the need to write a custom-made model checker: in this case it would not require complex translations and could be much faster. In summary, on one hand SPIN was much faster in model-checking our Mars robot scenario, but on the other hand the PROMELA translator took much longer to implement than the Java one, it also has many restrictions that can be easily dealt with in Java (e.g., the bounds on the size of the date structures), and the generated PROMELA model is so cumbersome that it is barely readable.

6   Related Work

Since Rao's original proposal [21], a number of authors have investigated a range of different aspects of AgentSpeak(L). In [10], an abstract interpreter for AgentSpeak(L) was formally specified using the Z specification language. Most of the elements in that formalisation had already appeared in [9]; this highlights the fact that AgentSpeak(L) is strongly based on the experience with the BDI-inspired dMARS system [15]. Some extensions to AgentSpeak(L) were proposed in [2], and an interpreter for the extended language was introduced. The extensions aim at providing a more practical programming language; the extended language also allows the specification of relations between plans and quantitative criteria for their execution. The interpreter then uses decision-theoretic task scheduling for automatically guiding the choices made by an agent's intention selection function. In [18], an operational semantics for AgentSpeak(L) was given following Plotkin's structural approach [20]; this is a more familiar notation than Z for giving semantics to programming languages. Later, that operational semantics was used in the specification of a framework for carrying out proofs of BDI properties of AgentSpeak(L) [4]. This was used in this work to define precisely how the BDI specifications to be verified against systems of multiple AgentSpeak(L)-like agents are interpreted. In [4], The particular combination of asymmetry thesis principles [23] satisfied by any AgentSpeak(L) agent was shown in that paper. This is relevant in assuring the rationality of agents programmed in AgentSpeak(L).

In [13], techniques were given for model-checking temporal epistemic properties of multi-agent systems; the target of that work was the SPIN model checker.
However, that work did not consider an agent's motivational attitudes, such
as desires and intentions. Perhaps the closest work to ours is that in [29] on
the MABLE multi-agent programming language and model-checking framework.
MABLE is a regular imperative language (an impoverished version of C), extended with some features from Shoham's agent-oriented programming framework [25]. Thus, agents in MABLE have data structures corresponding to beliefs,
desires, and intentions, and can communicate using KQML-like performatives.
MABLE is automatically translated into PROMELA, much like AgentSpeak(F) in
this work. Claims about the system are also written in a $\mathcal{LORA}$-like language,
which is also translated into SPIN's LTL framework for model checking.

We now mention some of the papers in this volume which are related to
ours. In [7], recent extensions to 3APL are presented. The agent-oriented programming language we used here was quite influential in the design of other
BDI-based programming languages, including 3APL. The work presented in [8]
is quite relevant for adding planning from first principles within agent-oriented
languages (recall that mostly such languages assume the existence a library of
partially instantiated plans which the agent uses). In particular, they look at the
problem of deliberation under incomplete information, more specifically under
the presence of sensing and consequently updating belief bases from perception of
the environment (a setting that underlies most agent programming languages).
Finally, in [24], an improved proxy architecture for the coordination of teams of
agents is presented. This is a continuation on the long line of work on STEAM.
They provide a fully-fledged framework for developing teams of agents, which are
themselves also based on concepts such as goals and plans; the aspects related
to teams and coordination is particularly more advanced in their approach then
other approaches to developing agent-based systems. However, their work has no
formal basis as agent programming languages such as AgentSpeak(L) and 3APL
have.

7   Conclusions

We have introduced a framework for the verification of agent programs written in
an expressive logic programming language against BDI specifications. We do so
by transforming AgentSpeak(F) code into either PROMELA (as reported in [3]) or
Java, and transforming BDI specifications into LTL formulæ, then using either
SPIN or JPF2 to model check the resulting system. AgentSpeak(L) is a practical
BDI programming language with a well-defined theoretical foundation, and we
here contribute to the missing aspect of practical AgentSpeak(L) verification.

Model checking techniques have only recently begun to find a significant
audience in the multi-agent systems community. Rao and Georgeff developed
basic algorithms for model-checking BDI logics [22], but the authors proposed
no method for generating BDI models from programs. In [1], a general approach
for model-checking multi-agent systems was proposed, based on the branching

temporal logic CTL together with modalities for BDI-like attitudes. However, once again no method was given for generating models from actual systems, and so the techniques given there could not easily be applied to verifying real multi-agent systems.

The statistics of our case study in Section 5.2 show that our AgentSpeak(F) model in PROMELA and Java are highly demanding in terms of memory and processing time. Future work will attempt to improve the efficiency of the models by optimisations on the PROMELA and Java code that is automatically generated. We may also consider the implementation of a custom-made model checker for AgentSpeak(F), and we plan to combine our approach with deductive verification so that we can handle larger applications. Further, it would be interesting to add extra features to our approach to agent verification (e.g., handling plan failure, allowing first order terms, allowing variables in the property specifications), as far as the complexity of model checking would allow. Finally, we also plan as future work to verify more ambitious applications, such as autonomous spacecraft control (along the lines of [12, 11]).

Acknowledgements

This research was supported by a Marie Curie Fellowship of the European Community programme *Improving Human Potential* under contract number HPMF-CT-2001-00065.

References

1. M. Benerecetti and A. Cimatti. Symbolic model checking for multi-agent systems. In *Proceedings of the Model Checking and Artificial Intelligence Workshop (MoChArt-2002), held with 15th ECAI, 21–26 July, Lyon, France*, pages 1–8, 2002.
2. R. H. Bordini, A. L. C. Bazzan, R. O. Jannone, D. M. Basso, R. M. Vicari, and V. R. Lesser. AgentSpeak(XL): Efficient intention selection in BDI agents via decision-theoretic task scheduling. In C. Castelfranchi and W. L. Johnson, editors, *Proceedings of the First International Joint Conference on Autonomous Agents and Multi-Agent Systems (AAMAS-2002), 15–19 July, Bologna, Italy*, pages 1294–1302, New York, NY, 2002. ACM Press.
3. R. H. Bordini, M. Fisher, C. Pardavila, and M. Wooldridge. Model checking AgentSpeak. In J. S. Rosenschein, T. Sandholm, W. Michael, and M. Yokoo, editors, *Proceedings of the Second International Joint Conference on Autonomous Agents and Multi-Agent Systems (AAMAS-2003), Melbourne, Australia, 14–18 July*, pages 409–416, New York, NY, 2003. ACM Press.
4. R. H. Bordini and Á. F. Moreira. Proving the asymmetry thesis principles for a BDI agent-oriented programming language. In J. Dix, J. A. Leite, and K. Satoh, editors, *Proceedings of the Third International Workshop on Computational Logic in Multi-Agent Systems (CLIMA-02), 1st August, Copenhagen, Denmark*, Electronic Notes in Theoretical Computer Science 70(5). Elsevier, 2002. URL: <http://www.elsevier.nl/locate/entcs/volume70.html>. CLIMA-02 was held as part of FLoC-02. This paper was originally published in Datalogiske Skrifter number 93, Roskilde University, Denmark, pages 94–108.

5. R. H. Bordini, W. Visser, M. Fisher, C. Pardavila, and M. Wooldridge. Model checking multi-agent programs with CASP. In W. A. Hunt Jr. and F. Somenzi, editors, *Proceedgins of the Fifteenth Conference on Computer-Aided Verification (CAV-2003), Boulder, CO, 8–12 July*, number 2725 in Lecture Notes in Computer Science, pages 110–113, Berlin, 2003. Springer-Verlag. Tool description.

6. E. M. Clarke, O. Grumberg, and D. A. Peled. *Model Checking*. The MIT Press: Cambridge, MA, 2000.

7. M. Dastani, B. van Riemsdijk, F. Dignum, and J.-J. C. Meyer. A programming language for cognitive agents: Goal directed 3apl. In this volume.

8. G. de Giacomo, Y. Lesperance, H. J. Levesque, and S. Sardiña. On deliberation under incomplete information and the inadequacy of entailment and consistency-based formalizations. In this volume.

9. M. d'Inverno, D. Kinny, M. Luck, and M. Wooldridge. A formal specification of dMARS. In M. P. Singh, A. S. Rao, and M. Wooldridge, editors, *Intelligent Agents IV–Proceedings of the Fourth International Workshop on Agent Theories, Architectures, and Languages (ATAL-97), Providence, RI, 24–26 July, 1997*, number 1365 in Lecture Notes in Artificial Intelligence, pages 155–176. Springer-Verlag, Berlin, 1998.

10. M. d'Inverno and M. Luck. Engineering AgentSpeak(L): A formal computational model. *Journal of Logic and Computation*, 8(3):1–27, 1998.

11. M. Fisher and C. Ghidini. The ABC of rational agent modelling. In C. Castelfranchi and W. L. Johnson, editors, *Proceedings of the First International Joint Conference on Autonomous Agents and Multi-Agent Systems (AAMAS-2002), 15–19 July, Bologna, Italy*, pages 849–856, New York, NY, 2002. ACM Press.

12. M. Fisher and W. Visser. Verification of autonomous spacecraft control – a logical vision of the future. In *Proceedings of the Workshop on AI Planning and Scheduling For Autonomy in Space Applications, co-located with TIME-2002, 7–9 July, Manchester, UK*, 2002.

13. W. Hoek and M. Wooldridge. Model checking knowledge and time. In D. Bošnački and S. Leue, editors, *Model Checking Software, Proceedings of SPIN 2002 (LNCS Volume 2318)*, pages 95–111. Springer-Verlag: Berlin, Germany, 2002.

14. G. Holzmann. The Spin model checker. *IEEE Transaction on Software Engineering*, 23(5):279–295, May 1997.

15. D. Kinny. The distributed multi-agent reasoning system architecture and language specification. Technical report, Australian Artificial Intelligence Institute, Melbourne, Australia, 1993.

16. R. Machado and R. H. Bordini. Running AgentSpeak(L) agents on SIM_AGENT. In J.-J. Meyer and M. Tambe, editors, *Intelligent Agents VIII – Proceedings of the Eighth International Workshop on Agent Theories, Architectures, and Languages (ATAL-2001), August 1–3, 2001, Seattle, WA*, number 2333 in Lecture Notes in Artificial Intelligence, pages 158–174, Berlin, 2002. Springer-Verlag.

17. J. Mayfield, Y. Labrou, and T. Finin. Evaluation of KQML as an agent communication language. In M. Wooldridge, J. P. Müller, and M. Tambe, editors, *Intelligent Agents II–Proceedings of the Second International Workshop on Agent Theories, Architectures, and Languages (ATAL'95), held as part of IJCAI'95, Montréal, Canada, August 1995*, number 1037 in Lecture Notes in Artificial Intelligence, pages 347–360, Berlin, 1996. Springer-Verlag.

18. Á. F. Moreira and R. H. Bordini. An operational semantics for a BDI agent-oriented programming language. In J.-J. C. Meyer and M. J. Wooldridge, editors, *Proceedings of the Workshop on Logics for Agent-Based Systems (LABS-02), held in conjunction with the Eighth International Conference on Principles of Knowledge Representation and Reasoning (KR2002), April 22–25, Toulouse, France*, pages 45–59, 2002.

19. N. Muscettola, P. P. Nayak, B. Pell, and B. C. Williams. Remote agents: To boldly go where no AI system has gone before. *Artificial Intelligence*, 103:5–47, 1998.

20. G. D. Plotkin. A structural approach to operational semantics. Technical report, Computer Science Department, Aarhus University, Aarhus, 1981.

21. A. S. Rao. AgentSpeak(L): BDI agents speak out in a logical computable language. In W. Van de Velde and J. Perram, editors, *Proceedings of the Seventh Workshop on Modelling Autonomous Agents in a Multi-Agent World (MAAMAW'96), 22–25 January, Eindhoven, The Netherlands*, number 1038 in Lecture Notes in Artificial Intelligence, pages 42–55, London, 1996. Springer-Verlag.

22. A. S. Rao and M. P. Georgeff. A model-theoretic approach to the verification of situated reasoning systems. In *Proceedings of the Thirteenth International Joint Conference on Artificial Intelligence (IJCAI-93)*, pages 318–324, Chambéry, France, 1993.

23. A. S. Rao and M. P. Georgeff. Decision procedures for BDI logics. *Journal of Logic and Computation*, 8(3):293–343, 1998.

24. P. Scerri, D. V. Pynadath, N. Schurr, A. Farinelli, S. Gandhe, and M. Tambe. Team oriented programming and proxy agents: the next generation. In this volume.

25. Y. Shoham. Agent-oriented programming. *Artificial Intelligence*, 60:51–92, 1993.

26. A. Sloman and B. Logan. Building cognitively rich agents using the SIM_AGENT toolkit. *Communications of the Association of Computing Machinery*, 43(2):71–77, Mar. 1999.

27. W. Visser, K. Havelund, G. Brat, and S. Park. Model checking programs. In *Proceedings of the Fifteenth International Conference on Automated Software Engineering (ASE'00), 11-15 September, Grenoble, France*, pages 3–12. IEEE Computer Society, 2000.

28. M. Wooldridge. *Reasoning about Rational Agents*. The MIT Press, Cambridge, MA, 2000.

29. M. Wooldridge, M. Fisher, M.-P. Huget, and S. Parsons. Model checking multi-agent systems with MABLE. In C. Castelfranchi and W. L. Johnson, editors, *Proceedings of the First International Joint Conference on Autonomous Agents and Multi-Agent Systems (AAMAS-2002), 15–19 July, Bologna, Italy*, pages 952–959, New York, NY, 2002. ACM Press.

CLAIM: A Computational Language for Autonomous, Intelligent and Mobile Agents

Amal El Fallah-Seghrouchni and Alexandru Suna

LIP6 – University of Paris 6
8, Rue du Capitaine Scott
75015, Paris
{Amal.Elfallah,Alexandru.Suna}@lip6.fr

Abstract. This paper proposes a language called CLAIM : Computational Language for Autonomous Intelligent and Mobile agents. CLAIM allows designing Multi-Agent Systems that support both stationary and mobile agents. Agents designed thanks to CLAIM are endowed with cognitive capabilities (*e.g.* reasoning), are able to communicate with other agents and are mobile. The primitives of mobility are inspired from the ambient calculus. The CLAIM language is supported by a multi-platform system (SyMPA) compliant with the specifications of the MASIF standard (from OMG);*i.e.* agents can be distributed over several sites and can move from one to another with respect to MASIF specifications. this paper presents the main features of our language CLAIM, resumes the most significant aspects of SyMPA, shows the expressiveness of our language, and discusses the completeness of the mobility.

Keywords: Agent oriented programming, Mobile agents, Ambient calculus.

1 Introduction

Multi-Agent Systems (MAS) propose a credible paradigm to design distributed and co-operative systems based on the intelligent agents technology. During the last decade, several consortiums such as the FIPA or OMG have tended to propose a wide range of standards to cover the main aspects of MAS engineering. Most of these standards focus on generic platforms (*e.g.* MASIF), on the specifications of the communication (*e.g.* FIPA-ACL), or on modeling agents (AUML). Nevertheless, for a larger use of the MAS paradigm, specific programming languages are required. The success of object oriented programming (OOP) increases thanks to the development of dedicated languages supporting the OOP paradigm. Our work is motivated by two main objectives:

1) The MAS design needs a specific language (*i.e.* agent oriented) in order to help the designer to reduce the gap between the design and the implementation phases. The idea is to offer a declarative language that frees the designer from the most implementation aspects, *i.e.* the designer should think and implement in the same paradigm (namely through agents).

M. Dastani, J. Dix, A. El Fallah-Seghrouchni (Eds.): PROMAS 2003, LNAI 3067, pp. 90–110, 2004.
© Springer-Verlag Berlin Heidelberg 2004

2) The second motivation of our language is to meet the requirements of mobile computation (concerning mobile code that moves between devices, such as applets, agents, etc.) which becomes popular due to the recent developments in the mobile code paradigm and enabling programming technologies. In fact, the physical distribution of the systems and of their computation over the net (*e.g.* World Wide Web) naturally calls for mobility (agents' migration from a node to another), as a way of flexibly managing latency and bandwidth and appeals for co-operation between the system's entities.

Many existing agent-based systems are suitable for representing intelligent agents endowed with cognitive skills (reasoning, planning, decision making, etc.) but lack clear standards to deal with mobility and distribution. This work aims to homogeneously combine in an unified language, the advantages of the intelligent agents (in particular autonomy and cognitive skills) with those of the concurrent languages such as the ambient calculus which has been recently proposed [3, 4] as a theoretical framework for distributed and mobile objects/agents.

This paper is organized as follows: the second section presents the related work concerning the agent oriented programming languages and the languages for programming mobile and concurrent processes/agents. The third section provides the specifications of our language-CLAIM: the syntax and a informal semantics. It presents the agent's definition and details its components. An example is also given to illustrate the specifications. The fourth section is dedicated to the platform we developed to support the CLAIM language. The fifth section discusses the expressiveness of CLAIM comparing to other agent oriented programming languages and the completeness of our mobility implementation. The sixth section concludes our paper and outlines our perspectives.

2   Related Work

In order to meet the requirements of mobile and intelligent agents, the language we propose - CLAIM - combines elements from the agent oriented programming languages (for representing agents' intelligence and communication) with elements from the concurrent languages for representing agents' mobility. The chosen formalism is the ambient calculus.

2.1   Agent Oriented Programming Languages

In the literature there are several agent oriented programming (AOP) languages that allow representing agents' intelligence, autonomy and interactions. We shall briefly present the main characteristics of the most significant AOP languages.

AGENT-0 [17] agents have a mental state composed of: *beliefs*, that represent the state of the world, the mental state and the capabilities of the agent and of the other agents, from the agent's point of view, at certain times, *capabilities*, representing what the agent can do at certain times and *decisions(choices) and commitments* that determine the agent's actions, in accordance with its beliefs and with its anterior decisions. The agent's behaviour in AGENT-0 consists in reading the current messages, updating the mental state and executing the commitments for the current time.

Although AGENT-0 presents many useful elements, especially for agents' mental state and reasoning, there is no planning, parallelism, nor mobility.

Two extensions of AGENT-0 have been proposed, **Agent-K** [6], which uses KQML for agents' communication and **PLACA** [18], which allows the planning. But AGENT-0's problems rest: no parallelism and no mobility.

In **AgentSpeak** [22], the agents are autonomous, distributed and have a *mental state* that includes beliefs, desires (goals), plans and intentions, a reactive and proactive (goal-directed) *behaviour*, they *communicate* through messages and have a *concurrent execution* of plans. Although in AgentSpeak an agent has a complex mental state, powerful reasoning capabilities, plans that are concurrently performed, the language does not support the agents' mobility.

VIVA [20] combines agent oriented programming elements with concepts from Prolog and SQL. A VIVA agent is composed of a *mental state* (containing *beliefs*, *tasks* and *current intentions*), an *event queue* for receiving messages and the *behaviour* represented by a set of *action rules* and a set of *reaction rules*. However, it is not possible to represent open agent systems and there is no planning, parallelism nor mobility.

3APL [10] is a programming language for intelligent agents that combines the imperative and logic programming. An agent has a *mental state* composed of *beliefs, desires, plans* and *intentions*, a *goal directed* behaviour and *reasoning capabilities* realized by the *practical reasoning rules*. In 3APL, the agents can execute several plans in parallel. However, the language is focused on one static agent's reasoning. There are no communication primitives and no mobility.

The **dMARS** [11] agents are BDI (Beliefs-Desires-Intentions) agents. A dMARS agent contains *beliefs* - the agent's information about the world, *desires (goals)* - agent's tasks, *intentions* - the desires chosen to be achieved, an *event queue* and a *plan library* - agent's set of plans. A plan contains *the invocation condition, the context, the maintenance condition* and *the body* - the actions to be executed. Although dMARS offers many useful element for agent reasoning and an agent can have several plans executed in parallel, the language is focused on one agent description and it is difficult to implement interaction protocols or the mobility.

We can conclude about the studied AOP languages that they allow representing agents' intelligence and reasoning, that several have plans executed in parallel and communication primitives. However, in none of these languages is possible to represent agents' **mobility**. CLAIM utilize cognitive elements for representing agents' mental state and reasoning.

2.2   Languages for Representing Agents' Mobility

There are many languages concerned with the representation of agents' or processes' mobility and concurrency. They have a well defined operational semantics useful for the verification of the system's behaviour. But none of these languages allows an explicit representation of the agents' goals, knowledge or reasoning.

For representing agents' migration, we endowed CLAIM with mobility primitives inspired from the **ambient calculus** [3, 4].

An ambient is a bounded place where the computation happens. An ambient has a name used to control the access to the ambient, a set of local processes and a set of sub-ambients. The ambients form a tree structure, being hierarchically organized. The ambients can move in and out of other ambients. An ambient moves as a whole, with all its components. For the migration, the ambients use the main mobility capabilities: **in** (an ambient enters, with all its sub-ambients and processes, another ambient, which must be in the same "neighbourhood" to execute the capability), **out** (an ambient exits, with all the sub-ambients and processes, its current parent) and **open** (an agent opens the bounds of one of its sub-ambients; all the processes and the sub-ambients of the opened ambient become sub-components of the former). There are also some additional mobility capabilities, such as **acid, mv in** or **mv out**. There are communication primitives. But the communication happens only inside an ambient.

The **safe ambients** [12] formalism is an extension of the ambient calculus which tries to avoid the interferences in the ambients. A permission asking mechanism, based on co-actions, is used. An agent cannot enter, exit or open an ambient without its permission.

The **SEAL calculus** [19] is a distributed variant of the Π-calculus, with mobility primitives, and security and control elements for the resources access. The *seals'* representation is also inspired from the ambient calculus.

Telescript [21] is the first commercial programming language for mobile agents. The agents can move from a place to another, can call other agent's procedures and have a concurrent execution. There are security elements, very important in the context of the mobile agents. However, **Telescript** agents do not have explicit goals nor reasoning capabilities.

April [13] is a symbolic programming language that allows defining concurrent processes in a distributed environment. The processes communicate through messages that start different actions. **April++** [5] is an object oriented extension where it is possible to create clones of objects, that can migrate. Although an agent is mobile, has a knowledge base, capabilities activable by messages and a concurrent execution, there is no explicit representation of its goals nor plans.

Obliq [2] is an object oriented language for distributed computation, where the objects have methods and fields with values, can migrate and can have clones.

NormandPict [23] is a concurrent language, inspired from the Π-calculus, with primitives for agents' creation, communication and migration.

KLAIM [15] is also a concurrent language, based on the Linda language, with operators for building processes, for migration and coordonation mechanisms.

Several others languages have been proposed for representing concurrent mobile processes (**MTTC** [16], **Jocaml** [7], **MobileML** [9], etc.).

All these languages allow more or less representing concurrent processes, that can communicate and migrate in a distributed environment. They have well defined operational semantics. But in none of these languages it is possible to represent intelligent agents, with explicit believes, plans, goals or reasoning.

3   CLAIM's Specification

A CLAIM agent is an autonomous, intelligent and mobile entity that can be seen as a bounded place where the computation happens (similar to ambients) and has a list of local processes and a list of sub-agents. In addition, an agent has mental components such as knowledge, capabilities, goals, that allow a forward or backward reasoning and a goal driven behaviour.

In CLAIM, agents and classes of agent can be defined using:

> **defineAgent** *agentName* {
>   **authority=null;** | *agentName* ;
>   **parent=null;** | *agentName* ;
>   **knowledge=null;** | { *(knowledge;)+*}
>   **goals=null;** | { *(goal;)+*}
>   **messages=null;** | { *(queueMessage;)+*}
>   **capabilities=null;** | { *(capability;)+*}
>   **processes=null;** | { *(process* |)* *process* }
>   **agents=null;** | { *(agentName;)+*}
> }
> **defineAgentClass** *className* (*(arg,)**) {...}

An agent who belongs to a specified class is created using the primitive:

> **newAgent** *name:className* (*(arg,)**)

In CLAIM we can use variables to replace agents' names, messages, capabilities signatures, etc. A variable is noted as: *?x*. There are global (for a class) or local (to a capability) variables.

We defined for an agent several components inspired from the agent-oriented languages and the ambient calculus. The components we propose allow representing the agents' mental state, communication and mobility.

3.1   Agent's Components

The **authority** component represents the name of the agent that has created the current agent. It is necessary for security reasons (*e.g.* for authentication). The *authority* keyword can be used in the agent's capabilities.

The **parent** component represents the name of the parent of the current agent. The agents are hierarchically organized, like the ambients in the ambient calculus. When an agent is created, its parent and its authority are the same; after the migration, its parent will change, but its authority will always be the same. The *parent* keyword can be used in the agent's capabilities.

The **knowledge** component represents the agent's information about the other agents (*i.e.* about theirs capabilities or their classes) or about the world. This knowledge base is a set of elements of *knowledge* type, defined as follows:

> *knowledge ::= agentName(capabilitySignature,message,effect)*
> | *agentName:className*
> | *proposition*

The **goals** component represents the agent's current goals. We shall see that CLAIM allows defining two types of reasoning: forward and backward reasoning. To satisfy its goals, an agent uses a backward reasoning.

The **messages** component represents the agent's current messages queue. Each agent has a queue for storing the arrived messages. The messages are processed in their arrival order and are used to activate capabilities. A queue message contains the sender of the message and the arrived message:

queueMessage ::= agentName > message

The **sender** keyword can be used in the agent's capabilities to indicate the sender of the current capability's activation message. An agent can send messages to an agent (*unicast*), to all the agents in a class (*multicast*), or to all the agents in the system (*broadcast*), using the primitive:

send(*receiver,message), where the receiver can be:

- **this** - the message is sent to itself;
- **parent** or **authority** - the message is sent to the agent's current parent or authority;
- **agentName** - the message is sent to the specified agent;
- **all** - the message is sent to all the agents in the system;
- **?Ag:className** - the message is sent to all the agents - instances of the specified class of agents;

In CLAIM there are three types of messages:

1. a *proposition*, used to activate agent's capabilities;
2. the **messages concerning the knowledge**: these messages are used by agents to exchange information about their knowledge and capabilities:
- **tell**(*knowledge) - to inform an agent about some knowledge; the specified knowledge is added in the agent's knowledge base.
- **askAllCapabilities**() - an agent requests all the capabilities of another agent; The later inform the first agent about all its capabilities, using the **tell** communication primitive.
- **askIfCapability**(*capabilitySignature) - an agent asks another agent if it has the specified capability; If the later has this capability, it confirms using the **tell** communication primitive.
- **achieveCapability**(*capabilitySignature) - an agent asks another agent to perform the specified capability; if its condition is verified, it is executed.
- **lostCapability**(*agentName,capabilitySignature) - this message is sent by an agent when it has lost the specified capability, to all the agents in the system that have in their knowledge base an information about this capability; this information is removed from the knowledge base.
3. the **mobility messages** are used by the system in the mobility operations. They cannot be used by the agents' programmers for security reasons. These messages are used for asking, according or not according the open, exit or enter permission: **openBy**(), **openOK**(), **openNotOK**(), **wantOut**(*mobilityArg), **outOK**(*mobilityArg), **outNotOK**(*mobilityArg), **wantIn**(*mobilityArg), **inOK**(*mobilityArg), **inNotOK**(*mobilityArg).

In the ambient calculus, the only condition for the mobility operations is a structure condition (*e.g.* for the *enter* operation, the involved agents must be on the same level in the agents' hierarchy). In CLAIM, we kept this condition, but we added the mobility messages for an advanced security and control. The mobility arguments will be explained later in this paper.

The **capabilities** component represents the actions an agent can do in order to achieve its goals or the services that it can offer to the other agents. The component consists in a set of elements of *capability* type. A *capability* has a message of activation, a condition, the process to execute in case of activation and a set of possible effects:

capability ::= capabilitySignature {
   message=null; | *message;*
   condition=null; | *condition;*
   do *{ process }*
   effects=null; | *{ (effect;)+ }*
}

To execute a capability, the agent must receive the activation message and verify the condition. If the message is **null**, the capability is executed whenever the condition is verified. If the condition is **null**, the capability is executed when the message is received. A condition can be a Java function that returns a *boolean*, an achieved effect, a condition about agent's knowledge or sub-agents, or a logical formula:

condition ::= **Java(***objectName.function(args)***)**
     | *agentName.effect*
     | **hasKnowledge(** *knowledge* **)**
     | **hasAgent(** *agentName* **)**
     | **not(** *condition* **)**
     | **and(** *condition,(condition)+* **)**
     | **or(** *condition,(condition)+* **)**

The **processes** component represents the agent's current processes executed in parallel. A process can be a sequence of processes, an instruction, a variable's instantiation, a function defined in another programming language (in this version an agent can call only Java methods), the creation of a new agent, a mobility operation or a message transmission:

process ::= process.process
     | *instruction*
     | *?x = (value |* **Java(***objectName.function(args)***)))**
     | **Java(***objectName.function(args)***)**
     | **newAgent** *agentName:className((arg,)*)*
     | **open** *(agentName)*
     | **acid**
     | **in** *(mobilityArg,agentName)*
     | **out** *(mobilityArg,agentName)*
     | **moveTo** *(mobilityArg,agentName)*
     | **send** *(receiver,message)*

In this version of CLAIM, we defined two instructions:

forAllKnowledges*(knowledge)* { *process* } - execute the process for all agent's knowledge that satisfy a criteria (*e.g.* all agent's knowledge about a certain agent).

forAllAgents*(agentName)* { *process* } - execute the process for all the agent's sub-agents that satisfy a criteria (*e.g.* all the agent's sub-agents that belong to a certain class of agents).

The mobility primitives have the same utilization as in the ambient calculus and are used by an agent for opening the borders of one of its sub-agents (***open***), for opening its own borders (***acid***), for entering an agent form the same level (***in***), for leaving the current parent (***out***) or for migrating into another agent (***moveTo***).

An important problem is the migration's granularity, and the question is "who can migrate?". We specify this using the mobility argument and it is possible the migration of the agent itself, of a clone of the agent or of a process:

mobilityArgument = ***this*** | ***clone*** | *process*

The **agent** component represents the agent's current sub-agents.

3.2   Agent's Reasoning

The CLAIM language offers to the agents' designer the possibility to define two types of reasoning for the agents: forward reasoning (activate corresponding capabilities when the messages arrive) and backward reasoning (execute capabilities in order to achieve the goals).

The ***forward reasoning*** represents the reactive behaviour of a CLAIM agent. Its steps are:

- get a message from the queue (the first or using a selection heuristic);
- find the capabilities that have this message of activation (pattern matching);
- verify the conditions of the chosen capabilities;
- activate the verified capabilities and execute the corresponding process; let us note that more than one capability can be activated.

The ***backward reasoning*** represents the goal driven bevahiour of a CLAIM agent, which will be based on planning mechanisms. Its steps are:

- get a goal from the list of goals (the first or using a selection heuristic);
- find the capabilities that allow to achieve this goal;
- verify the conditions of the chosen capabilities; if the condition is an agent's effect, add this effect in its list of goals; if the condition is other agent's effect, ask the execution of the corresponding capability;
- activate the verified capabilities and execute the corresponding process.

3.3   An Informal Representation of the Reduction Rules

The operational semantics for CLAIM is very complex, due to the richness of agents' definitions. Our current work focuses on finding a suitable formalism for representing CLAIM's semantics and on defining all the reduction rules. In this sub-section we shall intuitively present the semantics elements and the reduction rules for a mobility operation (**in**).

A CLAIM program is a set of running agents, a set of definitions of classes and a set of pairs of agents and their corresponding classes.

$$\Pi = < A, \Delta, R>$$

A CLAIM agent contains the components presented in the syntax. We consider that $\alpha, \beta, \pi, ...$ are agents' names and that $\rho_1, \rho_2, ...$ are propositions. The other notations will be explained when they are presented. We also consider that $a_1, a_2, ...$ are agents (with all the components) belonging to A.

$a_1 = < \alpha, \pi, \beta, K, G, G', M, C, P, S, E>$, where:

- α is the agent's name;
- π is the name of the agent's parent;
- β is the authority (the name of the agent that created this agent);
- K is the knowledge base; a knowledge can be, as defined in the section 3.1., a proposition or an information about another agent:

$\quad k_i = \rho_i$, or $k_i = < \alpha_i, s_i, m_i, E_i >$, or $k_i = \alpha_i : cl_i$
- G is the agent's set of current goals;
- G' is the agent's set of treated goals (considered for achievement);
- M is the agent's message queue, a set of pairs representing the sender and the message:

$\quad$ M=$\{\alpha_1 > m_1, \alpha_2 > m_2, ...\}$;
- C is the agent's list of capabilities. Each capability is composed of the signature, the message of activation, the condition, the process to execute and the eventual effects:

$\quad c_i = < s_i, m_i, \Omega_i, p_i, E_i >$
- P is the list of the agent' concurrent running processes;
- S is the set of the names of the agent's sub-agents;
- E is the list of achieved goals or effects.

We defined using this informal representation all the reduction rules corresponding to agents' execution. Due to the lack of space, we shall present only the reduction rules corresponding to a successful **in** mobility operation.

$\Pi = <A, \Delta, R>, A = \{a_1, a_2, ..., a_n\}, n \geq 3, Ev_i = \{K_i, G_i, G'_i, E_i\}$

****the agent α executes the process of entering the agent β****
$a_1 = < \alpha, \pi, \gamma_1, Ev_1, M_1, C_1, P_1 \bigcup \{\boldsymbol{in(this, \beta)}\}, S_1 >$
$a_2 = < \beta, \pi, \gamma_2, Ev_2, M_2, C_2, P_2, S_2 >$
$a_3 = < \pi, \pi_3, \gamma_3, Ev_3, M_3, C_3, P_3, S_3 \bigcup \{\alpha, \beta\}>$

**** α asks the enter permission to β ****
$a_1 = < \alpha, \pi, \gamma_1, Ev_1, M_1, C_1, P_1 \bigcup \{\boldsymbol{send(\beta, wantIn(this))}\}, S_1 >$
$a_2 = < \beta, \pi, \gamma_2, Ev_2, M_2, C_2, P_2, S_2 >$
$a_3 = < \pi, \pi_3, \gamma_3, Ev_3, M_3, C_3, P_3, S_3 \bigcup \{\alpha, \beta\}>$

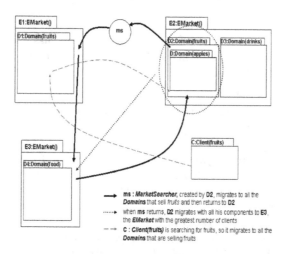

Fig. 1. The EMarket application

**** β *received the message from* α ****
$a_1 = < \alpha,\pi,\gamma_1,Ev_1,M_1,C_1,P_1,S_1 >$
$a_2 = < \beta,\pi,\gamma_2,Ev_2,M_2\bigcup\{\alpha >$***wantIn(this)***$\},C_2,P_2,S_2 >$
$a_3 = < \pi,\pi_3,\gamma_3,Ev_3,M_3,C_3,P_3,S_3\bigcup\{\alpha,\beta\}>$

**** β *gives to* α *the enter permission* ****
$a_1 = < \alpha,\pi,\gamma_1,Ev_1,M_1,C_1,P_1,S_1 >$
$a_2 = < \beta,\pi,\gamma_2,Ev_2,M_2,C_2,P_2\bigcup\{$***send(*** $\alpha,$***inOK(this)***$\},S_2 >$
$a_3 = < \pi,\pi_3,\gamma_3,Ev_3,M_3,C_3,P_3,S_3\bigcup\{\alpha,\beta\}>$

**** α *received the message from* β ****
$a_1 = < \alpha,\pi,\gamma_1,Ev_1,M_1\bigcup\{\beta >$***inOK(this)***$\},C_1,P_1,S_1 >$
$a_2 = < \beta,\pi,\gamma_2,Ev_2,M_2,C_2,P_2,S_2 >$
$a_3 = < \pi,\pi_3,\gamma_3,Ev_3,M_3,C_3,P_3,S_3\bigcup\{\alpha,\beta\}>$

**** α *becomes a sub-agent of* β ****
$a_1 = < \alpha,\beta,\gamma_1,Ev_1,M_1,C_1,P_1,S_1 >$
$a_2 = < \beta,\pi,\gamma_2,Ev_2,M_2,C_2,P_2,S_2\bigcup\{\alpha\}>$
$a_3 = < \pi,\pi_3,\gamma_3,Ev_3,M_3,C_3,P_3,S_3\bigcup\{\beta\}>$

3.4   An e-Commerce Example

CLAIM can be used in different domains. We've already defined a web data
searching example in [8]. We shall present next an electronic commerce application represented in CLAIM, which emphasizes the agents' reasoning and mobility
and the usefulness of the hierarchical representation of the agents (Figure 1). Let
us note that the knowledge base of the agents is empty at the beginning, but it
will evolve during the execution.

The **EMarket** class represents an electronic market. An **EMarket** agent has several domains that sell different products. The class has capabilities for creating and adding new domains and for answering to the clients' questions about the existing products.

```
defineAgentClass EMarket() {
    authority=null;    parent=null;    knowledge=null;
    goals=null;    messages=null;
    capabilities={
    addNewDomain(?AgD,?pr) {
capability for creating a new domain selling the product indicated as parameter
        message=addNewDomain(?AgD,?pr);
        condition=null;
        do{ newAgent ?AgD:Domain(?pr).
          send(this,tell(?AgD:Domain(?pr))).
          send(?AgD,askIfCapability(sell(?pr))) }
        effects=null;
    }
    newDomainArrived(?AgD,?pr) {
capability for updating the knowledge base when a new domain with the specified
product arrives
        message=newDomainArrived(?AgD,?pr);
        condition=null;
        do{ send(?AgD,askIfCapability(sell(?pr)))}
        effects=null;
    }
    acceptDomain(?prod) {
capability for answering to a MarketSearcher's query, if it accepts a new domain
        message=needClients(?prod);
        condition=Java(EM.needDomain(?prod));
        do{ send(sender,hasClients(?prod)) }
        effects=null;
    }
    answerClient() {
capability for answering to a client's query. The query is sent to all its domains
        message=needProduct(?prod);
        condition=null;
        do{ forAllAgents(?AgD:Domain(?prod)){
          send(?AgD,clientNeedProduct(sender,?prod))}}
        effects=null;
    }
  }
  processes=null;    agents=null;
}
```

The **Domain** class represents a domain in an electronic market. A domain can have sub-domains. This class has capabilities for creating and adding new sub-domains and for answering to the clients' questions about the products it sells. Also, when a **Domain** detects that the number of clients is decreasing, it can create a **MarketSearcher** agent that searches for another electronic market with sufficient clients and ready to host other domains. Then, the domain migrates with all its sub-components in this new market.

```
defineAgentClass  Domain(?prod) {
    authority=null;     parent=null;
    knowledge={hasProduct(?prod);}
    goals=null;     messages=null;
    capabilities={
      addNewSubDomain(?AgD,?pr) {
```
capability for creating a new sub-domain selling the specified product
```
          message=addNewDomain(?AgD,?pr);
          condition=null;
          do{newAgent ?AgD:Domain(?pr).
            send(parent,newDomainArrived(?AgD,?pr))}
          effects=null;
      }
      newDomainArrived(?AgD,?pr) {
```
capability for updating the knowledge base when a new sub-domain with the specified product arrives
```
          message=newDomainArrived(?AgD,?pr);
          condition=null;
          do{send(parent,newDomainArrived(?AgD,?pr))}
          effects=null;
      }
      clientNeedProduct1() {
```
capability for answering to a client's query, if it has the searched product
```
          message=clientNeedProduct(?Ag,?pr);
          condition=hasKnowledge(hasProduct(?pr));
          do{send(?Ag,haveProduct(?pr))}
          effects=null;
      }
      clientNeedProduct2() {
```
capability for answering to a client's query, if the domain does not have the searched product. The message is sent to all its sub-domains
```
          message=clientNeedProduct(?Ag,?pr);
          condition=not(hasKnowledge(hasProduct(?pr)));
          do{forAllAgents(?sAg:Domain(?pr)){
            send(?sAg,clientNeedProduct(?Ag,?pr))}}
          effects=null;
      }
      sell(?pr)
```
capability for selling a product to a client

```
    createMarketSearcher(?pr) {
capability for creating a MarketSearcher agent, when the number of clients is
not sufficient
      message=null;
      condition=Java(EM.needClients(?pr,parent));
      do{newAgent ms:MarketSearcher().
        send(ms,search(?pr))}
      effects=null;
  }
    goToNewMarket() {
capability for migrating to a new market, with all its sub-domains, when the
MarketSearcher come back with the gathered data
      message=bestMarket(?pr, ?bestEM);
      condition=null;
      do{moveTo(this, ?bestEM).
        send(?bestEM,newDomainArrived(this, ?pr))}
      effects=null;
    }
  }
  processes=null;    agents=null;
}
```

A **MarketSearcher** agent migrates to all the EMarket agents and counts the number of clients. Then, it goes back to the domain that has created it and send to this one the name of the electronic market with the greatest number of clients.

```
defineAgentClass MarketSearcher() {
  authority=null;    parent=null;    knowledge=null;
  goals=null;    messages=null;
  capabilities={
    search(?pr) {
capability for searching EMarket agents
      message=search(?prod);
      condition=null;
      do{send(?AgEM:EMarket(),needClients(?prod))}
      effects=null;
    }
    knowMarkets() {
capability for updating the knowledge base when the EMarket agents answer to
its query
      message=hasClients(?prod);
      condition=null;
      do{send(this,tell(sender:Emarket())).
        Java(EM.wait(15)).send(this,migrate()).
        send(this,tell(migrated()))}
      effects=null;
    }
```

```
    migrate() {
capability for migrating to all the known markets and counting the number of
clients
        message=migrate();
        condition=not(hasKnowledge(migrated()));
        do{ ?nrC=0. ?bM=authority.
          forAllKnowledge(?E:EMarket()){
            moveTo(this, ?E).
            ?bM=Java(EM.findBestEM(?E, ?bM, ?nrC)).
            ?nrC=Java(EM.cntClients(?E, ?bM, ?nrC))}.
          send(this, return(?product, ?bM))}
        effects=null;
    }
    return()
capability for returning to the domain that has created it and giving to this one
the result of its search
        message=return(?pr, ?bestEM);
        condition=null;
        do{ moveTo(this, authority).
          send(authority, bestMarket(?pr, ?bestEM)).acid}
        effects=null;
    }
  }
  processes=null;    agents=null;
}
```

A **Client** agent has as goal to buy a certain product. It has capabilities for
migrating to all the domains that sell the researched product and buying the
product.

```
defineAgentClass  Client(?product) {
    authority=null;    parent=null;    knowledge=null;
    goals={ have(?product);}
    messages=null;
    capabilities={
      searchProduct(?pr) {
capability for searching the product
        message=search(?pr);
        condition=null;
        do{ send(?AgI:EMarket(), needProduct(?pr)) }
        effects={ askedForProduct(?pr); }
    }
    foundProduct(?prod) {
capability for finding the domains that sell the searched product
        message=haveProduct(?prod);
        condition=null;
        do{ send(sender, askIfCapability(sell(?prod))).
```

Java(EM.wait(20)).send(this,goShopping(?prod)).
   send(this,tell(migrating())) }
  effects={ knowDomains(?prod); }
 }
  goShopping() {
capability for migrating to all the domains that sell the product and buying it, if the price is good
    message=goShopping(?prod);
    condition=not(hasKnowledge(migrating()));
    do{forAllKnowledges(?AgD(sell(?prod),?m,?ef)){
      moveTo(this,?AgD).send(?AgD,buy(?prod))}.
      moveTo(this,authority)}
    effects={have(?prod); }
   }
  }
  processes=null;   agents=null;
}

4 SyMPA, a Multi-platform System

To test and validate our approach, we developed SyMPA (French: Système Multi-Plateforme d'Agents) a multi-platform system that allows creating agents and classes of agents using CLAIM and visualizing the agents' behaviour, communication and mobility. For implementing SyMPA we used the Java language. A multi-platform system is a set of connected computers; on each computer there is an agent system (AS) that supports agents' creation, identification, management, execution and migration. We developed, using JavaCC, a compiler for verifying agents' definitions. There also exists in SyMPA a central system that provides management services. SyMPA's architecture is MASIF [14] compliant.

This architecture presents three levels that we shall present below, showing their compatibility with the MASIF architecture:

the central system: provides services for agents' and agents systems' management and localization. In MASIF, this corresponds to MAFFinder, an interface that provides methods for the management of agents, places and agent systems in a region. In SyMPA, the central system administrates (in this version) all the agents. In the future versions of SyMPA, the system administrator will be able to choose between different management solutions, in accordance with the current application.

the agent system: a platform that can create, identify, interpret, execute, transfer and terminate agents. It corresponds to the MASIF MAFAgentSystem interface. It provides an interface to define CLAIM agents and classes, an interpret to verify the definitions' syntax and methods for definitions' and multi-agent system's management.

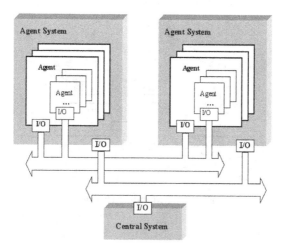

Fig. 2. SyMPA's Architecture

the agent: an autonomous, intelligent and mobile entity, defined using the CLAIM language. Each agent is uniquely identified in the system, but unlike MASIF, we can have clones of an agent. Like the ambients in *ambient calculus*, the agents form hierarchies. With this representation, a MASIF place becomes just an agent that has several sub-agents. For each agent there is a process called *PAgent* that provides methods for agent's state management, represented in a shared-memory zone. Also, *PAgent* launches several other processes:
- a graphical interface, utilized to visualize agent's behaviour, communication and mobility;
- a process that executes in parallel agent's current processes;
- a process that performs the agent's forward reasoning, by listening the arriving messages, selecting the corresponding capabilities, verifying their conditions and updating the current processes;
- a process that performs the agent's backward reasoning, by trying to execute the capabilities that allow to achieve the agent's goals.

In order to assure the efficiency and the security of the interactions between the central system and the agent systems, between the agent systems, and between the agents, we proposed communication protocols corresponding to agents' operations. Also, we use cryptographic mechanisms during communication. Each message is encrypted before the transmission and decrypted at the destination. We've seen in the presented example that the agents use for migration the ***moveTo*** mobility operation. Actually, this operation is a sequence of exit (***out***) and enter (***in***) operations executed in order to pass the agents' hierarchies. we shall present below (see Fig.3) one of the mobility protocols we propose, the one corresponding to the enter operation (***in***) between two different systems. The operational semantics of a part of this protocol was presented in the section 3.3.

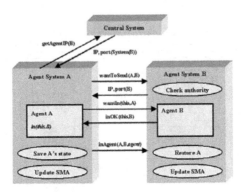

Fig. 3. A Mobility Protocol

The steps of this protocol are:

- the A's AS asks from the central system the IP and the communication port of the B's AS;
- the central system sends to the A's AS the demanded information (if any);
- the A's AS sends to the B's AS the permission to send A to B;
- the B's AS verifies the A's authority;
- the B's AS sends to the A's AS the B's communication port number (if it accepts to receive A);
- A asks from B the enter permission;
- B gives this permission (if it accepts to receive A);
- the A's AS saves the A's state, sends A to the B's AS and updates the local MAS;
- the B's AS receives A, restores its state and updates the local MAS;

5   Expressiveness and Mobility Completeness in CLAIM

Two very important characteristics of the language we propose are the generality and the expressiveness. We can represent agents' reasoning, communication and mobility. To evaluate the expressiveness of our language, we compare it to other agent oriented programming languages (see section 2.1). We made abstraction on the mobility aspects (not provided in these languages) and we translated in CLAIM applications written in other agent-oriented programming languages: *Airline Reservation* from Shoham's AGENT-0 [17], a *"bolts making"* scenario from AgentSpeak [22], and FIPA[1] protocols. we shall present next the FIPA *Contract Net Protocol* translated in CLAIM. In this protocol there are two classes of agents, *Initiator* and *Participant*.

defineAgentClass Initiator() {
  authority=null;   parent=null;   knowledge=null;
  goals=null;   messages=null;
  capabilities={

---
[1] www.fipa.org

```
  callForProposals() {
    message=callForProposal();
    condition=null;
    do{send(?Ag:Participant(),cfp())}
    effects=null; }
  rejectProposal() {
    message=propose();
    condition=Java(Init.reject(sender));
    do{send(sender,rejectProposal())}
    effects=null; }
  acceptProposal() {
    message=propose();
    condition=Java(Init.accept(sender));
    do{send(sender,acceptProposal())}
    effects=null; }
  }
  processes={send(this,callForProposal())}
  agents=null;
}

defineAgentClass Participant() {
  authority=null;     parent=null;     knowledge=null;
  goals=null;     messages=null;
  capabilities={
    refuseCFP() {
      message=cfp();
      condition=Java(Part.notAccept(sender));
      do{send(sender,refuse())}
      effects=null; }
    notUnderstood() {
      message=cfp();
      condition=Java(Part.notUnderstood());
      do{send(sender,notUnderstood())}
      effects=null; }
    acceptCFP() {
      message=cfp();
      condition=Java(Part.accept(sender));
      do{send(parent,propose(this))}
      effects=null; }
    failure() {
      message=acceptProposal();
      condition=Java(Part.failure());
      do{send(sender,failure())}
      effects=null; }
    done() {
      message=acceptProposal();
```

```
      condition=Java(Part.done());
      do{send(sender,informDone())}
      effects=null; }
   ref() {
      message=acceptProposal();
      condition=Java(Part.ref());
      do{send(sender,informRef())}
      effects=null; }
   }
   processes=null; agents=null;
}
```

In [1] , Luca Cardelli presents the desirable properties of the implementation of the reduction relation for the ambient calculus: *liveness, soundness and completeness*. it also gives an algorithm for achieving the *completeness*, the strongest and the most difficult to satisfy property.

In our language, the agents' representation is inspired from the ambient calculus. In our implementation of the mobility operations (**open, in, out, moveTo**) we defined an algorithm to satisfy the *completeness*, as presented below.

The agents are hierarchically organized. The mobility operations modify this hierarchy. The idea behind the algorithm is to have a coherent migration. For each mobility operation, the structure condition must be verified (*e.g.* for **in**, the involved agents must be on the same level in the hierarchy). This condition normally involves two agents, that can be on different machines. When the structure condition is verified, the mobility process can begin. First, in order that no other process modifies the position in the hierarchy of the agent that executes the mobility operation, all its other running processes are blocked. Its state is saved. Then, the agent asks the permission to the other involved agent to execute the mobility operation. If the later gives this permission, it also blocks all its running processes. After the mobility operation is successfully achieved, all the processes of the involved agents are resumed.

```
  algorithm MobilityOperation
Input : agent, MAS
while (not MAS.structureCondition()) do wait(t1)
if (MAS.structureCondition()) then
   agent.suspendAllProcesses()
   agent.saveState()
   agent.askPermission()
   while (not agent.receivePermission() ) do wait(t2)
   if (agent.receivePermission()) then
      MAS.update()
      while (not MAS.endUpdating()) do wait()
      agent.restoreState()
      agent.resumeAllProcesses()
   end if
```

else
  agent.removeProcess(currentMobilityOperation)
  agent.restoreState()
  agent.resumeAllProcesses()
  end else
end if

6   Conclusion and Perspectives

In this paper we argue that the MAS design needs specific languages (*i.e.* agent oriented) in order to help the designer to reduce the gap between the design and the implementation phases. Our main goal is two-folds. Firstly, we aim to offer a declarative language that frees the designer from the most implementation aspects, *i.e.* the designer should think and implement in the same paradigm (namely through agents). Secondly, we want our language to meet the requirements of mobile computation which becomes popular due to recent developments in the mobile code paradigm and enabling programming technologies.

To satisfy our goal, we combined, in an unified language called CLAIM, the advantages of the intelligent agents with those of the ambient calculus (particularly suitable for mobile computation). This allowed us to join in the same framework, computational aspects (communication, mobility, processing) and cognitive features (knowledge, goals and reasoning) of agents.

To experiment and validate our CLAIM, we developed a multi-platform system (SyMPA) compliant with the MASIF standard (OMG specifications). Hence, CLAIM agents can be distributed over several platforms and can move from one to another with respect to the MASIF specifications.

Our current work focuses on the operational semantics of CLAIM and the introduction of the security primitives as intrinsic elements of our language. We are also studying fault tolerance mechanisms for SyMPA.

Acknowledgements

Part of this work was done in the context of a LAFMI[2] project. We would like to thank our partners in this project, especially Patrick Baillot and Christophe Fouqueré from LIPN - University Paris 13.

References

1. Luca Cardelli - Mobile Ambients Synchronization, *SRC Technical Note*, Digital Equipment Corporation System Research Center, 1997.
2. Luca Cardelli - Obliq: A Language with Distributed Scope *SRC Technical Note*, Digital Equipment Corporation System Research Center, 1995.
3. Luca Cardelli, A.D. Gordon - Mobile Ambients, in *Foundations of Software Science and Computational Structures*, Maurice Nivat (Ed.), Lecture Notes in Computer Science, Vol. 1378, Springer, pages 140-155, 1998.

---

[2] http://lafmi.imag.fr/

4. Luca Cardelli - Abstractions for Mobile Computation, in *Secure Internet Programming: Security Issues for Mobile and Distributed Objects*. Lecture Notes in Computer Science, Vol. 1603, Springer, pages 51-94, 1999.
5. K. L. Clark, N. Skarmeas and F. McCabe - Agents as Clonable Objects with Knowledge Base State. *in Proc. of ICMAS96*, AAAI Press, 1996.
6. Winton H. E. Davies, Peter Edwards - Agent-K: An Integration of AOP and KQLM, *Proceedings of the CIKM'94 Workshop on Intelligent Agents*, 1994.
7. S. Conchon, F. Le Fessant - Jocaml: Mobile Agents for Objective-Caml *In ASA/MA'99*, IEEE Computer Society, pages 22-29, 1999
8. A. El Fallah-Seghrouchni, A. Suna - An Unified Framework for Programming Autonomous, Intelligent and Mobile Agents, *To appear in the proceedings of CEEMAS'03*, LNAI, Springer-Verlag, 2003
9. M. Hashimoto, A. Yonezawa - MobileML: A Programming Language for Mobile Computation *Coordination Models and Languages*, pages 198-215, 2000
10. K.V.Hindriks, F.S.deBoer, W.van der Hoek, J.J.Ch.Meyer - Agent Programming in 3APL, *Intelligent Agents and Multi-Agent Systems*, Vol. 2, pages 357-401, 1999.
11. M. d'Inverno, D. Kinny, M. Luck, M. Wooldridge - A Formal Specification of dMARS, *In Intelligent Agents IV:Procedings of the Fourth International Workshop on Agent Theories, Architectures and Languages*, Singh, Rao and Wooldridge(eds.), Lecture Notes in AI, 1365, pages 155-176, Springer-Verlag, 1998.
12. F. Levi, D. Sangiori - Controlling Interference in Ambients, *Proceedings of the 27th ACM SIGPLAN-SIGACT symposium on Principles of programming languages*, p.352-364, 2000.
13. F.G. McCabe, K.L. Clark - April Agent PRocess Interaction Language *Intelligent Agents: Theories, Architectures, and Languages*, LNAI volume 890, 1994
14. D. Milojicic, M. Breugst, I. Busse, J. Campbell, S. Covaci, B. Friedman, K. Kosaka, D. Lange, K. Ono, M. Oshima, C. Tham, S. Virdhagriswaran, J. White - MASIF, The OMG Mobile Agent System Interoperability Facility, 1998.
15. R. DeNicola, G. Ferrari, R. Pugliese - KLAIM: a Kernel Language for Agents Interaction and Mobility *IEEE Transactions on Software Engineering, 24(5)*, pages 315-330, 1998
16. P. Sampath - Modelling Multi-agent Reactive Systems *Proceedings of ICLP'02*, LNCS, Springer-Verlag, 2002
17. Yoav Shoham - Agent Oriented Programming, *Artificial Intelligence (60)*, pages 51-92, 1993.
18. Rebecca S.Thomas - The PLACA agent programming language, *Proceedings of the workshop on agent theories, architectures, and languages on Intelligent agents*, pages 355-370, 1995.
19. J. Vitek, G. Castagna - Towards a Calculus of Secure Mobile Computations, *IEEE Workshop on Internet Programming Languages*, 1998
20. Gerd Wagner - VIVA Knowledge-Based Agent Programming, Preprint (on-line at: www.inf.fu-berlin.de/ wagner/VIVA.ps.gz), 1996.
21. J. White - Mobile agents, *In Software Agents, Bradshaw, J. Ed.*, MIT Press, 1997
22. D.Weerasooriya, Anand S. Rao, K. Ramamohanarao - Design of a Concurrent Agent-Oriented Language, *Intelligent Agents. Proceedings of First International Workshop on Agent Theories, Architectures and Languages (ATAL'94)*, number 890 in LNAI, Springer Verlag, 1994.
23. P.T. Wojciechowski, P.Sewell - Normand Pict: Language and Infrastructure Design for Mobile Agents, *In Proceedings of ASA/MA*, 1999

A Programming Language
for Cognitive Agents Goal Directed 3APL

Mehdi Dastani, M. Birna van Riemsdijk,
Frank Dignum, and John-Jules Ch. Meyer

Institute of Information and Computing Sciences
Utrecht University
The Netherlands

Abstract. This paper presents the specification of a programming language for cognitive agents. This programming language is an extension of 3APL (An Abstract Agent Programming Language) and allows the programmer to implement agents' mental attitudes like beliefs, goals, plans, and actions, and agents' reasoning rules by means of which agents can modify their mental attitudes. The formal syntax and semantics of this language is presented as well as a discussion on the deliberation cycle and an example.

1 Introduction

In research on agents, besides architectures, the areas of agent theories and agent programming languages are distinguished. Theories concern descriptions of (the behavior of) agents. Agents are often described using logic [9, 15]. Concepts that are commonly incorporated in such logics are for instance knowledge, beliefs, desires, intentions, commitments, goals and plans.

It has been argued in the literature that it can be useful to analyze and specify a system in terms of these concepts [5, 12, 20]. If the system would however then be implemented using an arbitrary programming language, it will be difficult to verify whether it satisfies its specification: if we cannot identify what for instance the beliefs, desires and intentions of the system are, it will be hard to check the system against its specification expressed in these terms. This is referred to by Wooldridge as the problem of ungrounded semantics for agent specification languages [19]. It will moreover be more difficult to go from specification to implementation if there is no clear correspondence between the concepts used for specification and those used for implementation.

To support the practical development of intelligent agents, several programming languages have thus been introduced that incorporate some of the concepts from agent logics. First there is a family of languages that use actions as their starting point to define commitments (Agent-0, [14]), intentions (AgentSpeak(L), [10]) and goals (3APL, [6]). All of these languages however lacked an important element of BDI ([11]) or KARO ([16]) like (declarative) logics, which incorporate a declarative notion of goals. Having the notion of goals separate from structures

M. Dastani, J. Dix, A. El Fallah-Seghrouchni (Eds.): PROMAS 2003, LNAI 3067, pp. 111–130, 2004.
© Springer-Verlag Berlin Heidelberg 2004

built from actions, has the advantage that one can describe pro-active behavior of an agent. To bridge this gap, in [17], the language Dribble was proposed which constitutes a synthesis between the declarative and the procedural approaches, combining both notions in one and the same programming language. Dribble is however a propositional language without variables, which severely limits its programming power. In this paper, we propose an extension of the language 3APL, inspired by Dribble, with declarative goals *and* first order features. Furthermore, whereas in Dribble one can use goals for plan selection only, in this extension of 3APL we add rules for reasoning with goals. We will refer to the extension of 3APL presented in this paper, simply with the same name 3APL.

In the extended version of 3APL we consider the notion of procedural goals (used in [6]), to be reduced to that of plans, which are selected to achieve declarative goals. So, this version of 3APL provides formal constructs to implement an agent's beliefs, goals and plans. Of course, to solve the problem of ungrounded semantics for 3APL agents one should be able to implement an agent's intentions as well. However, in this paper for simplicity reasons we concentrate only on declarative goals. A discussion on the notion of intention and how to incorporate it in 3APL is discussed in [4]. In order to implement the dynamic behavior of 3APL agents, one needs formal constructs by means of which goals and plans are selected, plans executed, reasoning and planning rules are applied, etc. The language which is needed to implement such issues is called the deliberation language [3]. The behavior of 3APL agents can be implemented by means of a deliberation cycle which is an expression of the deliberation language. More details on the formal specification of the deliberation language can be found in [3].

In the next section we introduce the syntax of the extended version of 3APL and indicate some of the important (new) features. In section 3 we describe the operational semantics of 3APL using state transitions. In section 4 we indicate a number of issues to be dealt with at the deliberation level of goal directed agents. In section 5 we give an example to illustrate the use of the various programming constructs of 3APL. We give some conclusions and areas for further research in section 6.

2   Syntax

2.1   Beliefs and Goals

The *beliefs* of a 3APL agent describe the situation the agent is in. The beliefs of 3APL agents are specified by its belief base, which contains information the agent believes about the world as well as information that is internal to the agent. The *goals* of the agent on the other hand, denote the situation the agent wants to realize. It is specified by an agent's goal base, which contains information about its preferences. The beliefs and goals of 3APL agents can be specified in terms of a base language which is a first-order language. The terms of the base language represent the domain objects and its formulae represent the relations between the domain objects. In the sequel, a language defined by inclusion is the smallest set containing the specified elements.

Definition 1. *(base language) Let $Var, Func$, and $Pred$ be the sets of domain variables, functions and predicates, respectively. Let $n \geq 0$. The terms of the base language, $Term$, are defined as follows, where functions with no arguments are constants:*

- *if $x \in Var$, then $x \in Term$,*
- *if $f \in Func$ and $t_1, \ldots, t_n \in Term$, then $f(t_1, \ldots, t_n) \in Term$.*

The base language L contains only atomic formulae and is defined as follows:

- *if $p \in Pred$ and $t_1, \ldots, t_n \in Term$, then $p(t_1, \ldots, t_n) \in L$,*

In the following, we will use the standard notion of a *ground formula*. This is a formula not containing variables. Furthermore, a *closed formula* is a formula in which all variables are bound by a quantifier. The belief and goal bases are defined in terms of the expressions of the base language.

Definition 2. *(belief and goal base language) Let $\psi, \psi_1, \ldots, \psi_n \in L$ be ground formulae and let $\phi, \phi_1, \ldots, \phi_n \in L$. The belief base language, BB, and the goal base language, GB, of a 3APL agent are sets of formulae defined on the base language L as follows:*

- *$\psi, \forall_{x_1, \ldots, x_n}(\phi_1 \wedge \ldots \wedge \phi_n \rightarrow \phi) \in BB$,*
- *$\psi_1 \wedge \ldots \wedge \psi_m \in GB$*

where $\forall_{x_1, \ldots, x_n}(\varphi)$ denotes the universal closure of the formula φ for every variable $x_1, \ldots, x_n$ occurring in φ.

In the rules which will be defined in the sequel, one needs to be able to refer to formulae that are derivable from the belief base or goal base. Therefore, we define the following belief query and goal query languages on top of the base language.

Definition 3. *(belief and goal queries) Let L be the base language. Then, the belief query language L_B with typical formula β and the goal query language L_G with typical formula κ are defined as follows:*

- *if $\phi_1, \ldots, \phi_n \in L$, then $\top$, $\mathbf{B}(\phi_1 \wedge \ldots \wedge \phi_n)$, $\neg\mathbf{B}(\phi_1 \wedge \ldots \wedge \phi_n) \in Disjunction$,*
- *if $\delta, \delta' \in Disjunction$, then $\delta \overset{\rightarrow}{\vee} \delta' \in Disjunction$,*
- *if $\delta \in Disjunction$, then $\delta \in L_B$,*
- *if $\beta, \beta' \in L_B$, then $\beta \overset{\rightarrow}{\wedge} \beta' \in L_B$,*

- *if $\phi_1, \ldots, \phi_n \in L$, then $\top$, $\mathbf{G}(\phi_1 \wedge \ldots \wedge \phi_n) \in L_G$,*
- *if $\kappa, \kappa' \in L_G$, then $\kappa \overset{\rightarrow}{\wedge} \kappa' \in L_G$.*

The belief query language is a kind of conjunctive normal form, where formulas of the form $\mathbf{B}(\phi_1 \wedge \ldots \wedge \phi_n)$ are the "atoms". As will become clear in the sequel when we define the semantics of belief and goal queries (see definition 15), the "disjunction" and "conjunction" operators are not commutative. To indicate this, we use the special symbol $\overset{\rightarrow}{\vee}$ and $\overset{\rightarrow}{\wedge}$, respectively.

The goal query language does not include negation. The main reason for this is the use of such query expressions in the 3APL language. In particular, such a query can occur in the goal revision rules, which intuitively modify existing goals, i.e. they modify only goal expressions without negation.

2.2 Plans

In order to reach its goals, a 3APL agent adopts *plans*. A plan is built from basic elements. The basic elements can be *basic actions*, *tests* on the belief base or *abstract plans* (sometimes called achievement goals [6]).

As in the languages GOAL and 3APL, basic actions specify the capabilities with which an agent should achieve a certain state of affairs. The effect of the execution of a basic action is not a change in the world, but a change in the belief base of the agent.

A test action checks if a certain formula is derivable from the beliefbase.

An abstract plan cannot be executed directly in the sense that it updates the belief base of an agent. Abstract plans serve as an abstraction mechanism like procedures in imperative programming. If a plan consists of an abstract plan, this abstract plan could be transformed into basic actions through reasoning rules.

As abstract plans can be transformed into basic actions and basic actions are executed in a domain, both basic actions and abstract plans can be parameterized with terms that denote the domain objects. To be more specific, abstract plans are plan names which can be parameterized with terms (denoting domain objects). We thus use a set of plan names $PName = \{q_1, q_2, \ldots\}$ which are used to define the set of abstract plans $AP = \{q(t_1, \ldots, t_n) \mid q \in PName, t_1, \ldots, t_n \in Term, n \geq 0\}$ with typical element ρ. Moreover, we assume a set of basic action names $AName = \{a_1, a_2, \ldots\}$ which are used to define the set of basic actions $Act = \{a(t_1, \ldots, t_n) \mid a \in AName, t_1, \ldots, t_n \in Term, n \geq 0\}$ with typical element α.

Definition 4. *(plans) Let $\beta \in L_B$. The plan language L_P consists of the following elements:*

- *basic action: $Act \subseteq L_P$,*
- *test: $\beta? \in L_P$,*
- *abstract plan: $AP \subseteq L_P$,*
- *if $\beta?, \pi \in L_P, \alpha \in Act, \rho \in AP$, then $\alpha; \pi$, $\beta?; \pi$, $\rho; \pi \in L_P$,*
- *composite plans: if $\pi, \pi_1, \pi_2 \in L_P$, then*
  if β then π_1 else π_2 fi, if β then π_1 else π_2 fi; $\pi \in L_P$, *and*
  while β do π_1 od, while β do π_1 od; $\pi \in L_P$.

We use E to denote the empty plan, which is an empty list and we identify $E; \pi$ with π. In the sequel, we will use $\circ$ to indicate that a plan is a sequential composition of two plans, i.e. $\pi_1 \circ \pi$ denotes a plan in which π_1 is a plan followed by the second plan π (π_1 is the prefix of the plan $\pi_1 \circ \pi$).

2.3 Rules

We propose various rules to reason with goals and plans and to select plans. These rules are conditionalized by beliefs.

Definition 5. *(rules) Let* $\beta \in L_B$, $\kappa, \kappa_h, \kappa_b \in L_G$, *and* $\pi, \pi_h, \pi_b \in L_P$. *We define sets of reasoning rules to revise goals and plans, and to select plans. These rules are called goal revision rules (GR), plan revision rules (PR), and plan selection rules (PS), respectively.*

- $\kappa_h \leftarrow \beta \mid \kappa_b \in GR$,
- $\pi_h \leftarrow \beta \mid \pi_b \in PR$,
- $\kappa \leftarrow \beta \mid \pi \in PS$.

The *goal revision rules* are used to revise, generate or drop goals. For example, the goal revision rule $\mathbf{G}(on(x, y)) \leftarrow \mathbf{B}(tooHeavy(x) \wedge notHeavy(z)) \mid \mathbf{G}(on(z, y))$ can be used to revise one of an agent's goals: it informally means that if the agent desires to have block x on block y, but it believes that x is too heavy while z is not heavy, then it should revise its goal and aim to have block z on block y. The goal revision rules can also be used to generate, extend or drop goals by using the following general forms, respectively:

- $\top \leftarrow \beta \mid \kappa_b$ for goal generation,
- $\kappa_h \leftarrow \beta \mid \kappa_h \overset{\rightarrow}{\wedge} \kappa_b$ for goal extension,
- $\kappa_h \leftarrow \beta \mid \top$ for dropping goals,

The *plan selection rules* are used to generate plans to achieve goals. They are similar to the goal rules of Dribble. For example, the plan selection rule $\mathbf{G}(on(x, z)) \leftarrow \mathbf{B}(on(x, y)) \mid move(x, y, z)$ states that if the agent desires to have block x on block z, but it believes that x is on block y, then it plans to move x from y and put it on z. The belief condition thus indicates when the plan could be selected to achieve the specified goal. Plan selection rules can also be used to model reactive behavior with rules of the form $\top \leftarrow \beta \mid \pi$.

Finally, the *plan revision rules*, which are similar to the practical reasoning rules of 3APL, are used to revise and drop plans. For example, the plan revision rule $move(x, y, z) \leftarrow \neg\mathbf{B}(clear(x)) \mid on(u, x)?; move(u, x, Fl); move(x, y, z)$ informally means that if the agent plans to move block x from block y onto block z, but it cannot move x because (it believes that) there is a block on x, then the agent should revise its plan by finding out which block (u) is on x, moving u onto the floor, and finally moving x from y onto z.

2.4 Plan Safety and Rule Safety

In this subsection, we will explain and define the concepts of plan safety and rule safety, which will be used to ensure that applying rules cannot result in an unground goalbase or beliefbase (containing atomic formulae with variables that are not bound), and ill-defined plans (containing actions with variables that are not bound). As these notions are syntactic, they are defined in this section. The definitions in this section do not have to be mastered by the reader in order for him/her to understand the general ideas of the semantics.

In the sequel, we will assume that all rules are *safe*. The idea of the requirement of rule safety starts with the concept of *plan safety* (definition 8). The intuition behind the notion of a safe plan is that variables in the basic actions occurring in the plan should either be bound by a substitution or they should be preceded by a test through which a binding will be computed. The reason for this requirement is that it is not clear what it means to execute a basic action with variables without a binding. For example, it is not clear how to specify the semantics of the basic action $move(x, y)$ in a sensible way if x and y are variables without a binding. We require the same condition on variables that occur in abstract plans, as these can be transformed into basic actions using plan revision rules.

In order to define the concept of a safe plan, we define a function yielding the so-called safe variables of a belief query. This function takes a belief query formula and yields the variables that will be bound by any substitution under which the query would succeed (see definition 11 for the definition of a (ground) substitution and see definition 15 for the semantics of a belief query under a substitution). The idea thus is, that this function returns those variables of a belief query, that will definitely get a "value" if the query succeeds.

The reason that not all variables in a belief query will get a value if the query succeeds, is that we can pose queries such as $\neg\mathbf{B}(p(x))$. Informally, this query will succeed if the agent does not believe that $p(x)$ holds, i.e. there is no possible value a for x, such that the agent believes $p(a)$. A query such as $\mathbf{B}(p(x))$ however, will always return a value for x, if the query succeeds. We can furthermore pose queries such as $\mathbf{B}(p(x)) \overset{\rightarrow}{\vee} \mathbf{B}(q(y))$, which will succeed if either a value a for x can be found such that the agent believes $p(a)$, or alternatively if no such value can be found, if a value b for y can be found such that the agent believes $p(b)$. The definition of the function $safeVar$ for belief queries reflects these considerations.

Below, we also specify functions yielding the safe variables of goal queries and of plans. These are needed in the definition of the notion of a safe rule and will be explained later in more detail.

Definition 6. *(variables, safe variables) We define $Var_f(e)$[1] to be the set of variables occurring in the syntactic expression e. Moreover, the function $safeVar : L_B \rightarrow \wp(Var)$ is then defined as follows.*

$$
\begin{aligned}
safeVar(\mathbf{B}(\phi)) &= Var_f(\phi) \\
safeVar(\neg\mathbf{B}(\phi)) &= \emptyset \\
safeVar(\beta \overset{\rightarrow}{\vee} \beta') &= safeVar(\beta) \cap safeVar(\beta') \\
safeVar(\beta \overset{\rightarrow}{\wedge} \beta') &= safeVar(\beta) \cup safeVar(\beta')
\end{aligned}
$$

We assume a similar function $safeVar : L_G \rightarrow \wp(Var)$ for goal queries. For plans, we define the following function $safeVar : L_P \rightarrow \wp(Var)$ with $\alpha \in Act$, $\rho \in AP$ and $\pi, \pi' \in L_P$, where π' is not of the form $\alpha; \pi$ or $\rho; \pi$.

---

[1] Note that we used Var in definition 1 to denote the set of variables of the base language. In this definition, Var_f is a function yielding the set of variables occurring in some expression. We use the subscript f to denote that we are referring to the function Var_f.

$$safeVar(\alpha; \pi) = Var_f(\alpha) \cup safeVar(\pi)$$
$$safeVar(\rho; \pi) = Var_f(\rho) \cup safeVar(\pi)$$
$$safeVar(\pi') \quad = \emptyset$$

The function can be generalized, yielding a function $safeVar : \wp(L_B \cup L_G \cup L_P) \rightarrow \wp(Var)$ *as follows:* $safeVar(Expr) = \bigcup_{e \in Expr} safeVar(e)$.

In order to be able to define the notion of a safe plan, we also need the concept of free variables of a plan. The free variables of a plan π are those variables occurring in abstract plans or basic actions in π, that are not "preceded" by a test through which these variables will be bound for certain. In the specification of the free variables of a plan, we thus use the definition of the safe variables of a belief query. For example, in the plan $\mathbf{B}(p(x))?; do(x)$ the variable x in the basic action do will have a value after the execution of the test preceding this action, since x is in the set of safe variables of $\mathbf{B}(p(x))$. Below, we define a function yielding the free variables of a plan.

Definition 7. *(free variables of a plan) Let* $\alpha \in Act$, $\rho \in AP$, $\pi, \pi_1, \pi_2 \in L_P$ *and* $\beta \in L_B$. *Let the functions* Var_f *and* $safeVar$ *be as in definition 6. The function* $Free : L_P \rightarrow \wp(Var)$ *is then defined as follows.*

$$
\begin{aligned}
Free(E) &= Var_f(E) \\
Free(\alpha; \pi) &= Var_f(\alpha) \cup Free(\pi) \\
Free(\rho; \pi) &= Var_f(\rho) \cup Free(\pi) \\
Free(\beta?; \pi) &= Free(\pi) \setminus safeVar(\beta) \\
Free(\texttt{if } \beta \texttt{ then } \pi_1 \texttt{ else } \pi_2 \texttt{ fi}; \pi) &= (Free(\pi_1) \setminus safeVar(\beta)) \cup \\
&\quad\ Free(\pi_2) \cup Free(\pi) \\
Free(\texttt{while } \beta \texttt{ do } \pi_1 \texttt{ od}; \pi) &= Free(\pi_1) \cup Free(\pi)
\end{aligned}
$$

A safe plan now is defined as a plan without free variables.

Definition 8. *(safe plan) Let* $\pi \in L_P$ *be a plan. The plan* π *is safe if and only if* $Free(\pi) = \emptyset$.

As plans can be transformed using plan revision rules, we have to add a requirement on these rules, making sure that plan safety is preserved under plan revision. Furthermore, new plans can be adopted using plan selection rules. Therefore, we need a requirement on these rules as well, ascertaining that only safe plans are adopted. Finally, we also need a requirement on goal revision rules for the following reason. The goals in the body of goal revision rules are added to the goal base. The goal base should be ground, so we have to make sure that all variables in the goals that will be added, are substituted by a value. This is reflected in the safety requirement for goal revision rules.

Definition 9. *(safe rules)*

– *A goal revision rule* $\kappa_h \leftarrow \beta \mid \kappa_b \in GR$ *is safe,*
  if $Var_f(\kappa_b) \subseteq safeVar(\{\kappa_h, \beta\})$.

- *A plan selection rule $\kappa \leftarrow \beta \mid \pi \in PS$ is safe,*
  if $Free(\pi) \subseteq safeVar(\{\kappa, \beta\})$.
- *A plan revision rule $\pi_h \leftarrow \beta \mid \pi_b \in PR$ is safe,*
  if $Free(\pi_b) \subseteq safeVar(\{\pi_h, \beta\})$.

2.5   A 3APL Configuration

Above, the beliefs, goals, plans, and reasoning rules of a 3APL agent were defined. To program a 3APL agent means to specify its initial beliefs, goals, and plans, and to write sets of goal revision rules, plan selection rules and plan revision rules. This is formalized in the specification of a 3APL agent.

Definition 10. *(3APL agent) A 3APL agent is a tuple $\langle \sigma_0, \gamma_0, \Pi_0, GR, PS, PR \rangle$ where σ_0 is the initial beliefbase, γ_0 is the initial goalbase, Π_0 is the initial planbase, GR is a set of goal revision rules, PS is a set of plan selection rules, and PR is a set of plan revision rules.*

The beliefs, goals, and plans are the elements that change during the execution of the agent while the reasoning rules remain unchanged during the execution of the agent. Together with a fourth *substitution* component, these elements constitute a 3APL configuration. This substitution part of the configuration is used to store values or bindings associated with first order variables.

Definition 11. *((ground) substitution) A substitution θ is a finite set of the form $\{x_1/t_1, \ldots, x_n/t_n\}$, where $x_i \in Var$ and $t_i \in Term$ and $\forall i \neq j : x_i \neq x_j$. θ is called a ground substitution if all t_i are ground terms.*

Definition 12. *(binding, domain, free variables) Let $\theta = \{x_1/t_1, \ldots, x_n/t_n\}$ be a ground substitution. Each element x_i/t_i is called a binding for x_i. The set of variables $\{x_1, \ldots, x_n\}$ is the domain of θ and will be denoted by $dom(\theta)$. The variables occurring in some syntactic expression e that are not bound by some substitution θ, i.e. that are not in $dom(\theta)$, are called the free variables of e and this will be denoted by $Free_\theta(e)$.*

Below, we define what it means to apply a substitution to a syntactic expression. We will need this in the sequel.

Definition 13. *(application of substitution) Let e be a syntactic expression and let θ be a ground substitution. Then $e\theta$ denotes the expression where all occurrences of variable x in e for which $x/t \in \theta$ are simultaneously replaced by t.*

Definition 14. *(configuration) A configuration of a 3APL agent is a tuple $\langle \sigma, \gamma, \Pi, \theta \rangle$, where $\sigma \subseteq BB$ is the belief base of the agent, $\gamma \subseteq GB$ is the goal base of the agent, $\Pi \subseteq L_P \times L_G$ is the plan base of the agent[2] and θ represents a ground substitution that binds domain variables to domain terms. Finally, the goal base in a configuration is such that for any goal $\phi \in \gamma$ it holds that $\sigma \not\models \phi$, i.e. the goal ϕ is not entailed by the agent's beliefs.*

---

[2] Note that with each plan the (initial) goal to be achieved by the plan is associated.

In this definition, we have defined Π as consisting of plan-goal formula pairs. The goal for which a plan is selected is recorded with the plan, because this for instance provides the possibility to drop a plan of which the goal is reached. Furthermore, goals may be revised or dropped and one might want to remove a plan associated with a goal which has been dropped, from the plan base.

The rationale behind the condition on the goal base is the following. The beliefs of an agent describe the state the agent is in and the goals describe the state the agent wants to realize. If an agent believes ϕ is the case, it cannot have the goal to achieve ϕ, because the state of affairs ϕ is already realized.

3   Semantics

We define an operational semantics for 3APL in terms of a transition system ([8]). A transition system is a set of derivation rules for deriving transitions. A transition is a transformation of one configuration into another and it corresponds to a single computation step.

3.1   Semantics of Belief and Goal Formulae

In order to define the semantics of the various rules, we first need to define the semantics of the belief and goal queries.

Definition 15. *(semantics of belief and goal queries) Let* $\langle \sigma, \gamma, \Pi, \theta \rangle$ *be an agent configuration,* $\delta, \delta' \in Disjunction$, $\mathbf{B}\phi, \beta, \beta' \in L_B$ *and* $\mathbf{G}\phi, \kappa, \kappa' \in L_G$. *Let* τ, τ_1, τ_2 *be ground substitutions.*

$$\langle \sigma, \gamma, \Pi, \theta \rangle \models_\emptyset \top$$
$$\langle \sigma, \gamma, \Pi, \theta \rangle \models_\tau \mathbf{B}\phi \quad \Leftrightarrow \sigma \models \phi\tau$$
$$\text{where } Var_f(\phi) = dom(\tau)$$
$$\langle \sigma, \gamma, \Pi, \theta \rangle \models_\emptyset \neg\mathbf{B}\phi \quad \Leftrightarrow \neg\exists\tau : \langle \sigma, \gamma, \Pi, \theta \rangle \models_\tau \mathbf{B}\phi$$
$$\langle \sigma, \gamma, \Pi, \theta \rangle \models_\tau \delta \overrightarrow{\vee} \delta' \Leftrightarrow \langle \sigma, \gamma, \Pi, \theta \rangle \models_\tau \delta \text{ or}$$
$$(\forall\tau' : \langle \sigma, \gamma, \Pi, \theta \rangle \not\models_{\tau'} \delta \text{ and } \langle \sigma, \gamma, \Pi, \theta \rangle \models_\tau \delta')$$
$$\langle \sigma, \gamma, \Pi, \theta \rangle \models_\tau \beta \overrightarrow{\wedge} \beta' \Leftrightarrow \exists\tau_1, \tau_2 : \langle \sigma, \gamma, \Pi, \theta \rangle \models_{\tau_1} \beta \text{ and } \langle \sigma, \gamma, \Pi, \theta \rangle \models_{\tau_2} \beta'\tau_1$$
$$\text{where } \tau_1 \cup \tau_2 = \tau$$

$$\langle \sigma, \gamma, \Pi, \theta \rangle \models_\emptyset \top$$
$$\langle \sigma, \gamma, \Pi, \theta \rangle \models_\tau \mathbf{G}\phi \quad \Leftrightarrow \gamma \models \phi\tau \text{ and } \sigma \not\models \phi\tau$$
$$\text{where } Var_f(\phi) = dom(\tau)$$
$$\langle \sigma, \gamma, \Pi, \theta \rangle \models_\tau \kappa \overrightarrow{\wedge} \kappa' \Leftrightarrow \exists\tau_1, \tau_2 : \langle \sigma, \gamma, \Pi, \theta \rangle \models_{\tau_1} \kappa \text{ and } \langle \sigma, \gamma, \Pi, \theta \rangle \models_{\tau_2} \kappa'\tau_1$$
$$\text{where } \tau_1 \cup \tau_2 = \tau$$

Belief and goal queries can be posed in a configuration. The result of these queries is, like in logic programming, not just "succeeded" or "failed", but the query will also return a substitution τ (if it succeeds under this τ). A belief or goal query formula can thus hold in a configuration under some substitution τ. We will now explain the semantics of the belief and goal queries in more detail.

A formula of the form $\mathbf{B}\phi$ holds in a configuration with belief base σ under a substitution τ, iff ϕ with τ applied to it, follows from σ. We require that τ is such, that it binds all and nothing but the variables in ϕ. Suppose for example that $\phi = p(x, y)$ and that (only) $p(a, b)$ follows from σ. We then want our substitution to return, for instance, the binding a for x *and* the binding b for y. We furthermore do not want τ to bind any variables that do not occur in ϕ.

A formula of the form $\neg\mathbf{B}\phi$ holds in a configuration with belief base σ, iff there is no possible substitution τ such that $\mathbf{B}\phi$ follows from the configuration. If for example the formula $\neg\mathbf{B}(p(x))$ holds, it should not be possible to substitute some value a for x, such that $p(a)$ follows from σ. The evaluation of a negative "literal" will thus always yield an empty substitution.

A formula of the form $\delta \overset{\rightarrow}{\vee} \delta'$ holds in a configuration under a substitution τ, iff δ or otherwise δ' holds under τ. The idea is, that if for example a query $\mathbf{B}(p(x)) \overset{\rightarrow}{\vee} \mathbf{B}(q(y))$ is posed, the left part of the formula, i.e. $\mathbf{B}(p(x))$, is checked first. If this query $\mathbf{B}(p(x))$ succeeds, we conclude that the orginial query succeeds and we do not have to check the second part of the original query. If the first part fails however, we need to then check the second part. This definition of the semantics of $\overset{\rightarrow}{\vee}$ renders it a non-commutative operator. Take for example the formula $\mathbf{B}(p(x)) \overset{\rightarrow}{\vee} \mathbf{B}(q(y))$ and suppose that $\sigma = \{p(a), q(b)\}$. The formula $\mathbf{B}(p(x)) \overset{\rightarrow}{\vee} \mathbf{B}(q(y))$ holds in a configuration with belief base σ under $\tau = \{x/a\}$. The formula $\mathbf{B}(q(y)) \overset{\rightarrow}{\vee} \mathbf{B}(p(x))$ on the other hand, holds under $\tau = \{y/b\}$. They both fail under $\tau = \{y/b\}$.

A formula of the form $\beta \overset{\rightarrow}{\wedge} \beta'$ holds in a configuration under a substitution τ, iff β holds under some substitution τ_1 and β' with τ_1 applied to it, holds under some substitution τ_2. The operator $\overset{\rightarrow}{\wedge}$ is therefore not commutative. These τ_1 and τ_2 should be such that together they form substitution τ. For example, let $\sigma = \{p(a), q(b, c)\}$ and suppose that we evaluate the following formula in a configuration with belief base σ: $\neg\mathbf{B}(p(x)) \overset{\rightarrow}{\wedge} \mathbf{B}(q(x, y))$. We first evaluate $\neg\mathbf{B}(p(x))$, which means that there should exists no substitution τ such that $\mathbf{B}(p(x))$ holds under this τ. However, $\mathbf{B}(p(x))$ holds under $\tau = \{x/a\}$ and the query thus fails. Now take the formula $\mathbf{B}(q(x, y)) \overset{\rightarrow}{\wedge} \neg\mathbf{B}(p(x))$. We first evaluate $\mathbf{B}(q(x, y))$, which holds under $\tau_1 = \{x/b, y/c\}$. We then apply τ_1 to $\neg\mathbf{B}(p(x))$, yielding $\neg\mathbf{B}(p(b))$. Now we evaluate $\neg\mathbf{B}(p(b))$, which holds if there is no substitution τ such that $\mathbf{B}(p(b))$ holds under τ. There is indeed no substitution under which this formula holds, so the query succeeds with $\tau = \{x/b, y/c\}$.

The semantics of $\mathbf{G}\phi$ is defined in terms of separate goals, as opposed to defining it in terms of the entire goal base. The idea is, that all logical consequences of a particular goal are also goals, but only if they are not believed [7].

3.2   Transition System

In the following, a set of derivation rules is proposed that specifies the semantics of various ingredients of 3APL. These rules specify the semantics of a 3APL agent with a set of goal revision rules GR, a set of plan revision rules PR, and a set of plan selection rules PS.

The first derivation rule specifies the execution of the plan base of a 3APL agent. The plan base of the agent is a set of plan-goal pairs. This set can be executed by executing one of the constituent plans. The execution of a plan can change the agent's configuration.

Definition 16. *(plan base execution) Let* $\Pi = \{(\pi_1, \kappa_1), \ldots, (\pi_i, \kappa_i), \ldots, (\pi_n, \kappa_n)\} \subseteq L_P \times L_G$ *and* $\Pi' = \{(\pi_1, \kappa_1), \ldots, (\pi_i', \kappa_i), \ldots, (\pi_n, \kappa_n)\} \subseteq L_P \times L_G$ *be plan bases,* θ, θ' *be ground substitutions. Let* $Free_\theta : \wp(L_P \times L_G) \to \wp(Var)$ *be the generalization of the function* $Free_\theta$ *of definition 12 to sets of plan-goal pairs and let* $V = Free_\theta(\Pi)$. *Then, the derivation for the execution of a set of plans is specified in terms of the execution of individual plans as follows.*

$$\frac{\langle \sigma, \gamma, \{(\pi_i, \kappa_i)\}, \theta \rangle_V \to \langle \sigma', \gamma', \{(\pi_i', \kappa_i)\}, \theta' \rangle}{\langle \sigma, \gamma, \Pi, \theta \rangle \to \langle \sigma', \gamma', \Pi', \theta' \rangle}$$

Transitions for individual plans are parameterized by the set of free variables V, i.e. those not bound by θ, of the entire plan base Π. This is necessary because in the transition rules for individual plans, sometimes reference needs to be made to this set.

In the following, we use the function $args : L_G \to \wp(\{\phi_1 \wedge \ldots \wedge \phi_n \mid \phi_1, \ldots, \phi_n \in L\})$ that removes the **G** modalities from a goal formula returning its goals from L, with $args(\top) = \emptyset$. For example, $args(\mathbf{G}(p(x)) \wedge \mathbf{G}(q(y))) = \{p(x), q(y)\}$. Now we will introduce the derivation rules for the execution of individual plans. We introduce derivation rules for two types of basic elements of plans: basic actions and tests. We do not introduce derivation rules for abstract plans, because abstract plans cannot be executed. They can only be transformed using plan revision rules (see definition 22).

Definition 17. *(basic action execution) Let* $\alpha \in Act$ *and let* $\mathcal{T} : (Act \times BB) \to BB$ *be a function that specifies the belief update resulting from the execution of basic actions, then the execution of a single action is specified as follows:*

$$\frac{\mathcal{T}(\alpha\theta, \sigma) = \sigma' \ \& \ \langle \sigma, \gamma, \{(\alpha, \kappa)\}, \theta \rangle \models_\emptyset \kappa}{\langle \sigma, \gamma, \{(\alpha, \kappa)\}, \theta \rangle_V \to \langle \sigma', \gamma', \{(E, \kappa)\}, \theta \rangle}$$

where $\gamma' = \gamma \backslash \{\phi \in \gamma \mid \sigma' \models \phi\}$.

The substitution θ is used to instantiate free variables in the basic action α. Furthermore, by definition 23, we know that κ must be ground. We can therefore specify that κ should hold under the empty substitution, as no variables need to be bound.

Note that the condition $\langle \sigma, \gamma, \{(\alpha, \kappa)\}, \theta \rangle \models \kappa$ guarantees that the action can only be executed if the goal for which α was selected is still entailed by the current configuration. This condition might be considered too strong. An alternative is, to remove the condition from this transition rule. The decision of whether to execute plans of which the goal is not entailed by the current configuration, could then be lifted to the deliberation cycle (see section 4). The function $\mathcal{T}$ is assumed to preserve consistency of the belief base (see definition 14). Note also that the effect of the execution of basic actions is first of all a belief update. If goals in the goal base are realized through the execution of the action, these goals are removed from the goal base.

The derivation rule for the execution of the test can bind the free variables that occur in the test formula for which no bindings have been computed yet.

Definition 18. *(test execution) Let $\beta \in L_B$ and let τ be a ground substitution.*

$$\frac{\langle \sigma, \gamma, \Pi, \theta \rangle \models_\tau \beta\theta}{\langle \sigma, \gamma, \{(\beta?, \kappa)\}, \theta \rangle_V \rightarrow \langle \sigma, \gamma, \{(E, \kappa)\}, \theta\tau \rangle}$$

In the semantics of composite plans and rules, we will need the notion of a variant. A syntactic element e is a variant of another element e' in case e can be obtained from e' by renaming of variables. We will use variants of plans or rules to avoid unwanted bindings between variables in those plans or rules and variables in the plan base (V) or in $dom(\theta)$.

The derivation rules for the execution of composite plans are defined recursively in the standard way below.

Definition 19. *(execution of composite plans) Let τ be a ground substitution. The following transitions specify the execution of different types of composite plans.*

$$\frac{\langle \sigma, \gamma, \{(\pi_1, \kappa)\}, \theta \rangle_V \rightarrow \langle \sigma', \gamma', \{(\pi_2, \kappa)\}, \theta' \rangle}{\langle \sigma, \gamma, \{(\pi_1 \circ \pi, \kappa)\}, \theta \rangle_V \rightarrow \langle \sigma', \gamma', \{(\pi_2 \circ \pi, \kappa)\}, \theta' \rangle}$$

$$\frac{\langle \sigma, \gamma, \Pi, \theta \rangle \models_\tau \beta\theta}{\langle \sigma, \gamma, \{(\text{if } \beta \text{ then } \pi_1 \text{ else } \pi_2 \text{ fi}, \kappa)\}, \theta \rangle_V \rightarrow \langle \sigma, \gamma, \{(\pi_1\tau, \kappa)\}, \theta \rangle}$$

$$\frac{\neg\exists\tau : \langle \sigma, \gamma, \Pi, \theta \rangle \models_\tau \beta\theta}{\langle \sigma, \gamma, \{(\text{if } \beta \text{ then } \pi_1 \text{ else } \pi_2 \text{ fi}, \kappa)\}, \theta \rangle_V \rightarrow \langle \sigma, \gamma, \{(\pi_2, \kappa)\}, \theta \rangle}$$

$$\frac{\langle \sigma, \gamma, \Pi, \theta \rangle \models_\tau \beta\theta}{\langle \sigma, \gamma, \{(\text{while } \beta \text{ do } \pi \text{ od}, \kappa)\}, \theta \rangle_V \rightarrow \langle \sigma, \gamma, \{(\pi\tau; \text{while } \beta \text{ do } \pi \text{ od}, \kappa)\}, \theta \rangle}$$

$$\frac{\neg\exists\tau : \langle \sigma, \gamma, \Pi, \theta \rangle \models_\tau \beta\theta}{\langle \sigma, \gamma, \{(\text{while } \beta \text{ do } \pi \text{ od}, \kappa)\}, \theta \rangle_V \rightarrow \langle \sigma, \gamma, \{(E, \kappa)\}, \theta \rangle}$$

Note that the goal associated with some plan is passed on unchanged through the transitions modifying this plan.

We will now define the transition rules for the reasoning rules. A goal revision rule $\kappa_h \leftarrow \beta \mid \kappa_b$ is applicable if its head is derivable from the agent's goal base and its condition is derivable from the agent's belief base. The application of the goal revision rule only affects the goal base of the agent, i.e. the goal base of the agent is revised according to the goal revision rule.

Definition 20. *(goal revision rule application) Let the rule* $\kappa_h \leftarrow \beta \mid \kappa_b$ *be a safe goal revision rule from* GR *and* τ_1, τ_2 *be ground substitutions. Then the transition rule for this safe goal revision rule is defined as follows:*

$$\frac{\langle \sigma, \gamma, \Pi, \theta \rangle \models_{\tau_1} \kappa_h \ \& \ \langle \sigma, \gamma, \Pi, \theta \rangle \models_{\tau_2} \beta\tau_1 \ \& \ \forall \phi \in args(\kappa_b) : \sigma \not\models \phi\tau_1\tau_2}{\langle \sigma, \gamma, \Pi, \theta \rangle_V \rightarrow \langle \sigma, \gamma', \Pi, \theta \rangle}$$

where $\gamma' = (\gamma \backslash \{\phi \in \gamma \mid \phi' \in args(\kappa_h) \text{ and } \phi \equiv \phi'\tau_1\tau_2\}) \cup \{\phi\tau_1\tau_2 \mid \phi \in args(\kappa_b)\}$.

The effect of the application of the safe goal revision rule is removing the goals that occur in the head of the rule (modulo the **G** operator) from the goal base. Furthermore, it adds the goals in the body of the rule (for all possible substitutions τ_1 and τ_2).

Note that we first check if the head of the rule (a goal query) is derivable from the agent configuration under a substitution τ, and then we check if the guard of the rule (a belief query) to which τ is applied, is derivable from the agent configuration. Doing the checks in this order (and not first belief query and then goal query) allows more goal rules to be applicable. To illustrate this, consider the rule $\mathbf{G}(g(x)) \leftarrow \neg\mathbf{B}(p(x)) \mid \kappa$ and suppose that $\sigma = \{p(a)\}$ and $\gamma = \{g(c)\}$. The proposed order of checks allows this rule to be applied while the reverse order does not. Note that we do not require a variant of the goal revision rule since the (updating) goals are ground.

A plan revision rule $\pi_h \leftarrow \beta \mid \pi_b$ is applicable if its head π_h unifies with the prefix of an agent's plan and its condition β is derivable from the agent's beliefs. We assume that the revised plan π_b is designed to achieve the same goal. Therefore, the goal associated with plan π_h in the plan base will be associated with the revised plan π_b as well. The application of a plan revision rule only affects the plan base of the agent, i.e. the plan to which the plan revision rule is applied, is revised. We first define the concept of a most general unifier.

Definition 21. *(most general unifier) Let* $\pi, \pi' \in L_P$. *A unifier for the pair* (π, π') *is a substitution* θ *such that* $\pi\theta \equiv \pi'\theta$, *i.e. such that the two plans are syntactically equal. A unifier* θ *is called the most general unifier for the pair, if for each unifier* θ' *of the pair, there exists a substitution* τ *such that* $\theta' = \theta\tau$.

Definition 22. *(plan revision rule application) Let* $\pi_h \leftarrow \beta \mid \pi_b$ *be a variant of a safe plan revision rule from* PR *such that no free variables in the rule occur in* V *or* $dom(\theta)$. *Let* η *be a most general unifier for* π *and* π_h *and let* τ *be a ground substitution.*

$$\frac{\langle \sigma, \gamma, \Pi, \theta \rangle \models_{\tau} \beta\eta \ \& \ \langle \sigma, \gamma, \{(\pi, \kappa)\}, \theta \rangle \models_{\emptyset} \kappa}{\langle \sigma, \gamma, \{(\pi, \kappa)\}, \theta \rangle_V \rightarrow \langle \sigma, \gamma, \{(\pi_b\eta\tau, \kappa)\}, \theta \rangle}$$

The effect of the application of the safe plan revision rule on the plan base is that the plan π is replaced by the body π_b of the plan revision rule instantiated with the substitution η, which results from matching the head of the rule with the plan, and with the substitution τ, which results from matching the condition of the rule with the belief base. Note that the substitution θ is not updated by the substitutions τ or η because the body of the rule is a variant and does not contain any variable occurring in Π or $dom(\theta)$. This implies that all bindings in τ or η are about new variables that occur only in the body of the rule. τ or η can therefore be applied directly to π_b. Note also that plan revision rules revise the prefix of plans.

A safe plan selection rule $\kappa \leftarrow \beta \mid \pi$ specifies that the goal κ can be achieved by plan π if β is derivable from the agent's beliefs. A plan selection rule only affects the plan base of the agent.

Definition 23. *(plan selection rule application) Let $\kappa \leftarrow \beta \mid \pi$ be a variant of a safe plan selection rule from PS such that no free variables in the rule (plan part of the rule) occur in V or $dom(\theta)$. Let also τ_1, τ_2 be ground substitutions.*

$$\frac{\langle \sigma, \gamma, \Pi, \theta \rangle \models_{\tau_1} \kappa \ \& \ \langle \sigma, \gamma, \Pi, \theta \rangle \models_{\tau_2} \beta\tau_1}{\langle \sigma, \gamma, \Pi, \theta \rangle_V \rightarrow \langle \sigma, \gamma, \Pi \cup \{(\pi\tau_1\tau_2, \kappa\tau_1)\}, \theta \rangle}$$

Note that the goal $\kappa\tau_1$ that should be achieved by the plan $\pi\tau_1\tau_2$ is associated with it. It is only this rule that associates goals with plans. The goal base of the agent does not change because the plan $\pi\tau_1\tau_2$ is not executed yet; the goals of agents may change only after execution of plans. We do not add substitutions τ_1, τ_2 to θ since this substitution should only influence the new plan π.

3.3   Semantics of a 3APL Agent

The semantics of a 3APL agent is derived directly from the transition relation $\rightarrow$. The meaning of a 3APL agent consists of a set of so called computation runs.

Definition 24. *(computation run) A computation run $CR(s_0)$ for a 3APL agent is a finite or infinite sequence $s_0, \ldots, s_n$ or $s_0, \ldots$ where s_i are configurations, and $\forall_{i>0} : s_{i-1} \rightarrow s_i$ is a transition in the transition system for the 3APL agent.*

Definition 25. *(semantics of a 3APL agent) The semantics of a 3APL agent $\langle \sigma_0, \gamma_0, \Pi_0, GR, PR, PS \rangle$ is defined iff the plans in Π_0 and the rules GR, PR and PS are safe. The semantics then is the set of computation runs $CR(\langle \sigma_0, \gamma_0, \Pi_0, \emptyset \rangle)$.*

4   Deliberation Cycle

In the previous sections we have described the syntax and semantics of 3APL. However, in order to run 3APL we also need an interpreter that determines the order in which rules are applied, when actions should be performed, when belief updates should be made, etc. This interpreter is not fixed in 3APL but is itself a program again. This deliberation module for 3APL without the declarative goals was described already in [3].

The addition of declarative goals will, however, substantially influence the deliberation cycle. Although a complete discussion of all issues falls outside the scope of this paper we describe some of the prominent topics to be dealt with during the deliberation.

First of all one has to make choices about which types of rules to apply at what moment in time. Do we apply goal revision rules (changing current goals) whenever applicable or do we only invoke those rules when it seems the current goals are not reachable using any possible plan and using any possible planning rule. The latter leads to what is called "blindly committed" agents in [11]. Some more moderate alternatives are also possible. E.g. create a plan for a goal (using an plan selection rule) and use the planning rules in order to perform this plan. If this leads to a stage where no planning rule can be used any more and the goal is not reached, then one can change the goal using a goal revision rule. So, this leads to a strategy where one plan is tried completely (including all possible rewrites depending on the situation) and if it fails the goal is abandoned.

At the deliberation level we also have to check the relation between plans and goals. Although we check whether a goal still exists during the plan execution and thus avoid continuing with a plan while a goal is reached (or dropped), we still keep the plan itself. It is up to the deliberation module to perform a kind of "garbage collection" and remove a left-over plan for a goal that no longer exists. If this would not be done the left-over plan would become active again as soon as the goal would be established at any later time.

The last issue that we will describe in this paper is that of having multiple (parallel) goals and/or plans. First one should decide whether only one or more plans can be derived for the same goal at any time. It seems not unreasonable to allow only one plan at the time for each goal, which coincides with the idea that we try different plans consecutively and not in parallel, because this might lead to a lot of unnecessary interventions between plans and also a waist of resources. If we allow only one current plan for each goal, the plans in the plan base will all be for different goals.

Also in this case one has to determine whether the plans will be executed interleaved or consecutively. Interleaving might be beneficial, but can also lead to resource contention between plans in a way that no plan executes successfully anymore. E.g. a robot needs to go to two different rooms that lay in opposite directions. If it has a plan to arrive in each room and interleaves those two plans it will keep oscillating around its starting position indefinitely. Many of the existing work on concurrent planning can, however, be applied straight away in this setting to avoid most problems in this area.

Although many issues arise at this level, they can all be reduced to determining the order in which the rules are applied. In [3] the basic constructs needed to program this level were indicated . The same constructs can be used to write programs to tackle the issues indicated above.

The semantics of a 3APL agent was specified in section 3.3. This definition could be extended to include a certain programmed deliberation cycle. The resulting semantics should then define a subset of the traces of the most general semantic specification of section 3.3. As we however did not formally specify the constructs with which the deliberation cycle can be programmed, we cannot formulate this extension of the definition.

5   Example

In this section we will discuss an example to illustrate the actual performance of a 3APL agent from its (formal) initial state to its final state. Our example agent has to solve the problem of building a tower of blocks. The blocks have to be stacked in a certain order: block C has to be on the floor, B on C and block A on B. Initially, the blocks A and B are on the floor, while C is on A. The only action an agent can perform, is to move a block x from some block y onto another block z or the floor (Fl) $(move(x, y, z))$. The action is enabled only if the block to be moved (x) and the block onto which x is moved (z) are clear. The result of the action is, that x is on z and not on y, block y becomes clear and block z is not clear anymore (assuming that z is not the floor, because the floor is always clear). In this example, we assume the agent only has one plan in its plan base regarding this task. Otherwise, different plans for this task could interfere with each other in unwanted ways as discussed in the previous section. Plan selection rules can thus only be applied if the relevant plan of the agent is empty. Let

$$\sigma_0 = \{on(A, Fl) \wedge on(B, Fl) \wedge on(C, A) \wedge clear(B) \wedge clear(C) \wedge clear(Fl)\}$$
$$\gamma_0 = \{on(A, B) \wedge on(B, C) \wedge on(C, Fl)\}$$
$$\Pi_0 = \emptyset.$$

A 3APL agent can solve the tower building problem with the following rules $(i \in PS, p_1, p_2 \in PR)$.

$i :$ $\mathbf{G}(on(x, z))$ $\leftarrow \mathbf{B}(on(x, y))$ $\mid move(x, y, z)$
$p_1 : move(x, y, z) \leftarrow \neg\mathbf{B}(clear(x)) \mid \mathbf{B}(on(u, x))?; move(u, x, Fl); move(x, y, z)$
$p_2 : move(x, y, z) \leftarrow \neg\mathbf{B}(clear(z)) \mid \mathbf{B}(on(u, z))?; move(u, z, Fl); move(x, y, z)$

The plan selection rule is used to derive the $move(x, y, z)$ action that should be executed to fulfil a goal $on(x, z)$. The preconditions of the move action are not checked in this rule, so it is possible that the derived action cannot be executed in a particular configuration. The plan revision rules can then be used to create a configuration in which this action *can* be executed. Note that the plan selection rule is used to select an action to fulfil a goal of the form $on(x, z)$. The initial goal base however contains a conjunction of $on(x, z)$ predicates. The plan selection rule is applicable to this conjunction, because a formula $\mathbf{G}\phi$ is true if ϕ is a logical consequence of a goal in the goal base, but only if ϕ is not believed by the agent.

 Plan revision rule p_1 can be applied to an action $move(x, y, z)$ if the condition that x is clear is not satisfied which means that the action cannot be executed. Rule p_2 can be applied if z is not clear. The plan revision rules with head $move(x, y, z)$ construct a plan to create a configuration in which the move action can be executed. Rule p_1 for example specifies that if x is not clear, a $move(x, y, z)$ action should be replaced by the plan $\mathbf{B}(on(u, x))?; move(u, x, Fl); move(x, y, z)$: first bind u to the block that is on top of x, then clear x by moving u, then move x.

In the initial configuration of the agent $\langle \sigma_0, \gamma_0, \emptyset, \emptyset \rangle$, three possible substitutions of plan selection rule i can be computed: $\tau = \{x/A,\ y/Fl,\ z/B\}$ or $\{x/B,\ y/Fl,\ z/C\}$ or $\{x/C,\ y/A,\ z/Fl\}$ (yielding $move(A, Fl, B)$, $move(B, Fl, C)$ or $move(C, A, Fl)$). Suppose the first substitution is chosen. After application of this plan selection rule, the plan of the agent becomes the plan in the consequent of the rule after application of τ. The goal $on(A, B)$ is moreover associated with the plan, resulting in the following plan base (other components of the initial configuration do not change):

$$\Pi = \{(move(A, Fl, B), \mathbf{G}(on(A, B)))\}.$$

The plan cannot be executed because the preconditions of the action are not satisfied in this configuration (block A is not clear). The plan selection rule cannot be applied because the current plan of the agent for the goal is not empty. The only applicable rule is the plan revision rule p_1 where $\eta = \{x/A, y/Fl, z/B\}$, resulting in the following plan base:

$$\Pi = \{(\mathbf{B}(on(u, A))?; move(u, A, Fl); move(A, Fl, B), \mathbf{G}(on(A, B)))\}.$$

The only option is to execute the test. The substitution $\tau = \{u/C\}$ is computed and added to the empty substitution of the current configuration: $\theta = \{u/C\}$. Then the action $move(C, A, Fl)$ is executed (the substitution θ is applied to the action). The modified components of the agent's configuration are as follows:

$\sigma \models on(A, Fl) \wedge on(B, Fl) \wedge on(C, Fl) \wedge clear(A) \wedge clear(B) \wedge clear(C) \wedge$
    $clear(Fl)$,
$\Pi = \{(move(A, Fl, B), \mathbf{G}(on(A, B)))\}$,
$\theta = \{u/C\}$.

In the above configuration, the action $move(A, Fl, B)$ is executed. After a number of other test and action executions and rule applications, the agent reaches the final configuration. In this configuration, the goal is reached and thus removed from the goal base:

$\sigma_F \models on(A, B) \wedge on(B, C) \wedge on(C, Fl) \wedge clear(A) \wedge clear(Fl)$,
$\gamma_F = \emptyset$,
$\Pi_F = \emptyset$,
$\theta_F = \{u/C, v/A\}$.

During the execution, a substitution θ_F is computed with $v \in dom(\theta_F)$. We assume variable u of plan revision rule p_1 was renamed to v in the creation of a variant of p_1. The example execution shows that the 3APL agent can reach its initial goal. The agent will however not always take the shortest path. The length of the path depends on which choices are made if multiple substitutions can be computed for the plan selection rule.

In this example, we did not use any goal revision rule in order to keep it simple. However, in a domain where blocks for instance have weights, a goal revision rule could be added to drop goals involving blocks which are too heavy. Suppose the belief base of an agent contains a formula $\forall x, n : weight(x, n) \wedge (n > 3) \rightarrow tooHeavy(x)$ to indicate that a block x is too heavy for this agent if its weight exceeds 3 and suppose it contains the formula $weight(A, 5)$. The following goal revision rule could then be used to drop for instance a goal $on(A, B) \wedge$

$on(B, C)$ (a second rule would of course have to be added for the y-part of an $on(x, y)$ formula).

$g : \mathbf{G}(on(x, y)) \leftarrow \mathbf{B}(tooHeavy(x)) \mid \top$

The substitution $\eta = \{x/A, y/B\}$ is computed and goals of which $on(A, B)$ is a logical consequence, are dropped.

6   Related Work

Declarative goals were already added to a propositional version of 3APL in [17]. In this paper, we added declarative goals to the first-order version of 3APL. Moreover, plan selection rules were introduced to generate plans for declarative goals and goal rules are introduced to reason with goals.

Although the notion of declarative goals has been investigated many times in theoretic research on cognitive agents (see for example [2, 9]), it has received less attention in agent programming languages. An example of a programming language in which the notion of declarative goals is incorporated is the language GOAL [7]. However, this language lacks the notion of plans, which makes this language unsuitable to serve as a programming language. It nevertheless served as the starting point for the 3APL extensions discussed in [17].

A few other programming languages have also claimed to incorporate the notion of declarative goals, which we will review below briefly. In research on AgentSpeak(L), the issue has been addressed in [1], in which a BDI logic for AgentSpeak(L) is defined. In this logic, the notion of desire (or goal, as these concepts are often identified) is defined in terms of achievement goals. These achievement goals however are part of the procedural part of an AgentSpeak(L) agent, i.e. they can occur in a sequence of actions or in a plan as we call it. Achievement goals are not a separate component of an AgentSpeak(L) agent. In this way, it is difficult to decouple plan failure (or execution) from goal failure (or achievement) (see [18]). The interesting aspect of the use of declarative goals is precisely this decoupling: all kinds of unpredictable things can happen during plan execution and the execution of the plan might not have the desired result. In 3APL, the goal will remain in the goal base in this case and a new plan can be selected to try to achieve the goal once more. This is the reason why it *is* interesting for agents to explicitly incorporate desired end-states and it *is not* for normal procedural programs. A normal procedural program does not operate in a dynamic and unpredictable environment and if programmed right, the execution of it will have the desired result.

In the context of the agent programming language Golog, declarative goals are discussed in [13]. In this paper, the issue of acting rationally in the presence of prioritized goals is discussed. A set of prioritized goals and a high-level non-deterministic Golog program are used to produce a ready-to-execute plan, whose execution will respect both the given program and the set of goals. These goals are thus used to guide the generation of an executable low-level plan from a high-level plan. In 3APL on the contrary, goals are used to *select* a high- or low-level plan through the application of plan selection rules. In case of the selection of a high-level plan, this plan is transformed into a low-level plan while it is being executed, using plan revision rules. If the plan fails to reach the goal, the goal will remain in the goal base. It will probably depend on the characteristics of the problem at hand (dynamic versus static environment etc.) which approach is more suitable.

The issue of goal revision during execution has, as far as we know, not been addressed in the languages discussed above.

7   Conclusion and Future Research

In this paper we have described the syntax and semantics of an agent programming language that includes all the classical elements of the theory of agents. I.e. beliefs, goals and plans (or intentions). We thus conjecture that it should be possible to verify whether a 3APL program satisfies a given specification in terms of beliefs, goals and plans. It should moreover be easier to go from analysis and specification in terms of these concepts to implementation. These are however issues that remain for future research.

Another issue for future research could perhaps be to relate the Golog approach to declarative goals ([13]) to our approach.

An interpreter for the basic form of 3APL is already implemented and extensions are currently being programmed. The interpreter will enable us to evaluate the effectiveness of the language for problems of realistic complexity.

In this paper we only sketched a number of issues for the deliberation cycle of 3APL agents. Especially determining the balance between reactive and pro-active behavior and how to capture this in programming structures on the deliberative level will be an important issue for further research.

References

1. R. H. Bordini and A. F. Moreira. Proving the asymmetry thesis principles for a BDI agent-oriented programming language. *Electronic Notes in Theoretical Computer Science*, 70(5), 2002.
   http://www.elsevier.nl/gej-ng/31/29/23/125/23/29/70.5.008.pdf.
2. P. Cohen and H. Levesque. Intention is choice with commitment. *Artificial Intelligence*, 42:213–261, 1990.
3. M. Dastani, F. de Boer, F. Dignum, and J.-J. Meyer. Programming agent deliberation: An approach illustrated using the 3apl language. In *Proceedings of The Second Conference on Autonomous Agents and Multi-agent Systems (AAMAS'03)*, pages 97–104, Melbourne, 2003.
4. M. Dastani, F. Dignum, and J.-J. Meyer. Autonomy and agent deliberation. In *Proceedings of The First International Workshop on Computatinal Autonomy - Potential, Risks, Solutions (Autonomous 2003)*, Melbourne, Australia, 2003.
5. D. Dennet. *The intentional stance*. The MIT Press, Cambridge, 1987.
6. K. Hindriks, F. de Boer, W. van der Hoek, and J.-J. Ch. Meyer. Agent programming in 3APL. *Int. J. of Autonomous Agents and Multi-Agent Systems*, 2(4):357–401, 1999.

7. K. Hindriks, F. de Boer, W. van der Hoek, and J.-J. Ch. Meyer. Agent programming with declarative goals. In N. Jennings and Y. Lesperance, editors, *Intelligent Agents VI - Proceedings of ATAL'2000*, LNAI-1757. Springer, Berlin, 2001.
8. G. Plotkin. A structural approach to operational semantics. Technical report, Aarhus University, Computer Science Department, 1981.
9. A. Rao and M. Georgeff. Modeling rational agents within a BDI-architecture. In J. Allen, R. Fikes, and E. Sandewall, editors, *Proceedings of the Second International Conference on Principles of Knowledge Representation and Reasoning (KR'91)*, pages 473–484. Morgan Kaufmann, 1991.
10. A. S. Rao. AgentSpeak(L): BDI agents speak out in a logical computable language. In W. van der Velde and J. Perram, editors, *Agents Breaking Away (LNAI 1038)*, pages 42–55. Springer-Verlag, 1996.
11. A. S. Rao and M. Georgeff. BDI Agents: from theory to practice. In *Proceedings of the First International Conference on Multi-Agent Systems (ICMAS-95)*, pages 312–319, San Francisco, CA, June 1995.
12. A. S. Rao and M. P. Georgeff. BDI-agents: from theory to practice. In *Proceedings of the First Intl. Conference on Multiagent Systems*, San Francisco, 1995.
13. S. Sardina and S. Shapiro. Rational action in agent programs with prioritized goals. In *Proceedings of the second international joint conference on autonomous agents and multiagent systems (AAMAS'03)*, pages 417–424, Melbourne, 2003.
14. Y. Shoham. Agent-oriented programming. *Artificial Intelligence*, 60:51–92, 1993.
15. W. van der Hoek, B. van Linder, and J.-J. Ch. Meyer. An integrated modal approach to rational agents. In M. Wooldridge and A. Rao, editors, *Foundations of Rational Agency*, Applied Logic Series 14, pages 133–168. Kluwer, Dordrecht, 1998.
16. B. van Linder, W. van der Hoek, and J.-J. Ch. Meyer. Formalizing abilities and opportunities of agents. *Fundamenta Informaticae*, 34(1,2):53–101, 1998.
17. M. B. van Riemsdijk, W. van der Hoek, and J.-J. Ch. Meyer. Agent programming in Dribble: from beliefs to goals with plans. In *Proceedings of the second international joint conference on autonomous agents and multiagent systems (AAMAS'03)*, pages 393–400, Melbourne, 2003.
18. M. Winikoff, L. Padgham, J. Harland, and J. Thangarajah. Declarative and procedural goals in intelligent agent systems. In *Proceedings of the eighth international conference on principles of knowledge respresentation and reasoning (KR2002)*, Toulouse, 2002.
19. M. Wooldridge. *An introduction to multiagent systems*. John Wiley and Sons, LTD, West Sussex, 2002.
20. M. Wooldridge and N. R. Jennings. Intelligent agents: Theory and practice. HTTP://www.doc.mmu.ac.uk/STAFF/mike/ker95/ker95-html.h (Hypertext version of Knowledge Engineering Review paper), 1994.

Team Oriented Programming and Proxy Agents: The Next Generation

Paul Scerri[1], David V. Pynadath[2], Nathan Schurr[2], Alessandro Farinelli[2], Sudeep Gandhe[2], and Milind Tambe[2]

[1] Carnegie Mellon University
pscerri@cs.cmu.edu
[2] University of Southern California
pynadath@isi.edu, {schurr,farinelli,gandhe,tambe}@usc.edu

Abstract. Coordination between large teams of highly heterogeneous entities will change the way complex goals are pursued in real world environments. One approach to achieving the required coordination in such teams is to give each team member a *proxy* that assumes routine coordination activities on behalf of its team member. Despite that approach's success, as we attempt to apply this first generation of proxy architecture to larger teams in more challenging environments, some limitations become clear. In this paper, we present initial efforts on the next generation of proxy architecture and Team Oriented Programming (TOP), called Machinetta. Machinetta aims to overcome the limitations of the previous generation of proxies and allow effective coordination between very large teams of highly heterogeneous agents. We describe the principles underlying the design of the Machinetta proxies and present initial results from two domains.

1 Introduction

Exciting emerging applications require hundreds or thousands of robots, agents and people (RAPs) to coordinate to achieve their joint goals. In domains such as military operations, space or disaster response, coordination between large numbers of agents can revolutionize our ability to achieve complex goals. Such domains are characterized by widely distributed entities with limited communication channels between them. The environments often change dynamically and will in some cases be hostile.

An emerging standard for creating robust, highly heterogeneous teams is an architecture that uses semi-autonomous *proxy agents* to create an homogeneous coordination layer "above" the highly heterogeous agents [18]. By providing each agent with a proxy that has teamwork knowledge we raise the coordination ability of the agent-proxy pair to the level at which the rest of the team is operating. Via the use of adjustable autonomy [9], the amount of coordination ability that proxy actually provides (and the amount which the agent provides) is dynamically adjusted to the particular context of the agent at that point in time. The proxies manage the coordination, performing the routine operations that are

M. Dastani, J. Dix, A. El Fallah-Seghrouchni (Eds.): PROMAS 2003, LNAI 3067, pp. 131–148, 2004.
© Springer-Verlag Berlin Heidelberg 2004

required for cooperation; e.g., informing others when plans are completed, and assisting in the handling of exceptional situations; e.g., finding RAPs to fulfill roles due to failures or overloading. The proxies also assist in making adjustments to the plan the group is following when required. The proxies also perform more routine tasks, such as information sharing, that ensure the continued smooth operation of the team, while freeing the agent from engaging in these activities. One approach to achieving the required coordination in teams for such domains, is to give each team member a *proxy* that assumes routine coordination activities on behalf of its team member [11].

The relatively homogeneous proxies allow developers to write *Team Oriented Programs* (TOPs) which are executed according to the coordination algorithms the programmer knows the proxy is using [12]. For example, TEAMCORE proxies implement the STEAM interpretation of teamwork [17]. Programmers creating TOPs need not concern themselves with specifying low level coordination details. Instead, they specify the activities of the team with high level primitives such as *roles* and *team plan operators*. Writing TOPs at this high level of abstraction makes it feasible for a programmer to quickly specify complex team activities. A variety of interesting applications have shown the utility of the proxy based teams architecture, e.g., the Electric Elves [1] and interactions with autonomous systems for space missions [15].

Despite their successes, the first generation proxy architectures suffer from three key limitations when handling: scale, dynamism, and effective integration of humans in agent teamwork. First, in small-scale teams, agents can be allocated to roles by hand prior to starting up team activities; although limited reallocation can occur at run-time. Unfortunately, in large-scale teams, off-line allocation of agents to roles by hand is difficult. Second, a high level of dynamism in the environment requires that agents' role allocation and reallocation strategy must often be integrated into one unified fluid algorithm, rather than as two separate phases (allocation and reallocation) as seen in existing architectures. Furthermore, agents must consider role reallocation not only under catastrophic failures (as was done previously), but must be willing to give up current roles to take up new precious opportunities. Third, as we build increasingly heterogeneous teams, and particularly include humans in the loop, we must enable the proxies to tap into human expertise when coordinating key situations. Previous research on teamwork has allowed agents and humans to work together, but the human participation was limited to domain level activities. Proxies should be able to use human enterprise for both domain activities and coordination.

In this chapter, we present initial efforts on the next generation of TOP and proxy architecture, called Machinetta. Machinetta aims to overcome the limitations of the previous generation of proxy and allow effective coordination between very large teams of highly heterogeneous agents. To achieve this, Machinetta embodies several new design principles. To address the first two limitations discussed above, Machinetta has a fluid, integrated role allocation and reallocation algorithm. Within this algorithm, agents attempt to continually allocate and reallocate themselves to new tasks. When new tasks/opportunities arise, or when agents' capabilities decline substantially, agents reconsider their current commitments to roles; thus, agents may change roles even without catastrophic failures. This new integrated algorithm enables a much more flexible response to dynamic environments.

Many heuristics used by a team fail under some circumstances. However, the answer is not simply to replace current coordination algorithms with new ones. If a big enough team is put into a complex enough environment there are, despite our best efforts, bound to be situations where any coordination algorithms perform very poorly or breaks altogether. A key idea in Machinetta is to acknowledge that such problems are going to occur and build in mechanisms for meta-reasoning to handle those situations. This is achieved by making as much of the coordination process as possible explicit, thus making it easier to monitor the coordination and understand when problems occur. For example, we use a role allocation algorithm [14] that represents each role to be allocated as an explicit role. If the role of allocating the role goes unachieved for some period of time, i.e., because the standard role allocation algorithm does not succeed in allocating it, the team can detect this situation and recursively invoke meta-reasoning about a "role allocation role".

With respect to involving humans in coordination (and not just in domain-level tasks), the meta-reasoning capability provides a helpful mechanism. In particular, when meta-reasoning about coordination, agents can appeal to human input. However, humans could provide input that may not necessarily be in agreement with choices made by the coordination algorithm. Thus, given the possibility of such arbitrary changes by humans to coordination algorithms, the algorithms must be robust to decisions that are "wrong" according the algorithm. For example, a human may arbitrarily (so far as the proxies are concerned) decide to terminate a plan and the proxies must implement this decision.

The final change in direction for the new generation of proxy is the properties that we aim to prove for the key algorithms. With relatively small teams, establishing properties such as optimality is important. However, proofs of such algorithm properties typically rely on assumptions such as the underlying situation not changing while the algorithm is executing. While such assumptions are very reasonable for small teams, they are not so interesting for very large teams where the assumptions will never be met. The critical point is that large enough teams in complex enough environemts will be in a constant state of change. For example, in a large team for disaster recovery in a large city, some team member will always be completing, abandoning or beginning a task. The inherent, continuous dynamics makes other algorithmic properties interesting. For example, the "stability" of the system – will one team member's failure to complete a role lead to many role reallocations or will the effects be limited? Another interesting property would be to show that certain events will never happen, or happen only with a very low probability. For example, we may be able to prove that some team member will always eventually accept a role, if its priority is above some threshold. Our current approach is to use the theory of dynamic patterns [7] to model and understand the system's properties.

In the remainder of this chapter we present Machinetta in detail, showing how it embodies the principles discussed above. We also present a graphical development environment for specifying Machinetta plans. We show preliminary results from using Machinetta in two domains, a fire fighting domain and a distributed sensor domain.

2 Proxies

Machinetta proxies are lightweight, domain-independent software modules, capable of performing the activities required to work cooperatively within a larger team on TOPs. The proxies are implemented in Java and are designed to run on a number of platforms including laptops and handheld devices. A proxy's software is made up of five components (see Figure 1):

Communication: communication with other proxies
Coordination: reasoning about team plans and communication
State: the working memory of the proxy
Adjustable Autonomy: reasoning about whether to act autonomously or pass control to the RAP
RAP Interface: communication with the RAP

Each component abstracts away details allowing other components to work without considering those details. For example, the RAP interface component is aware of what type of RAP it is connected to and the methods of interacting with the RAP, while the adjustable autonomy component deals with the RAP as an abstract entity having particular capabilities. Likewise, the communication component will be tailored to the RAP communication abilities, e.g., wireless or wired, but the coordination component will only be told available bandwidth and cost of communication.

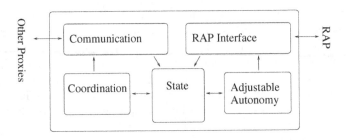

Fig. 1. Proxy software architecture.

A critical component in deploying the proxies is the mechanism by which they interact with their RAPs. The adjustable autonomy component is responsible for deciding what interaction should happen with the RAP, but the RAP interface component manages that interaction. The RAP interface component is the only part of the proxy that needs to be designed for a specific type of RAP. These components are very diverse, matching the very diverse RAPs. For example, the RAP interface for a person playing the role of fire chief in the disaster rescue domain is a large graphical interface, while for the agents, a simple socket communicating a small, fixed set of messages is sufficient. Since the proxies interact closely with their RAPs, it is desirable to have them in close physical proximity. For mobile RAPs, the proxies can be run on handheld devices that communicate wirelessly with robots or, in the case of a person in the field, via a graphical interface on the handheld device.

2.1   Proxy Algorithms

The proxy's overall execution is message driven. When a message comes in from its RAP or from another proxy, a new *belief* is added to the proxy's *state*. The beliefs in the state constitute the proxy's knowledge of the status of the team and the environment. The state operates as a blackboard, with components writing information to the blackboard and others reacting to information written to the blackboard. Any change to the state triggers two reasoning algorithms: *Coordination* (Algorithm 1) and *Adjustable Autonomy* (Algorithm 2). Either of these algorithms may in turn change the belief state, which will once again trigger the algorithms.

Algorithm 1 shows the Coordination algorithm, which instantiates the theory of *joint commitments* [3] as operationalized by STEAM. The functions, *establishJointCommitment* and *endJointCommitment* establish or terminate commitments by communicating with other proxies when a new belief triggers the start or end of a team plan. In the algorithm, the function *communicate?* returns true if the capability or role progress information should be communicated to others. This function encapsulates previous work on determining policies for communicating such information with team members [10].

Algorithm 1: Coordination
COORDINATION($\mathbf{B_{in}}$)
(1)   **foreach** $b \in \mathbf{B_{in}}$
(2)   **if** b is *CapabilityInformation* or *Role Progress*
(3)   **if** *communicate?*(b)
(4)   *sendToOthers*(b)
(5)   **else if** *startTeamPlan* α?(b)
(6)   *establishJointCommitment*(α)
(7)   ALLOCATEROLE*role*(α)
(8)   **else if** *endTeamPlan* α?(b)
(9)   *endJointCommitment*(α)
(10) **return** $\mathbf{B_{out}}$

The Adjustable Autonomy algorithm (Algorithm 2) is responsible for managing the interactions between the proxy and the RAP. In the algorithm, the function *tellRAP?* determines if there is value in sending this particular piece of information received from another proxy to the RAP. The *shouldRAPbeAsked?* is the "core" of adjustable autonomy reasoning and is responsible for deciding whether or not this particular coordination decision should be handled autonomously by the proxy or by the RAP. The *if* statement beginning on Line 2 shows the basic processing that the proxy performs when its RAP is offered a new role. First, it decides whether to act autonomously. If so, it decides whether or not to accept the role on behalf of the RAP (see next section for more detail).

Algorithm 2: Adjustable Autonomy
ADJUSTABLEAUTONOMY($\mathbf{B_{in}}$)
(1)   **foreach** $b \in \mathbf{B_{in}}$
(2)   **if** b is *role offer*
(3)   **if** RAP is capable of role
(4)   **if** *shouldRAPbeAsked?*
(5)   Ask RAP
(6)   **else if** accept autonomously?
(7) $B_{out} \leftarrow$ *role accepted*
(8)   **else**
(9) $B_{out} \leftarrow$ *role rejected*
(10)   **else if** b is a new role
(11)   send role to RAP
(12) **return** $\mathbf{B_{out}}$

3   Executing Team Oriented Plans

Within Machinetta, team plans provide an explicit representation of the joint goals held by all team members. As such, they allow the team members to scope their reasoning and concentrate on only those tasks that are directly relevant to the team's currently active goals. Due to its intended use as a domain-independent coordination architecture, Machinetta makes minimal assumptions about the nature of team plans. In other words, the team plans provided by the architecture are a skeleton of execution that the system designer then fleshes out with the intended domain-specific behavior (e.g., as part of a specific RAP behavior that triggers off team plans).

As in the original STEAM-based Teamcore architecture [11], we implement the joint goals of the TOP via reactive team plans. Active team plans take the form of beliefs within the proxies' state. This explicit representation enables the underlying architecture to reason about the means of ensuring coherent plan execution. Because each proxy maintains separate beliefs about these joint goals, the architecture can detect (in a distributed manner) any inconsistencies among team members' plan beliefs. The architecture's primary responsibility regarding coherent team beliefs about active goals is to synchronize the initiation and termination of team plans. Perhaps more importantly, the proxy must also ensure that the team makes progress toward achieving its active joint goals. The proxies themselves have no ability to achieve goals at the domain level; instead, they must ensure that all of the requisite domain-level capabilities are brought to bear by instantiating the appropriate roles and filling them with the appropriate RAPs. Section 3.1 describes the initiation of team plans, Section 3.2 describes the instantiation of the associated roles, and Section 3.3 describes the termination of team plans.

3.1   Plan Initiation

Machinetta's proxy-based infrastructure ensures that the team will synchronize itself appropriately in initiating a new team plan. Thus, the team programmer need not program such synchronization actions, because the proxies (through the *establishJointCommitment* procedure in Algorithm 1) ensure such synchronization, so all team members will agree on the set of active team plans.

The most common mechanism for creating team plans is to write a "team plan template". Such a template represents a class of possible plan instantiations. We thus save on specification effort, since writing one team plan template replaces the specification of many individual plans themselves. For example, we can write one template to represent a generic plan of "Fight a fire at building x", rather than writing hundreds of plans of the form "Fight a fire at building 1", "Fight a fire at building 2", "Fight a fire at building 3", etc.

When the preconditions of a plan template match the proxy's current state of beliefs (i.e., when $startTeamPlan\ \alpha$ is true), a new plan belief is instantiated with the specific details of the particular precondition match. This team plan belief can then trigger domain-specific behavior through the interface with a proxy's specific RAP. The proxies dynamically instantiate plans when, during the course of execution, their current states match a plan's required trigger conditions. The preconditions specify those trigger conditions, templates against which the proxies try to match active belief objects in their proxy state. Because we cannot anticipate all of the possible structures that a belief object may take on, we perform this matching by converting the belief object into some canonical string representation.

The preconditions may also include coordination constraints among team plans. For example, subgoal relationships translate into an additional precondition on child plans (e.g., if α_1 is a subgoal of α_0, then there is a precondition for α_1 requiring a current plan belief α_0). We can also specify temporal constraints between parallel subgoals (e.g., if α_1 must complete before α_2 begins, then there is a precondition for α_2 requiring a current plan belief α_1 that has been completed). Thus, the architecture can automatically translate coordination constraints specified at the abstract plan level into specific preconditions at the coordination policy level.

Upon successfully triggering a new plan, the proxies perform the *establishJointCommitment* procedure specified by their coordination policy. For example, in the initial stages of development, we used a naive communication policy that established commitments by requiring communication of all beliefs. Because all of the proxies are truthful and because we assume perfect communication, such a policy necessarily achieves mutual belief of active team plans. We have also implemented the STEAM policy [17] as a communication policy that is able to more flexibly balance the costs and benefits of communication during the establishment of a new commitment.

3.2   Role Instantiation

Roles are slots for specialized execution that the team may potentially fill at runtime. Upon instantiation of a newly triggered plan, the proxies also instantiate any associated roles, subject to the specific triggers. The specification of such roles is domain-specific, and may include appropriate role relationships, such as *AND*, *OR*, and *role-dependency* relationships (using STEAM semantics [17]). The initial plan specification may name particular RAPs to fill these roles, but more typically, the roles are instantiated unfilled. These unfilled roles are then subject to role allocation, as specified by the ALLOCATEROLE call in Algorithm 1.

3.3   Plan Termination

As in the original Teamcore architecture [11], the TOP includes each plan's termination conditions, under which a team plan is achieved, irrelevant or unachievable. Such explicit specification ensures common knowledge of such conditions, so that the team can terminate the goal coherently. Machinetta then automatically uses the termination conditions as the basis for automatically generating the communication necessary to jointly terminate a team plan.

Postconditions are roughly identical to preconditions, except for the obvious difference that the conditions contained within a postcondition refer to plan termination rather than initiation. Furthermore, the conditions are not matched against arbitrary beliefs, but rather against only those beliefs stored within the relevant container belief object (e.g., a plan). There is another key difference, in that we differentiate among three different types of termination states. In particular, we distinguish whether a plan terminated because it has become achieved, unachievable, or irrelevant (following the STEAM semantics [17]).

When a proxy's current beliefs match the postconditions of a currently active team plan (i.e., *endTeamPlan* α is true), the proxy triggers the plan termination phase of Algorithm 1. Again, our developmental coordination policy simply communicated the terminated plan belief (along with the domain-specific that triggered the termination) to all of the team members. We have also implemented the STEAM policy as an alternate *endJointCommitment* procedure that is capable of communicating only selectively.

4   Specifying Team Oriented Plans

As a step towards realizing Team Oriented Programming paradigm, we have built a Java based Graphical User Interface (GUI) to facilitate domain experts to specify these TOPs. We view a TOP consisting of three parts: team organization hierarchy and descriptions of individual agents and their capabilities. These are specified using the tool in form of diagrams and are finally converted to beliefs each agent should hold to start with. These beliefs are described in XML. We have designed a XML scheme that can specify reactive plans and constraints between them, also different roles and capabilities of agents. Current Machinetta work has focused on developing proxies capable of executing simple team plans and we are in the process of extending the capabilities of the proxies to incorporate all the aforementioned features. The key thing to note about our specifications of TOPs is what is not specified. Specifically, nothing about how the coordination should be performed is explicitly specified.

Our TOP specification interface has 3 views; the first is plan hierarchy where user can draw reactive plans with plans/subplans as nodes and links showing hierarchy between them. Each subplan can have preconditions and postconditions and plan body. The agents will instantiate a team plan when preconditions match with the environment. One can specify what information will be passed to the instantiated team plan while specifying preconditions. Figure 1 shows the use of tool to specify TOP for a Robocup Rescue scenario. By using hierarchy in plans we can break down a complex plan in parts as in this case fightFire can have two subplans to evacuate civilians, secure the area, extinguish the fire. When a particular subplan's success depends on coordination with other activity we can specify coordination constraints between them. For example, such constraints can be useful in specifying that activities of transport of civilians and securing the route for transport vehicles must be coordinated. Also AND/OR constraints between subplans can be specified, for example, while fighting a fire, evacuating people, securing an area and extinguishing fire, all actions should be done, failure in any subplan can result in failure of fightFire plan, thus the designs should use an AND constraint.

A subplan can be chosen by double-clicking it and pre and post conditions for it can be specified in the right subpanel. Conditions themselves have a set of keys and values of those keys which will trigger the plans. These keys are attributes of the *domain specific beliefs*. The GUI has facilities to specify such preconditions. Multiple preconditions can be specified which then are thought to be in disjunction. Postconditions are very similar and have a type associated with them for differentiating in achieved, unachievable and irrelevant cases. Returning parameters are the output keys passed to the instantiated team plan which have further information about the event that caused that plan to trigger. For example, FightFire plan is passed back information about location of FirePresent after the precondition is matched.

The second view is team organization hierarchy. The team hierarchy defines subteams as those teams that get more specialized down the tree. Thus the subteam FireEngines consists of engines that can fight chemical fire and engines that can fight electrical fires. The plan hierarchy nodes can be associated with a particular subteam via its name. As in this case only fireEngines subteam will be assigned to extinguish-fire subplan. When the domain expert wants to assign

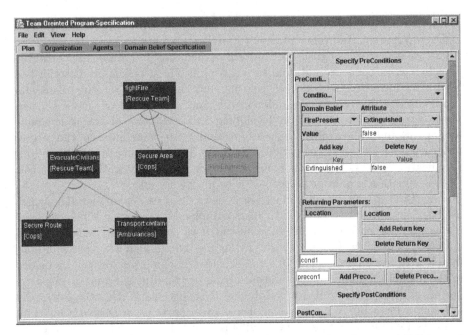

Fig. 2. Snapshot of tool showing team plan and user entering the preconditions and postconditions for ExtinguishFire subplan.

specific agents to specific tasks, this type of specification of teams and subteams can be useful. These can be used either as hints or constraints for role allocation.

The third view is a list of available domain agents and their capabilities. Capabilities are matched against requirements before agents are assigned to specific subteams. The last panel allows the user to specify the domain specific beliefs. We represent a domain specific belief as a key-value pair. For example, in the fire fighting domain, FirePresent belief has keys location and extinguished and corresponding values of where the fire is and its status, which the agent believes.

The last step is to save the TOPs specified graphically in XML documents as individual beliefs of agents. These beliefs consist of the team plans and the agents own capabilities. Hints or constraints for forming teams/subteams can be stored. Throughout the interface users are not allowed to input invalid specifications, such as specifying preconditions on non-existing keys. This simplifies validation procedure. Most of the XML generation is straight-forward. Currently the tool can handle the plan graphs which are tree-structured,, although it can be easily extended to any arbitrary plan graph.

5   Experiments

We have performed initial experiments in two domains. Each set of experiments and domain is aimed at testing one aspect of the Machinetta architecture.

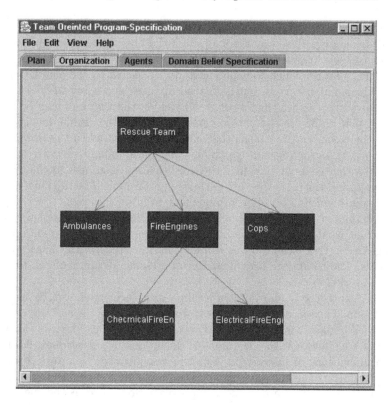

Fig. 3. Snapshot showing team organization hierarchy.

5.1   Fire Fighting

In our first experiment, we used a simulator of a fire fighting domain [14]. The aim of this experiment was to include a human fire chief in the loop to help the team of intelligent agent fire fighters assign themselves to fires. The experiment was designed to show that the basic approach of identifying problems in team coordination and referring them to an expert was effective. The key parameter varied in this experiment is when the expert was brought into help. In particular, the *maxAsked* parameter controls the number of team members that should be offered a role before asking for expert input. If *maxAsked*= 0%, a proxy whose team member cannot (or will not) take on the role, the role will be immediately referred to an expert. If *maxAsked*= 100%, the algorithm ensures that all potentially capable team members are offered the role once before giving up. At the extreme, a special setting of *maxAsked*= ∞ means that proxies repeatedly pass the role amongst themselves (with each getting offered the role multiple times) without ever giving up. Varying *maxAsked* throughout this range produces distinct algorithms that produce different loads on role-allocation expert (i.e., the fire chief).

The fire chief interface consists of two frames. One frame shows a map of the city, displaying labeled markers for all of the fires that have been found, the positions of each fire brigade, and the location of the role each fire brigade is assigned to. The fire chief does not have direct access to the simulation state through the simulator itself, but is instead updated according to only the messages received by the fire chief's proxy. Therefore, the fire chief may be viewing a delayed picture of the simulation's progress. The other frame displays a list of all of the role-allocation tasks that have been allocated to the fire chief. By clicking on a task, the relevant capability information about each fire brigade is shown. The right-side window lists the fire brigades' distances to the fire, their water levels, and the roles they are currently performing. The fire chief can then view this data and find an appropriate agent to fulfill the role.

We conducted tests with three different fire chiefs. Each completed several practice runs with the simulation prior to experiments in order to minimize any learning effects. Each scenario was run for 100 time steps, with each step taking 30 seconds. The total data presented here represents 20 hours of run-time with a human in the loop.

Table 1 shows the team's domain-level performance across each experimental configuration. The scoring function measures how much of the city was destroyed by fire, with higher scores representing worse performance. The table shows the mean scores achieved, with the standard deviations in parentheses. Examining our two dimensions of interest, we can first compare the two rows to examine the effect of increasing the complexity of the coordination problem. In this case, increasing the number of fire brigades improves performance, as one might expect when adding resources while keeping the number of initial tasks fixed.

Table 1. Domain-level performance scores.

# Brigades	$maxAsked=0\%$	$maxAsked=100\%$	$maxAsked=\infty$
3	58(3.56)	73(16.97)	74(0.71)
10	52(19.09)	42(14.00)	73(4.24)

However, we can dig a little deeper and examine the effect of increasing complexity on the fire chief's performance. In the simpler configuration, asking the fire chief earlier (i.e., $maxAsked=0$) improves performance, as the team gets a head start on exploiting the person's capabilities. On the other hand, in the more complex configuration, asking the fire chief earlier has the opposite effect. To better understand the effect of varying the point at which we assign roles to people, Table 2 presents some of the other statistics we gathered from these runs (mean values, with standard deviations in parentheses). With 3 brigades, if we count the mean number of roles taken on by the fire chief, we see that it stays roughly the same (401 vs. 407) across the two $maxAsked$ settings. In this case, asking the fire chief sooner, allows the team to exploit the person's capabilities earlier, without much increase in his/her workload. On the other hand, with 10 brigades, the fire chief's mean role count increases from 563 to 716, so although

Table 2. Role and fire-chief task metrics.

# Brigs.	*max* *Asked*	Domain Roles	Fire Chief Roles	Tasks Performed	% Tasks Performed
3	0%	116 (7.12)	401 (51.81)	27 (6.55)	23.29 (6.51)
	100%	146 (33.94)	407 (54.45)	24 (6.36)	16.02 (0.63)
10	0%	103 (38.18)	864 (79.90)	67 (2.83)	14.49 (2.13)
	100%	98 (42.40)	563 (182.95)	41 (8.38)	48.06 (19.32)

Table 3. Statistics for each Fire Chief.

Fire Chief	Score	Tasks Performed	% Performed
A	0.61	25	28%
B	0.59	40	56%
C	0.31	42	32%

the proxies ask the fire chief sooner, we are imposing a significant increase in the person's workload. Judging by the decreased average score in the bottom row of Table 1, the increased workload more than offsets the earlier exploitation of the person's capabilities. Thus, our experiments provide some evidence that increasing domain-level scale has significant consequences for the appropriate style of interaction with human team members.

Regardless of the variation of human behavior across scale, the data demonstrates that exploiting human capabilities can, in fact, improve overall team performance. We see this most clearly by examining the rightmost column of Table 1, which represents the results when the agents make all of the decisions. These scores are significantly worse than the leftmost data column, where the person is handed role-allocation roles immediately. Thus, the ability of our role-allocation algorithm to exploit the special coordination capabilities of people has provided a dramatic improvement in the performance of our team.

We can draw some additional conclusions about the heterogeneity introduced by people by clustering our statistics by person rather than by configuration. Each row in Table 3 represents the mean statistics of one of our three different fire chiefs. The "Tasks Performed" column counts the number of firefighting allocations performed by the fire chief, while the "% Performed" column measures that count against the number of total firefighting allocations assigned to the fire chief by the proxy architecture. Given the small sample size, we cannot draw any conclusions about a person's expected behavior. On the other hand, it *is* clear that we can expect a great deal of variance in behavior. For example, although fire chiefs A and B achieve roughly similar mean scores, they do so in very different ways. In fact, our proxies can expect fire chief A to be half as likely as fire chief B to respond to a task request. On the other hand, fire chief C is about equally likely as A to respond, and C performs roughly the same number of tasks as B, yet C achieves only half the score as the other two. Thus, it appears unlikely that we can easily classify people's capabilities, since, for even the relatively few dimensions measured here, our human fire chiefs show no generalizable characteristics.

5.2   Recharging 100 Robots

In our second domain, we have a large number of sensor robots (CSRs) distributed in some environment over and extended period. Over time the batteries on the CSR robots run down and they need to be collected for recharging by a CHR robot. The CSR robot is led to the recharging station by the CHR robot, hence must have some remaining battery power to be recharged. This scenario is part of DARPA's Software for Distributed Robotics program. Proxies running on CHR robots must cooperatively work out which CHR collects which CSR. In this set of experiments we aim to better establish the properties of the autonomous role allocation algorithm.

We have conducted several experiments in order to evaluate our approach, using a simulation of the distributed robotics domain. The simulator represents the building as a grid and the CHRs are able to move from grid location to grid location, pick up CSRs and recharge CSRs by moving them to a recharge station. While the details of robot control are not simulated, the uncertainty CHRs have about their position is modelled using a localization algorithm very similar to those used on real CHRs. In particular, the localization algorithm uses a well known markovian localization method [4], based on simulated landmarks in the building. Battery level in the CSRs decrease with uncertainty, thus it is not possible to predict its dynamic during the task execution.

We used two different kinds of simulation set up. In the first one, the experiments are conducted without using the proxies for the role assignment. The role allocation approach is implemented in a software module inside the simulator. In the second setting the proxies have been connected to the simulator and execute the same approach for the role assignment. While in the first set of experiments we mainly focused on investigating how different parameter settings for the environment affect the performance of our approach, the second experimental setting is used to validate the obtained results using the proxies framework.

In the first set of experiments, we tested four different algorithms: the allocation algorithm described in [14], an extension of this algorithm to handle dynamic capability estimation, a mechanism for the uncertainty handling, and finally the combination of these two extensions. We decided to vary the amount of CHRs that can have a degradation on their localization capability during the experiments and investigate how this parameter affects the different algorithms performance.

For the first set of experiments we used an environment with 24 CHRs and 47 CSRs and each experiment is 6000 simulation steps long. For each different parameter setting we performed five repetitions. The results obtained are reported in table 4 and in table 5. Table 4 show the results when five CHRs experience problems in their localization capability while table 5 reports the result with ten. In each table the first column shows the algorithm used, the second column shows the average battery level of CSRs over time. The third column shows the average of the minimum battery level of all the CSRs over time. In both the second and third columns, the averages exclude the battery levels of robots that have failed. The fourth column of the tables, show the number of CSR that com-

Table 4. Results for five CHR with localization problems.

Algorithm	Avg B. L.	Min B. L.	Fail	σ
Basic	0.644672	0.195902	13.6	2.8
Ovl Handl.	0.65997	0.223343	11.8	0.97
Unc Handl.	0.693892	0.229101	12.2	0.75
Ovl and Unc	0.684224	0.241805	9.8	1.47

Table 5. Results for ten CHR with localization problems.

Algorithm	Avg B. L.	Min B. L.	Fail	σ
Basic	0.633321	0.17654	20.6	2.58
Ovl Handl.	0.65293	0.215206	17.6	1.85
Unc Handl.	0.691214	0.221129	15.8	2.64
Ovl and Unc	0.691896	0.219198	16.2	2.79

Table 6. Results for the limited exchange.

Algorithm	Avg B. L.	Min B. L.	Fail	σ
Unc Hnd. 5	0.695983	0.238347	14.6	1.36
Unc Hnd. 10	0.699272	0.237091	17.6	2.87

Table 7. Results for the distributed setting.

Algorithm	Avg B. L.	Min B. L.	Fail	σ
Unc Handl.	0.699902	0.236674	12.5	1.65

pletely failed, i.e., the number of CSRs whose battery level falls to 0. Finally the last column shows the standard deviation computed over the five repetitions.

The results show that the overall performance of the team is negatively affected, when more CHRs have their localization capability degraded. When comparing results obtained using the overload handling algorithm with the basic algorithm, the number of failed CSRs were lower while both the average battery level and the average of the minimum battery level were improved. The improvement is similar both for the case when five and ten CHRs can have a degrading localization capability. Moreover, the overload handling algorithm results in a lower standard deviation from the average failure value, showing a better adaption to problematic situations.

Also the algorithm for uncertainty handling seems to improve the performance for the overall team. In particular for the result reported in table 4 we have a very low standard deviation, similar to the overload handling mechanism. However when the number of CHR that can have localization problems is higher we have actually a higher standard deviation but still acceptable results. The results reported in table 4 and 5 for the uncertainty handling algorithm, are obtained assuming that each CHR can ask and have a response at each simulation step from all its team mates when trying to exchange a role. This is a very strong assumption and it is not likely to be met in the real application. Therefore we performed an experiment limiting the number of team mates that can be queried during each time step. In table 6 we report the results for this set of experiments. The first row of the table refers to the case where five CHR can have their localization capability degraded, while the second row reports the results for ten. In both cases, the results are worst if compared with the respective row of table 4 and 5. These experiments show that the discussed approach could not be effective enough for our reference scenario, where the assumption made in the previous experiments could easily not be met.

In the second experimental setting we connected the proxies to the simulator. We decided to test the algorithm for the uncertainty handling, when five CHRs can have a degradation in their localization capability. All the parameters described in the previous set of experiments are used also in this set, except for the number of repetition that in this case is not five but two. These experiments have been conducted in order to see how the overall performance of the algorithm could be affected using the actual proxy framework. In particular for our scenario, a very important issue is the conflict that can possibly arise among the proxies' information on the actual world state, due to the asinchronicity of the message passing approach. The results reported in table 7 show that the algorithm performance seems not to be heavily affected by this issue, however the small number of experiments conducted does not allow to draw a statistically significant conclusion, and further investigations need to be done.

6   Related Work

Proxy-based integration architectures are not a new concept, however no previous architecture has been explicitly designed to have robots, agents and people in the same team. Jennings's GRATE* [5] uses a teamwork module, implementing a model of cooperation based on the joint intentions framework. Each agent has its own *cooperation level* module that negotiates involvement in a joint task and maintains information about its own and other agents' involvement in joint goals. Jones [6], Fong [16], Kortenkamp [8] and others have worked on improving collaboration between groups of robots and a single person, though these approaches to robotics teams have not explicitly used proxies. The Electric Elves project was the first human-agent collaboration architecture to include both proxies and adjustable autonomy [2]. COLLAGEN [13] uses a proxy architecture for collaboration between a single agent and user. Payne et al [19] illustrate how variance in an agent's interaction style with humans affects performance in domain tasks. Tidhar [20] used the term "team-oriented programming" to describe a conceptual framework for specifying team behaviors based on mutual beliefs and joint plans, coupled with organizational structures. His framework also addressed the issue of team selection [20] – team selection matches the "skills" required for executing a team plan against agents that have those skills.

7   Conclusions and Future Work

As seen in both domains, Machinetta shows promise in allowing complex teams to tackle the challenge of effective coordination. The main advantages to our approach become apparent when dealing with teams that display one or a combination of the characteristics: large scale, dynamic environment, and integration of humans. By connecting the Machinetta proxies with the graphical development tool for constructing team plans, the TOP programmer gains a good idea of what is going on in the plan and how to make effective changes in it in order to have the team behave more desirably. In the future, we plan on extending the features of both the graphical planning tool and Machinetta itself, while keeping the framework generalizable.

References

1. H. Chalupsky, Y. Gil, C. Knoblock, K. Lerman, J. Oh, D. Pynadath, T. Russ, and M. Tambe. Electric Elves: Applying agent technology to support human organizations. In *International Conference on Innovative Applications of AI*, pages 51–58, 2001.
2. Hans Chalupsky, Yolanda Gil, Craig A. Knoblock, Kristina Lerman, Jean Oh, David V. Pynadath, Thomas A. Russ, and Milind Tambe. Electric Elves: Agent technology for supporting human organizations. *AI Magazine*, 23(2):11–24, 2002.
3. Philip R. Cohen and Hector J. Levesque. Teamwork. *Nous*, 25(4):487–512, 1991.
4. Dieter Fox, Wolfram Burgard, and Sebastian Thrun. Markov localization for mobile robots in dynamic environments. *Journal of Artificial Intelligence Research*, 11:391–427, 1999.
5. N. Jennings. The archon systems and its applications. Project Report, 1995.
6. Henry L. Jones, Stephen M. Rock, Dennis Burns, and Steve Morris. Autonomous robots in swat applications: Research, design, and operations challenges. In *AUVSI '02*, 2002.
7. S. Kelso. *Dynamic Patterns: the self-organization of brain and behavior*. The MIT Press, 1995.
8. D. Kortenkamp, D. Schreckenghost, and C. Martin. User interaction with multi-robot systems. In *Proceedings of Workshop on Multi-Robot Systems*, 2002.
9. Dave Mulsiner and Barney Pell. Call for papers: AAAI spring symposium on adjustable autonomy. www.aaai.org, 1999.
10. David Pynadath and Milind Tambe. Multiagent teamwork: Analyzing the optimality and complexity of key theories and models. In *First International Joint Conference on Autonomous Agents and Multi-Agent Systems (AAMAS'02)*, 2002.
11. David V. Pynadath and Milind Tambe. An automated teamwork infrastructure for heterogeneous software agents and humans. *Journal of Autonomous Agents and Multi-Agent Systems, Special Issue on Infrastructure and Requirements for Building Research Grade Multi-Agent Systems*, page to appear, 2002.
12. D.V. Pynadath, M. Tambe, N. Chauvat, and L. Cavedon. Toward team-oriented programming. In *Intelligent Agents VI: Agent Theories, Architectures, and Languages*, pages 233–247, 1999.
13. C. Rich and C. Sidner. COLLAGEN: When agents collaborate with people. In *Proceedings of the International Conference on Autonomous Agents (Agents'97)*, 1997.

14. P. Scerri, D. V. Pynadath, L. Johnson, Rosenbloom P., N. Schurr, M Si, and M. Tambe. A prototype infrastructure for distributed robot-agent-person teams. In *The Second International Joint Conference on Autonomous Agents and Multiagent Systems*, 2003.

15. D. Schreckenghost, C. Thronesbery, P. Bonasso, D. Kortenkamp, and C. Martin. Intelligent control of life support for space missions. *IEEE Intelligent Systems Magazine*, 2002.

16. C. Thorpe T. Fong and C. Baur. Advanced interfaces for vehicle teleoperation: collaborative control, sensor fusion displays, and web-based tools. In *Vehicle Teleoperation Interfaces Workshop, IEEE International Conference on Robotics and Automation*, San Fransisco, CA, April 2000.

17. Milind Tambe. Agent architectures for flexible, practical teamwork. *National Conference on AI (AAAI97)*, pages 22–28, 1997.

18. Milind Tambe, Wei-Min Shen, Maja Mataric, David Pynadath, Dani Goldberg, Pragnesh Jay Modi, Zhun Qiu, and Behnam Salemi. Teamwork in cyberspace: using TEAMCORE to make agents team-ready. In *AAAI Spring Symposium on agents in cyberspace*, 1999.

19. Katia Sycara Terry Payne and Michael Lewis. Varying the user interaction within multiagent systems. In *Agents'00*, pages 412–418, 2000.

20. G. Tidhar, A.S. Rao, and E.A. Sonenberg. Guided team selection. In *Proceedings of the Second International Conference on Multi-Agent Systems*, 1996.

Developing Agent Interaction Protocols Using Graphical and Logical Methodologies

Shamimabi Paurobally[1], Jim Cunningham[2], and Nicholas R. Jennings[1]

[1] University of Southampton, School of Electronics and Computer Science,
Southampton SO17 1BJ, UK
{sp,nrj}@ecs.soton.ac.uk
[2] Imperial College, Computing Department, London SW7 2BZ, UK
rjc@doc.ic.ac.uk

Abstract. Although interaction protocols are often part of multi-agent infrastructures, many of the published protocols are semi-formal, vague or contain errors. Formal presentations can counter such disadvantages since they are amenable to verification of correctness. On the other hand, a diagrammatic representation of system structure is easier to comprehend. To this end, this paper bridges the gap between formal specification and intuitive development by: (1) proposing an extended form of propositional dynamic logic for expressing protocols completely, with clear semantics, that can be converted to a programming language for interaction protocols and (2) developing extended statecharts as a diagrammatic counterpart.

1 Introduction

Shared protocols and conversations facilitate interaction and coordination between agents towards achieving their goals. In this context, an interaction protocol defines the possible sequences of message exchange between agents in a group. Interaction protocols need to be clearly specified, validated and correctly implemented to enable reliable agent interactions. In the agent community, however, protocols are mostly specified in a diagrammatic or semi-formal methodology. Given this situation, there remains a need for formal specification and implementation tools for protocols, and for methods to verify, validate and reason about interaction protocols [11]. These methods should allow agents to be able to define, in a shared methodology, the protocols they are willing to engage in and to recognise other agents' protocols. Such a basis may also enable existing protocols to be extended into new and more detailed versions, or to be combined in order to better suit the prevailing context.

To this end, this paper proposes an extended form of Propositional Dynamic Logic (PDL) for presenting interaction protocols. The extended form of PDL that we outline is called ANML (Agent Negotiation Meta-Language). Interaction protocols in ANML are in the form of multi-modal theories, leading to an abstract theory of an interaction in a group. More specifically, we propose a program logic that can be used for specifying and validating the properties of

M. Dastani, J. Dix, A. El Fallah-Seghrouchni (Eds.): PROMAS 2003, LNAI 3067, pp. 149–168, 2004.
© Springer-Verlag Berlin Heidelberg 2004

a protocol [12]. From another angle, the ANML logic can be treated as close to an executable programming language for correctly implementing and executing interaction protocols. At the same time, we acknowledge that developers can understand the essence of an interaction protocol more quickly from a diagrammatic notation, given the human capacity for visual processing of spatial presentation. Therefore we accompany our extended PDL with extended statecharts to represent protocols diagrammatically. The aim is that protocols can be translated from extended statecharts to ANML and vice versa. A protocol in extended statecharts is the diagrammatic aspect for visual understanding whilst in ANML is the logical counterpart for verification and reasoning purposes. The translation is currently manual, but can be automated through an interpreter. ANML protocols facilitate verification, validation and other forms of reasoning including symbolic execution. We choose to extend statecharts for visual representation because they seem to exhibit the most adequate expressiveness, readability and intuitiveness for our purpose. To illustrate this point, we study the expressiveness of currently used notations like AUML and Petri nets. Although our work can also be applied to distributed systems protocols, there are two main distinctions between the latter protocols and interaction protocols. The first difference concerns the representation of an agent sending a message or executing a process, not found in program logic. The second difference is with respect to the state of an interaction which we consider as part of the beliefs of an agent and the group and the interaction protocol indicates how an agent's beliefs change with state transitions. In [15] we use our methodology to ensure the consistency in a shared interaction state.

Against this background, this paper advances the state of the art by identifying and answering the need for agent interaction protocols to be defined more formally than at present. ANML seems able to scale up and portray interactions between several agents while still fully specifying the details of a protocol. This, in turn, means that different agents may now represent, implement and interpret the same protocol without the risk of inconsistency between their mental states. At the same time, developers may use extended statecharts to convey a protocol to other users. We are also progressing towards executable libraries of protocols, which has not yet been achieved in multi-agent systems [14]. In this combined logical and graphical approach, there is a set of constructs that occurs in both the graphical and logical languages, implying an intersection between specification and implementation. In effect we are proposing a unified modeling and implementation language which reduces the amount of effort on the part of designers and programmers.

The remainder of the paper is organised in the following way. Section 2 discusses the requirements of a language for specifying protocols using a multi-lateral protocol for raising, amending and voting on motions as an example. Section 3 presents the syntax and semantics of ANML and its application in specifying the multi-lateral protocol. Section 4 compares diagrammatic notations such as AUML, Petri nets and statecharts. Section 5 presents extended statecharts as a graphical notation. Section 6 studies the translation between the logical and the graphical notation in a combined approach for specifying and implementing interaction protocols. Section 7 presents our conclusion.

2   Agent Interaction Protocols

A group of rational agents complies with an interaction protocol in order to engage in task-oriented sequences of exchanged messages. Thus, when an agent sends a message, it can expect a receiver's response to be among a set of messages indicated by the protocol and the interaction history. With a common interpretation of the protocol, each member of the group can also use the "rules" of the interaction in order to satisfy its own goals. In order to reach an implicit consensus about the possible states and actions in an interaction, it is necessary for the protocol itself to be correct (e.g. no contradictory states), unambiguous (e.g. possible actions are not vague), complete (e.g. no states are undefined) and verifiable (e.g. correctness properties can be verified). If a protocol does not exhibit these features, then with the difference in the participants' private beliefs, experience, intuition or culture, the agents may perform contradictory and unexpected actions leading to the possible breakdown of the interaction, the group, or encourage malicious behaviour and cause discontent.

The ability to express correct protocols, in turn, depends on the specification language or tool used to model the protocol. There are a number of requirements for a specification/implementation language or methodology for an interaction protocol. One of them is a formalisation which lends itself to verification, validation and execution tools.

2.1   Examplar Protocol

To illustrate the requirements of a specification methodology, we consider conventional rules of (formal) procedure as a protocol between two or more agents. The protocol presented here is of sufficient complexity for illustrating realistic interactions. It highlights the required expressiveness of a specification language. It is a multi-lateral protocol presenting the rules of procedure for submitting motions in a quorum, for seconding and amending these motions and for subsequent voting within a community of two or more agents.

An agent initiates a multilateral interaction, say $process\_m_1$, into a *pending* state of interaction, by raising motion m_1. The initiator can withdraw its motion m_1 or the motion may time out leading to a *withdrawn* state. Otherwise, from a *pending* state, a *seconded* state may be triggered by another participant seconding m_1. In the *seconded* state, a countdown to a vote timeout is activated. Any user may invoke the *amend* transition in the *seconded* state to replace the motion m_1 by m_2 or may call a transition to the *voting* state. The *amend* and *call* transitions are compound transitions (not atomic actions) themselves spawning sub-processes. On invoking an *amend* to replace m_1 by m_2, the group enters into a new instance of a multi-lateral process between the same agents, say $process\_m_2$, with the motion of whether to replace m_1 with m_2. If the multi-lateral interaction *process_m$_2$* succeeds in an *agreed* state, then the *seconded* state is re-entered in *process_m$_1$*, but with a new motion m_2 and the countdown to *voting* reinitialised. If *process_m$_2$* fails, then the amendment of m_1 with m_2 fails and the state remains *seconded* without any change. Similarly if the complex transition *call* to *voting* fails, the current state remains *seconded*. The *call* transition itself launches a separate multi-lateral process. In the *voting* state, vote processes occur until the time for voting is over or all participants have voted. If the proportion of "*yes*" votes is greater than the ceiling, then the protocol terminates successfully in an *agreed* state, otherwise the motion is *rejected*.

2.2   Requirements for a Protocol Language

The above natural language description of a multi-lateral protocol is hard to understand and is prone to misunderstandings, even when using variable names for clarity. From examining the multi-lateral protocol, we consider that a language for developing protocols is needed which can ideally meet the following requirements:

1. Provide a graphical representation for ready understanding of structure by developers.
2. Have an unambiguous formal specification language with clear semantics for verification.
3. Be close to an executable language for implementation purposes.
4. For relative tractability, maintain a propositional form for a formal language.
5. Provide a well-defined program logic for ensuring complete protocols and validating the properties of a protocol.
6. Allow a state automata like methodology for compatibility with existing methodologies and interaction protocols. For the sake of referring to a part of an interaction, the modeling language has to represent *both* the possible states and the possible actions.
7. Exhibit enough expressiveness for agent interactions and nested interactions.
8. Allow ease of reuse and abstraction of protocols.

3   Logical Approach: ANML

ANML is a language for specifying agent interaction protocols. It is based on Propositional Dynamic Logic (PDL), but without program assignment (similar to Hennessey-Milner logic [7] and related modal action logics). Dynamic logic [17] enables reasoning about the effect of programs on states of affairs, although in its primitive form it lacks process abstraction. However, Propositional Dynamic Logic [4] does allow the properties of complex processes to be expressed in terms of their constituent processes through modal connectives. This allows reasoning about the effect of processes on interaction states (and so PDL is adopted in our work). The minimal syntax of PDL operators expresses complex processes in terms of their sub-processes with modal connectives:

Formulae: $A ::= p \mid \perp \mid A_1 \rightarrow A_2 \mid [\alpha]A \mid \ldots$
Processes: $\alpha ::= \varpi \mid \alpha_1 ; \alpha_2 \mid \alpha_1 \cup \alpha_2 \mid \alpha^* \mid A? \mid null$

A formulae can contain derived connectives such as Boolean connectives $\wedge$, $\neg$, $\vee$, $\leftrightarrow$ or $\top$. The modal formula $\langle\alpha\rangle A$ is equivalent to $\neg([\alpha]\neg A)$.

The meta-variables p and ϖ denote, respectively, atomic formula (i.e. propositions) and atomic programs. The formula $[\alpha]A$ has the intended meaning: A holds after executing process α. This is the weakest precondition for α to terminate with A. The complex process $(\alpha_1 ; \alpha_2)$ denotes the sub-process α_1 followed by α_2, the process $(\alpha_1 \cup \alpha_2)$ is either α_1 or α_2 non-deterministically, α^* denotes zero or more iterations of process α. A state test operator "?" allows sequential composition to follow only if successful. A *null* process represents no execution while an *abort* process results in a failed state.

3.1 Extensions to PDL

The syntax of ANML is an adaptation of the program logic described in [17] and of PDL, with extensions to express multi-agent interactions. An agent can execute atomic actions or complex processes. Each atomic action constitutes a primitive process that may be combined into more complex ones. The processes performed by an agent trigger states of interaction which themselves can be organised into a hierarchy of parents and sub-states. This allows representation of complex actions and reasoning about computational aspects such as properties of protocols. ANML is defined over the types propositions, atomic processes, agents and as in [20] agent roles. We assume throughout that each atomic formula, agent and instance of an atomic process can be denoted by a distinct identifying term. Classical logic operators, list and set notations (e.g. $\cup$ and $\cap$) apply to formulae. The connectors in ANML *in addition to the above minimal set of PDL operators* are as follows:

An agent:	$oneAg ::= agent \mid agent : role$
Sets of agents	$gp ::= \epsilon \mid \{oneAg\} \mid gp_1 \cup gp_2$
Groups of agents:	$Ag\_group ::= oneAg \mid gp$
Set of states:	$States ::= \{A\} \mid \{A\} \cup States_1$
Formulae:	$A ::= A(Ag\_group) \mid \alpha_1 :: \alpha_2 \mid$
	$none\_of(States) \mid one\_of(States)$
Processes:	$\alpha ::= Ag\_group \bullet \alpha \mid \alpha?$

3.2 Informal Semantics of ANML

An agent group, Ag_group, is one agent or a set of agents, where an agent may be typed with a role for example $\{roger{:}retailer, bill{:}buyer\}$. A set of states is expressed as *States*. The state of a process, such as interaction, at an instance can be inferred from a formula over propositions, processes and agents holding at that instance. Simple and double implications between states define the relation between parent and possibly multiple sub-states. For example, in the formula (*rejected* → *closed*), the state *rejected* is a sub-state of *closed*. States may be hierarchical, groups of agents are not hierarchical but set operations may be applied to them. A state A can be parameterised by an agent or a set of agents as in the formula $A(Ag\_group)$ (or *rejected ({roger,bill})*).

The formula A holding after executing a process α is represented as the formula $[\alpha]A$ (e.g. *[offer]offered* is read as the state *offered* always holds after the process *offer*). In addition to testing atomic states (PDL allows tests on atomic states only), the process A? may also be defined when A is a compound formula and therefore in our methodology the test operator is used in its full generality over formulae. The meaning of a state parameterised by an agent depends on the rules and parameterisation of the protocol it occurs in. For example, state A_2 is parameterised in the protocol rule $A_1(Y) \leftrightarrow [X.\alpha]A_2(X)$.

The formula $(\alpha_1::\alpha_2)$ denotes that process α_1 is constrained to be of the same type as α_2. That is, all the states and transitions allowed in process α_1 can also be inferred from α_2 (e.g. *E-bay-auction :: English-auction*). The process α_1 is a different instance of the same class of process as α_2.

The operators *none_of* and *one_of* return *true* if, respectively, none of and exactly one of the states in their given sets of states are valid. They are used to express exclusivity between states and actions.

The executor of a process and that process are separated with a full stop (e.g. *r:retailer.display* means *retailer r* executes the *display* process). The role may be omitted and a joint process between two parties is denoted by the set of the two parties performing the process as in *{c, r}.shopping*. A process may be decomposed into a sequence of sub-processes, each possibly coupled with the agent or agents executing that sub-process, using the composition operator ";". For example, a negotiation process can be decomposed into the sub-processes of browsing, bargaining and paying. The process *(browsed(c)?; c.choose)* is the process *c.choose* if the test on *browsed(c)* succeeds, otherwise it fails. The test α? leads to the world holding after the execution of α, if the process α succeeds.

3.3   Formal Semantics of ANML

The semantics of ANML can be modelled through accessibility relations between possible worlds [11]. As for PDL, worlds are viewed as process states and accessibility relations as processes for state transitions. The semantics of the additional operators in ANML are based on a model denoted by $M = (W, R_\alpha, V)$. The set of worlds in the model are denoted by W.

R_α is a binary relation on W for each process α and reflects the intended meaning of process α, resulting in a uniquely determined standard model by inductively defining R_α for non-atomic processes α. For example, the relation $R_{Ag\_group.\alpha}$ maps world w_1 to world w_2 through an agent or a group executing process α. The function V represents an assignment of sets of possible worlds to propositions, where $V(p)$ is the set of worlds where atomic formula p holds, as an interpretation of the atoms in the model. The semantics of the ANML connectors are as follows, where $PROP$ is the set of propositions:

$M, w \models p$	iff $w \in V(p), p \in PROP$
$M, w \models [\alpha]A$	iff $\forall w_1 (wR_\alpha w_1$ implies $M, w_1 \models A)$
$M, w \models <\alpha>A$	iff $\exists w_1 (wR_\alpha w_1$ and $M, w_1 \models A)$
$M, w \models A(X)$	iff $M, w \models A$ and $X \in Ag\_group$
$M, w \models (\alpha_1 :: \alpha_2)$	iff $R_{\alpha_1} \subseteq R_{\alpha_2}$
$M, w \models none\_of(S_1)$	iff $\forall A(A \in S_1$ implies $M, w \not\models A)$
$M, w \models one\_of(S_1)$	iff $\exists A_1(A_1 \in S_1$ and $M, w \models A_1)$ and
	$\exists A_2((A_2 \in S_1 \text{and} M, w \models A_2)$ implies $A_1 \leftrightarrow A_2)$
$R_{Ag\_group.\alpha} \subseteq R_\alpha$	
$R_{A?} = \{(w, w) : M, w \models A\}$	
$R_{\alpha?} = \{(w_1, w_2) : (w_1, w_2) \in R_\alpha\}$	

For the formula $M, w \models A(X)$, the meaning of a state parameterised by an agent depends on the rules and synchronisation of the protocol it occurs in. The semantics of $M, w \models (\alpha_1 :: \alpha_2)$ states that all the worlds obtained through execution of process α_1 are elements of the set of worlds possible through performing α_2. The relation $R_{Ag\_group.\alpha}$ maps world w_1 to w_2 through an agent or a group executing process α. The set of worlds in the image of relation $R_{Ag\_group.\alpha}$ is a subset of the set of worlds in the image of R_α. In the case of two processes executed by two groups gp_1 and gp_2, where $gp_1 \subset gp_2$, and if the process α is the same instance, then $R_{gp_1.\alpha} = R_{gp_2.\alpha}$ On the other hand, if the two groups are performing different instances of process α, then no relation between the two processes $gp_1.\alpha$ and $gp_2.\alpha$ is derivable before execution. The success of a process is tested in $\alpha?$ by checking whether its consequential end state holds.

ANML inherits the axioms of a normal modal system and the underlying modal logics are decidable. Future work consists of analysing the complexity of ANML and its decidability. In addition, we have the axiom $(A(X) \rightarrow A)$ (e.g. offered(X) $\rightarrow$ offered). We assume that groups of agents in an interaction are finite sets and therefore our formalism does not embody quantification.

3.4   A Multi-lateral Protocol in ANML

The logical theory in figure 1 shows the application of ANML to represent the multi-lateral protocol in section 2.1. This theory can form the basis for further customisation for application or domain specific interactions. Here, axiom (1) ensures that a group of agents G adheres to a multi-lateral protocol in a process instance called *multilateral_process* to vote on a motion m. Double implication in the action-condition rules allows to infer the history of an interaction.

Axioms (2) to (7) define the relations between parent and sub-states. For example, the state of a multi-lateral interaction is either *motioned* or *closed*, but not both (axiom 1) or a *closed* state is either *agreed*, *rejected* or *withdrawn* (axiom 2). Axioms (5) to (7) ensure that when a parent state is false, none of its sub-states are true. An agent initiates a multilateral process into a *pending* state by raising a motion m (Axiom 8), ensuring the interaction cannot be arbitrarily re-started. The initiator can withdraw its motion m or the motion may time out into a *withdrawn* state (axiom 9). Otherwise from a *pending* state, a *seconded* state is triggered by another participant seconding the motion m (axiom 9).

$$\neg\ multi\_interaction\ \leftrightarrow\ [G.multilateral\_process_m]\ closed \tag{1}$$

$$multi\_interaction\ \leftrightarrow\ one\text{-}of\ (\{motioned\ ,\ closed\}) \tag{2}$$

$$closed\ \leftrightarrow\ one\text{-}of(\{agreed\ ,\ rejected\ ,\ withdrawn\}) \tag{3}$$

$$motioned\ \leftrightarrow\ one\text{-}of(\{pending,\ seconded,\ voting\}) \tag{4}$$

$$\neg\ multi\_interaction\ \leftrightarrow\ none\text{-}of(\{motioned\ ,\ closed\}) \tag{5}$$

$$\neg\ closed\leftrightarrow none\text{-}of(\{agreed, rejected, withdrawn\}) \tag{6}$$

$$\neg\ motioned\ \leftrightarrow\ none\text{-}of(\{pending,\ seconded,\ voting\}) \tag{7}$$

$$\neg\ multi\_interaction\ \leftrightarrow\ [\ X.motion_m]\ pending_m\,(X) \tag{8}$$

$$pending_m\,(X)\ \leftrightarrow\ ([Y.second_m]\ seconded_m\,(Y)\ \vee\ [timeout]withdrawn_m\ \vee$$
$$[X.withdraw_m]withdrawn_m)\ \wedge\neg(X{=}Y) \tag{9}$$

$$Y \in G\ \leftrightarrow\ (\ Y.amend_{m_1}\ ::\ G.multilateral\_process_{m_1}) \tag{10}$$

$$Y \in G\ \leftrightarrow\ (\ Y.call_{m_2}\ ::\ G.multilateral\_process_{m_2}) \tag{11}$$

$$seconded_m\,(X)\ \leftrightarrow\ ([timeout;G.vote_m]voting_m\,(G)\ \vee$$
$$([Y.amend_{m_1};agreed_{m_1}?;reinitialise]\ seconded_{m_1}\,(Y))\ \vee$$
$$([Y.call_{m_2};agreed_{m_2}?;G.vote_m]voting_m\,(G)))\ \wedge\neg(X{=}Y) \tag{12}$$

$$voting_m\,(G)\ \leftrightarrow\ [G.count_m;\ (\Sigma yes\text{-}votes \geq \tfrac{1}{2})?]\ agreed_m\ \vee$$
$$[G.count_m;\ (\Sigma yes\text{-}votes < \tfrac{1}{2})?]\ rejected_m \tag{13}$$

Fig. 1. Multi-lateral Protocol in ANML.

Axioms (10) and (11) define the processes $amend_{m_1}$ and $call_{m_2}$ as complex processes each launching a new *multilateral_process*, involving group G, with motions m_1 and m_2 respectively. In the $seconded_m$ state, when the countdown to voting has elapsed, the group votes on the motion m in the state $voting_m\,(G)$ (axiom 12). In the $seconded_m$ state, any agent may also invoke the complex $amend_{m_1}$ transition to replace the motion m by m_1. If the multi-lateral interaction spawned by the $amend_{m_1}$ process fails, then the state of the process *multilateral_process$_m$* remains $seconded_m$ without any change. Otherwise if the amendment of motion m succeeds by *multilateral_process$_{m_1}$* terminating in an $agreed_{m_1}$ state, then the $seconded_{m_1}\,(Y)$ state is entered in the *multilateral_process$_m$* interaction. The new motion is m_1 and the countdown to voting is reinitialised (axiom 12). Similarly the $Y.call_{m_2}$ process launches a multi-lateral interaction ($G.multilateral\_process_{m_2}$) with the motion m_2 being whether to vote immediately on the motion m.

In the $voting_m\,(G)$ state, depending on the number of "*yes*" votes, the multilateral interaction terminates successfully in an $agreed_m$ state, otherwise the motion m is *rejected* (axiom 13).

3.5   Analysing the Multi-lateral Theory

The theory in figure 1 is essentially propositional and may be analysed for completeness using tools such as model-checking or theorem proving. The logical theory of the above protocol in ANML is complete if it is consistent and all states are well-defined (either *true* or *false*). Here, we do not give the completeness proof for the ANML multi-lateral protocol, since this is not an objective of the paper. However, a completeness proof for a similar protocol can be found in [11].

The axiom $(A(X) \rightarrow A)$ in our framework ensures that there are no conflicts between a parent and its sub-states and in iterative actions, as found when using primitive statecharts in section 4.3. ANML also inherits the axioms and properties of PDL for decidability, soundness and completeness. We can use an axiomatisation of PDL when reasoning about protocols in ANML.

From analysing the properties of ANML, as above, to analysing the properties of the protocol, ANML is a program logic where the properties that a protocol can exhibit are defined as ANML axioms and the sequences of actions inferred from the theory of the protocol are analysed to show whether a property holds [12].

4   Graphical Methodologies

The ANML theory of the multi-lateral protocol in figure 1 defines all the possible states and actions in an interaction and therefore embodies the full details of the multi-lateral protocol. In addition, combined with a parser, ANML can act as a programming language for executing interaction protocols. However, as can be seen, although the theory facilitates automatic verification and validation, its structure may be hard to grasp. To assist comprehension, we propose the translation from a logical theory of a protocol into a diagrammatic notation for more intuitive human understanding.

From our experience in expressing and verifying protocols, we provide an analysis of the expressiveness of various methodologies for our purpose, including AUML, Petri nets and statecharts, since these are the most commonly used modelling methodologies. This analysis also stands as a comparison between the different notations and our approach for representing agent interaction protocols.

4.1   Specifying Protocols in AUML

Bauer et al. [1] have proposed AUML, (Agent Unified Modeling Language), as an extension of UML to define interaction protocols between agents. AUML is intended to be a graphical specification technique, which relies partly on FIPA ACL by using a subset of its communicative acts as messages.

An AUML Interaction Protocol (IP) diagram expresses a protocol in the form of a UML sequence diagram with extensions specific to AUML (as shown in Figure 2). Agents are assigned to roles, belong to classes and an IP diagram shows interactions between these agents along a timeline. An arrow indicates an unnested, asynchronous communication while a diamond means a decision point that can result in zero or more communications being sent (no diamonds – all threads are sent concurrently, an empty diamond – zero or more messages may be sent and a crossed diamond – exactly one message may be sent).

Advantages of AUML. The benefits of using AUML include the following:

– The process of an interaction over time is explicitly expressed through timelines, allowing a visual representation of events over time.

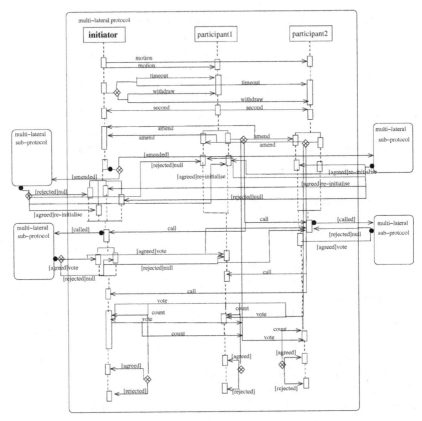

Fig. 2. The Multi-Lateral Protocol of section 2.1 in AUML.

- The exchange of messages between the different roles are shown explicitly as arrows.
- UML users are already familiar with most of AUML features.

Disadvantages of AUML. Despite both our understanding of the multi-lateral protocol from extensive analysis and past experience with the AUML notation [11], it took four hours to draw up the multi-lateral protocol in AUML using the *xfig* graphical tool. In this vein, we notice the following drawbacks of specifying protocols in AUML:

- Cluttered AUML diagrams are easy to misinterpret and a large amount of time and effort is required for developing and understanding reasonable interaction protocols in AUML.
- In fact, figure 2 is incomplete because we did not express several aspects including 1) the other agents in the protocol are passive, but vote; 2) agents sending a motion, its seconding, amendment, call and timeout may all be different. To do so would have led to six timelines and doubled the complexity of figure 2.

- A major drawback of AUML is the inability to bind roles, cardinalities, access agent identities or interacting as in a forum. As many timelines may be needed as the maximum number of messages exchanged and the number of participants.
- Conditions at decision points are undefined because an AUML diagram does not show states.
- Redundancy is hard to debug and modify. Actions that are possible by any agent have to be expressed on all the timelines.
- There is no easy way to express time-dependent actions such as timeouts, deadlines or ubiquitous messages like rejections at any time.
- There is no notion of history because states are not identified.
- Termination of the interaction is not obvious, especially when the threads of interaction are abbreviated to a single timeline.

Of course, there are ways to correct some of the deficiencies, but it remains hard to capture the m-n nature of agent interactions in a graphical notation like AUML. OCL [21] have been proposed as a textual representation of UML and could be extended for AUML diagrams. However OCL is essentially a constraint language, it has been subject to several criticisms amongst which is its lack of formality [19]. See [13] and [11] for a more detailed critique of AUML protocols.

4.2 Specifying Protocols in Petri Nets

Petri nets are another candidate for graphically modeling interaction protocols. In Petri nets, tokens are used to simulate and synchronise dynamic and concurrent activities and algebraic equations can be derived from Petri nets. The dynamics of a Petri net are a sequence of transition firings where tokens are taken away from input places to output places. Petri nets are used in a variety of applications including communication networks. However a weakness of Petri nets is the complexity problem; Petri-net-based models tend to become too large for analysis even for a modest-size system [8].

Interaction protocols expressed in Coloured Petri nets can be found in [2], [9] and [18]. The latter expresses in Petri nets some of the protocols proposed in AUML by FIPA [3]. Figure 3 is a coloured Petri net of the multi-lateral interaction according to the notation used in [9] and [2]. We have not shown the full details of the protocol so as not to render the diagram illegible.

Advantages of Petri Nets. Petri nets exhibit a number of useful features of which some worth mentioning are:

- Petri nets allow concurrency and synchronisation in the execution of threads.
- A large array of tools have been developed to detect conflicts and properties such as deadlocks or liveness and evaluate performance.
- There is a representation of states.
- Petri nets make less cluttered diagrams than AUML.

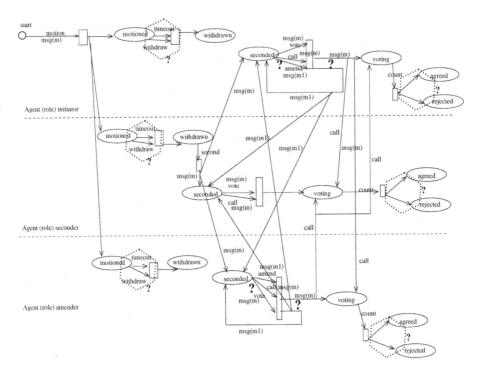

Fig. 3. Petri net of a Multi-Lateral Protocol (notation according to [9]).

Disadvantages of Petri Nets. However, we find that there are still limitations to the Petri net notation:

- Interaction protocols in Petri nets are still hard to read as can be seen in figure 3, in [2], [9] and [18] for a contract net protocol, a KQML register performative or a pair-wise negotiation.
- In figure 3, the dotted hexagons and bold "?" indicate parts of the Petri net where alternative actions and states cannot be expressed in the notation. For example, at the *seconded* place, an agent either executes an *amend, call* or *vote* action, but not all of them as indicated in the Petri net. The logical "∨" and ANML "∪" operators cannot be expressed in Petri nets. Thus, the ANML rule $R \leftrightarrow [c \cup e]S \vee [d]T$ cannot be expressed.
- Multiple Petri nets can be used for a protocol. In this case, a Petri net is assigned to each agent role, for example an initiator and a participant agent follow different Petri nets [18]. The collection of individual Petri nets associated with all the roles represents the entire interaction protocol, but this leads to issues about how the Petri nets are merged. There are also questions regarding reachability, consistency and mutually exclusive access to shared places between two or more Petri nets.

– A single Petri net can be used for a protocol by partitioning according to the role or identity of an agent (as shown with the horizontal dotted lines in figure 3) [9]. This still leads to a complex diagram. This raises the same problem as timelines in AUML where, here, a partition is required each time it is necessary to show a particular agent doing an action. Here ideally we should have five partitions for five different messages that can be sent by five different agents, yielding the same worst-case scenarios as for AUML.

– In each of the above cases, there is redundancy in repeating the same parts of a protocol for different agents or roles. This leads to diagrams which are unduly complicated and hard to read and suggests poor scalability.

– The notion of agents and execution of an action by an agent is not explicit in the notation.

– It is not easy to replace a piece of protocol by another Petri net [11] and thus Petri nets are not suitable for reusability and abstraction of protocols, including the replacement of sub-protocols.

It may seem that the Petri net in figure 3 is wrong, but this exactly reflects our comments regarding the disadvantages of using Petri net notation for our purpose. More specifically, because we have not found any notation in Petri net to express process alternation, this shortcoming gives rise to several errors in figure 3. These errors are compounded by the need to replicate the effects of transitions for each sub-net representing an agent or its role. For example, for agent role1, the transitions from the state *seconded*, an agent with that role can either amend the motion, call a vote or the voting process can begin after a countdown, but not more than two of them. We do not know how to represent this alternation in the Petri net and we show a "?" at this point. Our endeavour to nonetheless represent the multi-lateral protocol while having these open issues may bring about the remark that the protocol is wrong. It is effectively wrong since as shown here vote, call and amend all happen at the same time and trigger *both* the states *seconded* and *voting*. But we do not know how to correct this with the current notation. Likewise another error in the Petri net raises the question of how do we stop two agents (role1 and role2) each sending an amend or one agent sending a call while the other sends an amend.

The multi-lateral protocol does not only involve sending messages between two parties, but also broadcasting a message to the entire group. This is why we show that a message from an agent (or role) is sent to the rest of the agents in the other partitions. Thus amends and calls may be sent by any one agent to all the other agents. For example, agent role1 sends an amendment to agent role2 and agent role3 and similarly agent role2 may send amendment to agent role1 and agent role3. The same applies to the call for a vote where agent role1 sends a call to agent role2 and agent role3 or agent role2 may send a call to agent role1 and agent role3. These involve extensive crossing of the arrows representing all the possible messages and give rise to confusion, a complex diagram and the intuition that figure 3 is incorrect. In fact, we have omitted certain of these broadcast messages so as not to render the Petri net illegible. Thus, our conclusion is that

Petri nets (including high-level or coloured) are not ideal for representing agent interaction protocols because of weaknessess in expressiveness and scalability.

Petri Charts. Petri charts are presented in [6] and are based on Petri net and statechart notations. Petri charts introduce hierarchical net construction in Petri nets with subnets and super-places, allowing net refinements and composition. The approach in [6] focusses on Petri nets and adding to them the abstraction capabilities of statecharts. However, reversely how Petri net adds to statechart is not analysed. Even though Petri charts facilitate a modular approach to the construction of protocols, the above issue about the complexity of Petri nets for representing realistic protocols remain as can be seen in the Petri charts in [6]. The issues about representing agent roles with partitioning or seperate Petri nets still hold in Petri charts. Furthermore, to represent alternative actions at several states would require for each transition in a Petri net to contain a statechart, again increasing the complexity.

4.3   Specifying Protocols in Statecharts

Statecharts [5] are a graphical method to illustrate reactive behaviour and are an extension of conventional finite-state machines and state transition diagrams. This section discusses the desirability of statecharts for illustrating interaction protocols. To this end, figure 4 is a statechart of the multi-lateral protocol. From our experience with statecharts, we mention some general issues about using statecharts for interaction protocols.

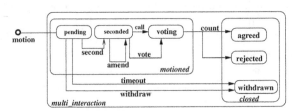

Fig. 4. Statechart of a Multi-Lateral Protocol (from [10]).

Advantages of Statecharts. The statechart notation possesses a number of advantages of interest for expressing protocols. Some of them are listed below:

- Figure 4 is clearer than its AUML and Petri nets counterparts.
- Augmenting statecharts to parameterise actions and states with agents is relatively simple and does not require new timelines (as in AUML), partitions or new Petri nets. Thus the statechart does not suffer from the drastic rise in complexity and redundancy with increase in the number of agents identified, contrary to AUML and Petri nets.
- States and processes are treated equally in statecharts, allowing an agent to refer and reason about the state of an interaction.
- Statechart notation is more amenable for extension for expressing agent interaction protocols graphically by adding in ANML constructs.

Disadvantages of Statecharts. Figure 4 does not show the full multi-lateral protocol because of the lack of expressiveness of the statechart notation in its original form.

- Statecharts do not portray the agents that are involved in exchanging messages and states that become valid do not contain information about which agent triggered the state.
- Compound transitions such as *amend, call* and *vote* that are themselves new multi-lateral processes are not shown in detail, nor are how their results affect the parent interaction shown.
- Incompleteness arises when a parent state can be valid without being in its sub-state [11].
- It must be ensured that entry actions are not possible once the interaction has begun, to prevent arbitrary restarting of the interaction.

Our choice for a graphical notation would be between Petri nets and statecharts. The factors that have influenced this decision, with respect to our requirements, include: 1) alternative actions are often part of an interaction and are expressible in statecharts but not in Petri nets 2) representing agents requires less effort in statecharts 3) hierarchies of states in statecharts facilitate abstraction, reuse and expressing nested protocols.

It may be remarked that the Petri net notation still has the ability to express concurrent actions and synchronisation between threads for firing a transition. In this paper, we specify the core syntax and semantics of ANML and extended statecharts enough for expressing realistic and sequential agent interactions. Our two methodologies can be extended as needs be for more expressiveness. In a more powerful ANML embracing the concurrent and synchronisation capabilities of Petri nets, places, transitions and arcs in Petri nets are respectively analogue to states, intermediate states and processes in ANML. The rules in ANML translate how the places and transitions are connected with arcs. Concurrent ANML reuses the operators from concurrent PDL [4]. The concurrent execution of processes α and β is expressed as "$\alpha \cap \beta$". More details on concurrent ANML can be found in [11].

Therefore we accompany our logical notation of extended PDL with extended statecharts as a graphical notation. After all, statecharts stem from Harel's research who has also contributed extensively to propositional dynamic logic. Statecharts are the natural graphical representation of PDL and vice versa. The contribution here is to extend these two notations for representing agent interaction protocols and fulfil the needs and open issues found in section 4.

5   Extending Statecharts

We render the portrayal of protocols in statecharts more complete by providing additional constructs to the statechart notation. Moreover, we add to statecharts, ANML constructs for dealing with agents performing actions, triggering states, nested protocols and synchronisation. Our extended statechart notation thus benefits from the same semantics as ANML because they both share a set of constructs. This allows developers to learn only one semantic specification for both the graphical (specification) and the logical (implementation-related) methodologies. To this end, figure 5 presents the additional constructs for extending statecharts. The arcs in the original statechart notation represent alternative actions, i.e. only one of the arcs is executed. Figure 5 shows how we augmented statecharts with ANML-like formulas and processes.

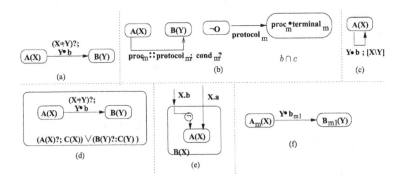

Fig. 5. Extended Statechart Notation.

Contrary to what may be perceived, the notations we add to statecharts are entirely new and derive from neither Petri nets nor Petri charts. PDL and statecharts have essentially been developed by Harel [5] to represent programs and reactive systems. Therefore, they are respectively logical and graphical counternotations with an intuitive link and translation between them. This is why we choose these two notations and our extensions to represent agent interaction protocols are exported to both notations. While it can be seen that statecharts and PDL are not new notations, it is our extensions to them which are new and represent our contribution. These extensions do not occur in the notations in section 4 and result from the deficiencies in the compared notations and the needs for expressing agent interaction protocols.

In more detail, figure 5(a) shows the parameterisation of the states A and B and the process b, where X and Y are two different agents or groups of agents. The process $(Y \bullet b)$ changes the state $A(X)$ to $B(Y)$, if the test $(X \neq Y)$? succeeds.

Figure 5(b) shows the nesting of protocols. The process $proc_m$, leading from state $A(X)$ to $B(Y)$, is a complex process that is constrained by the process $protocol_m$. The state $B(Y)$ is triggered if the condition $cond_m$ holds (which can be brought about by the process $proc_m$). The right hand side of the diagram 5(b) abstractly defines $protocol_m$.

In Figure 5(c), we solve the conflicts when two actions may lead to the same state, but with different agent parameters. Here the notation $[X\backslash Y]$ is read as the parameter X is replaced by the agent Y in state A, leading to $A(Y)$.

Figure 5(d) solves conflicts when a parent state consists of two different sub-states with different parameters. Here, from the condition $(A(X)?; C(X))? \vee (B(Y)?C(Y))$, the parent state is $C(X)$ if the sub-state $A(X)$ holds, otherwise $C(Y)$ if $B(Y)$ holds.

Figure 5(e) resolves the incompleteness in statecharts when a parent state can be valid without being in any of its sub-states. Here the arrow with a negation explicitly expresses that the process $X.b$ leads to the parent state $B(X)$, but not to the sub-state $A(X)$.

Figure 5(f) shows the subscripting of states (A and B) and process b with an identifier m or $m1$. This notation is useful in dealing with instances of a process that can occur several times in a single interaction as a result of nested processes.

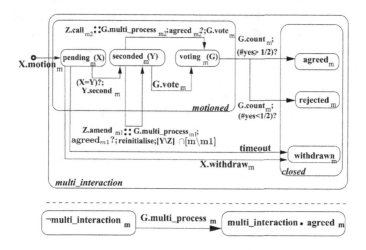

Fig. 6. Extended Statechart of a Multi-Lateral Protocol.

We can now represent all the details of the multi-lateral protocol in our extended statechart notation, as shown in figure 6. Even though figure 6 is complete, while figures 2 and 3 are incomplete, it can be seen that the extended statechart is far less cluttered and more readable, thus justifying our choice for extending statecharts.

6   A Combined Approach

Our combined approach consists of the extended forms of PDL and statecharts presented in the previous sections. Interaction protocols between agents can be specified and implemented using these methodologies, where a major advantage is the sharing of a set of constructs and their semantics for executing processes and triggering interaction states. This stands as a bridge between theory and application or specification and implementation of protocols. In this section, we discuss the combined approach.

6.1   Meeting the Requirements

We analyse whether the combined approach meets the requirements for a language for agent interaction protocols discussed in section 2.2. The aim stated in the premises of the paper is to propose an approach that specifies verifiable interaction protocols clearly and completely, and yet is close to an executable form. The extended statecharts notation fulfils the first requirement for a diagrammatic notation. In addition figure 6 is an example of the conciseness of the extended statecharts notation over AUML and Petri nets.

ANML is a formal language with specified syntax and semantics and verification and model checking may be applied on ANML protocols (requirement 2). Furthermore, implementation tools such as a parser or modal prolog systems could allow the execution of protocols in ANML (requirement 3). ANML is essentially propositional and useful logic-based theorems are applicable (requirement 4). Properties of a protocol can be specified as axioms in ANML and ANML protocols can be validated against these properties [12] (requirement 5).

Both extended statecharts and ANML adopt a state automata representation and express processes and states of an interaction (requirement 6). Furthermore, in both notations, we parameterise the processes and states with the agents or groups of agents performing and triggering them respectively. Generic actions may be typed with roles or the roles may be bound to identified agents without a significant increase in complexity. The combined approach is suitable in a multi-agent domain (requirement 7). Nested interactions are represented by the :: operator in both ANML and extended statecharts (requirement 7). Hierarchies of states allow abstraction and reuse of protocols (requirement 8).

6.2   Translating between Methods

Using a unified modeling/implementation language reduces the amount of effort on the part of designers and programmers. ANML and extended statecharts are linked through the ANML constructs used inside the statecharts. We can translate statecharts to ANML (corresponding to a translation from specification to an implementation-like language for execution, automated verification and validation) and from ANML to statecharts (for visual understanding). The translation can be shown to be lossless. Figure 6 and the theory in figure 1 are complementary; the former represents the multi-lateral protocol in extended statecharts and the latter in ANML.

In essence, a protocol in extended statecharts is a graphical visualisation of the set of rules in an ANML theory. ANML rules between states (parent and sub-states) correspond to the hierarchy of states in statecharts. ANML action-condition rules are translated into state transitions.

6.3   Modular Translation between Methods

We first provide a general translation from each extended statecharts in figure 5 to ANML. A translation from ANML to extended statecharts is similarly performed from the rules in this section to figure 5. The general PDL rule represents a state transition in statecharts $A \rightarrow [b]B$. Our new constructs translate litterally from ANML rules to annotations on the corresponding statecharts.

5	ANML representation
(a)	$A(X) \rightarrow ([Y.b]B(Y) \wedge X \neq Y)$
(b)	$\neg O \rightarrow [protocol_m](proc_m.terminal_m)$ (defining the overall protocol) $proc_m :: protocol_m$ ($proc_m$ is a process according to a protocol) $A(X) \rightarrow [proc_m; cond_m?]B(Y)$ (execution of $proc_m$)
(c)	$A(X) \rightarrow ([Y.b; [X \backslash Y]]A(Y)$ ie $A(X) \rightarrow ([Y.b]A(Y)$ (swapping role)
(d)	$C(X) \leftrightarrow one{-}of(A(X), B(X))$ $A(X) \rightarrow ([Y.b]B(Y) \wedge X \neq Y)$
(e)	$A(X) \rightarrow B(X)$ $[X.a]A(X)$ $[X.b](B(X) \wedge \neg A(X))$
(f)	$A_m(X) \rightarrow ([Y.b_{m1}]B_{m1}(Y))$

7   Conclusions

This paper has addressed the need for formalised and more expressive logical and graphical methodologies for precisely specifying and validating protocols and their properties for interaction between rational agents. Towards this end, we propose a combined approach consisting of extended PDL and extended statecharts. We specify a formal language, called ANML, based on PDL for representing and reasoning about agent interaction protocols. ANML can be developed into a language for programming libraries of protocols and logic-based theorems can be applied to ANML theories. The notations can also be applied to other protocols than multi-agent interactions, but our extensions allow us to consider the domain of agent executing actions.

We show the application of our language using an example multi-lateral protocol. Case studies of AUML, Petri nets and statecharts convince us that of all methods, statecharts are the closest to a completely expressive graphical notation. It seems that we can enhance statecharts to match the ANML formalism. Future work includes analysing the complexity and soundness of ANML, comparing with other logics such as action logics, event calculus and mu-calculus and combining with game theoretic strategies [16]

References

1. B. Bauer, J. P. Muller, and J. Odell. Agent UML: A Formalism for Specifying Multiagent Software Systems. In *Agent-Oriented Software Engineering*, pages 91–104, 2000.
2. R. Cost, Y. Chen, T. Finin, Y. Labrou, and Y. Peng. Modeling agent conversations with colored petri nets. In *Workshop on Specifying and Implementing Conversation Policies*, pages 59–66, 1999.
3. Foundation for Intelligent Physical Agents, http://www.fipa.org. *FIPA Agent Communication Language Specification*.

4. R. Goldblatt. *Logics of Time and Computation*. CSLI, 1987.

5. D. Harel and M. Politi. *Modeling reactive systems with statecharts*. McGraw-Hill, 1998.

6. T. Holvoet and P. Verbaeten. Petri charts: an alternative technique for hierarchical net construction. In *Proceedings of IEEE Conference on System, Man, and Cybernetics, October*, 1995.

7. R. Milner. *Communication and Concurrency*. Prentice Hall, 1989.

8. T. Murata. Petri nets: Properties, analysis, and applications. *IEEE*, 77(4):541–580, 1989.

9. M. Nowostawski, M. Purvis, and S. Cranefield. A layered approach for modelling agent conversations. In *2nd Int. Work. on Infrastructure for Agents, MAS, and Scalable MAS, Agents 2001*, 2001.

10. OMG. *Negotiation Facility Specification*. The Object Management Group, Inc., http://www.omg.org, 2002.

11. S. Paurobally. *Rational Agents and the Processes and States of Negotiation*. PhD thesis, Imperial College, 2002.

12. S. Paurobally and J. Cunningham. Safety and liveness of negotiation protocols. In *AISB2002 Convention on AI and the Simulation of Behaviour, Intelligent Agents in virtual market track.*, 2002.

13. S. Paurobally and R. Cunningham. Verification of protocols for negotiation between agents. In *ECAI-15*, pages 43–48, 2002.

14. S. Paurobally and R. Cunningham. Achieving common interaction protocols in open agent environments. In *Challenges in Open Agent Systems 2003 Workshop, 2nd Int. Joint Conf. on Autonomous Agents and Multi-Agent Systems*, 2003.

15. S. Paurobally, R. Cunningham, and N. R. Jennings. Ensuring consistency in joint beliefs of interacting agents. In *2nd Int. Joint Conf. on Autonomous Agents and Multi-Agent Systems*, pages 662–669, 2003.

16. S. Paurobally, P. J. Turner, and N. R. Jennings. Towards automating negotiation for m-services. In *AMEC V workshop, 2nd Int. Joint Conf. on Autonomous Agents and Multi-Agent Systems*, pages 124–131, 2003.

17. V. R. Pratt. Semantical considerations on Floyd-Hoare logic. In *Proceedings of 17th IEEE Symposium, Foundations of Computer Science*, pages 109–121, 1976.

18. M. K. Purvis, S. Cranefield, M. Nowostawski, and M. A. Purvis. Multi-agent system interaction protocols in a dynamically changing environment. In *Workshop on Toward Application Science: MAS Problem Spaces and their implementation to achieve globally coherent behaviour. AAMAS*, 2002.

19. M. Richters and M. Gogolla. On formalizing the UML object constraint language OCL. In *Proc. 17th International Conference on Conceptual Modeling (ER)*, volume 1507, pages 449–464. Springer-Verlag, 1998.

20. M. Strobel. Design of roles and protocols for electronic negotiations. *Electronic Commerce Research*, 3:335–353, 2001.

21. J. Warmer and A. Kleppe. Ocl: The constraint language of the uml. *Journal of Object-Oriented Programming*, 1999.

Norm Adoption and Consistency
in the NoA Agent Architecture

Martin J. Kollingbaum and Timothy J. Norman

Department of Computing Science, University of Aberdeen,
Aberdeen AB24 3UE, Scotland, UK
{mkolling,tnorman}@csd.abdn.ac.uk

Abstract. The behaviour of a norm-driven agent is governed by obligations, permissions and prohibitions. Agents joining a society or accepting a contract for the purpose of executing specific collaborative tasks usually have to adopt norms representing certain rules and regulations. Adoption of norms can cause problems – an agent maybe already hold norms that would be in conflict or *inconsistent* with new norms it adopts. How can it be shown that the set of norms is consistent to allow the agent to act according to the ideals that the norms specify? In general, the answer to such a question in a real-world situation is not simple. This paper addresses the problem of finding a pragmatic solution to the problem of norm consistency checking for practical reasoning agents in the context of the NoA Normative Agent Architecture.

1 Introduction

Norm-driven agents are motivated and influenced by norms in their behaviour. These norms are the obligations, permissions and prohibitions that determine their role within a society of agents. Incorporating normative concepts into an agent architecture allows the development of an agent with an explicit representation of its normative state. With that, normative agents know, besides their capabilities, what their rights and duties are within a society of agents. Obligations motivate or demand agents to perform a specific act or achieve a specific state of affairs. Prohibitions are obligations to *not* perform a specific act or to *not* achieve a state of affairs – a prohibited state of affairs may occur regardless of the behaviour of the agent influenced in such a way, but the agent must not bring it about of its own volition. Permissions allow that agent to achieve a specific state of affairs or to perform a specific action.

Adopting new norms is an essential activity for normative agents. Agents join societies and take on certain positions and roles by accepting rules and regulations or sign contracts comprising sets of norms to pursue collaborative tasks with other agents. Norm adoption means that new norms are integrated into the set of norms currently held by the agent. But there is a specific problem – the agent may already hold norms that would be in conflict or *inconsistent* with newly adopted norms. For example, a new obligation could demand an action that is actually forbidden by the agent's currently held norms. For a normative agent, it is important to consider (and have means to investigate) the impact of such an adoption on its normative state. For a decision on whether or not to adopt a new norm (if, of course, the agent has a choice) the agent must, at least, determine how such an adoption influences the consistency of its current set of norms. The following questions must be addressed:

M. Dastani, J. Dix, A. El Fallah-Seghrouchni (Eds.): PROMAS 2003, LNAI 3067, pp. 169–186, 2004.
© Springer-Verlag Berlin Heidelberg 2004

- Under what circumstances is it appropriate for an agent to adopt a new obligation, permission or prohibition?
- What effect does the adoption of a new norm have on the agent's normative state?
- Is the newly adopted norm consistent with the norms currently held by the agent?

These questions are motivated by issues of conflicts between norms, the ability to automatically detect such conflicts and how to express and represent norms and the normative state of an agent. In general, these question are not easy to answer, although some cases are clear-cut. For example, an agent considering the adoption of an obligation to achieve p may already be prohibited from bringing about p. There are situations, however, where conflicts are less obvious. Suppose that all plans that could be chosen to achieve p have side-effects that conflict with one prohibition or another. In this case, the agent has to take into account not only the state p that, according to the norm, it is obliged to achieve, but also the various means (plans) at its disposal to achieve p.

The architecture of a normative agent plays an important role in how conflicts are detected, norms are represented, and how norm adoption takes place. The NoA agent architecture [13] is specifically constructed for the implementation of norm-governed agents and includes such mechanisms that are important for maintaining the normative state of an agent and for the adoption of norms. As a reactive planning architecture, it operates with prefabricated plans, which are enacted to fulfill obligations. NoA is used to describe and investigate issues of norm adoption and consistency in detail. Section 2 gives an overview of NoA, describing the NoA language as a means for specifying norms and plans, and its principal architecture. The focus of section 3 is on norm adoption and consistency; the main concern of this paper. Using the concepts introduced with the NoA architecture, the effects of norm adoption are outlined in detail. Section 4 complements the previous section by providing a discussion about further observations made in the context of norm adoption. Sections 5 reviews related work and section 6 presents conclusions.

2   NoA

Norm-governed agents require an architecture that allows an explicit representation and maintenance of their "normative state". Such a normative state is determined by the set of norms the agent currently holds – obligations, permissions and prohibitions. The NoA agent architecture [13] meets this requirement. The design of NoA reflects the fact that a norm-governed agent must be able to investigate how the selection of a specific plan and the execution of this plan, with its effects on the environment, would influence and change its current normative situation. It must "look ahead", and, if it is endowed with the ability to automatically construct plans to achieve its goals, it must search the space of possible plans to determine whether there exists one that fulfils the obligation without violating some other norm. Such a decision is, of course, costly and practical reasoning agents must be provided with appropriate heuristics to limit such an overhead [17,21]. Reactive planning architectures [7] provide a compromise between the flexibility of planning and the efficiency of purely reactive agents by requiring the designer to declare a fixed set of plan procedures, organised in a set of hierarchies, that are selected through a process of means-ends analysis [5,7]. This representation of the capabilities of an agent serves to restrict the search for applicable plans to just those that have the required effect. Thus, the complexity of the problem of searching for a plan is minimised, although at a concomitant loss of run-time flexibility.

To balance flexibility and efficiency, NoA is designed as a reactive planning architecture. As outlined before, it is important for a normative agent, especially a NoA agent, to reason about the "effects" of the execution of a plan. NoA agents adopt a heuristic (see section 3) to determine the consistency of a newly adopted norm with an existing set of norms by "looking ahead" and estimating probable outcomes of the execution of a set of plan options.

This requirement has influenced the design of the NoA plan and norm specification language (influenced by systems such as JAM [9] and Agentspeak(L) [4, 16, 20]) – plans are declared with explicit effect specifications. NoA has following main characteristics:

- *Multiple effects in the plan specification.* The NoA language in common with planning domain specification languages such as PDDL [8], but in contrast to languages such as JAM, allows all the effects of a plan to be explicitly declared in a plan specification. Any of these effects can be the reason for the agent to select a plan. This provides greater flexibility in the specification of agent capabilities, and enables a NoA agent to reason about side-effects occurring during the execution of a plan

- *Agents are motivated by norms.* Norms are important motivators for NoA agents to act. These norms capture states of affairs or actions the agent is obliged or permitted to achieve or perform, or prohibited from achieving or performing.

- *Distinction between states and actions.* The norms governing the behaviour of a NoA agent refer to either actions that are obligatory, permitted, forbidden, or states of affairs that are obligatory, permitted or forbidden [18]. This explicit distinction between achieving states of affairs and performing actions is reflected in the NoA language and accommodated in the design of the NoA architecture.

The NoA language enables an agent to be programmed in terms of plans and norms. The NoA architecture provides an executor for these plan and norm specifications. Both concepts are outlined in more detail in the following sections

2.1 NoA Language

The fact that NoA is based on a reactive planning architecture with normative extensions is reflected in the NoA language. This language serves two purposes:

- declaration of normative statements expressing obligations, permissions and prohibitions and contracts as sets of these norms; and

- declaration of agent capability in the form of pre-specified plans.

Normative statements formulated in this language express obligations, permissions and prohibitions of an agent:

- **Obligations** in NoA are goal / action generators – they motivate the achievement of a state of affairs or the performance of an action. Based on such a motivation, agents select an appropriate plan from their currently available behavioural repertoire. The language construct `obligation` is introduced to express obligations.

- **Prohibitions** are effectively obligations to not achieve a state of affairs or to not perform an action. A prohibition states that it is forbidden for the agent to achieve / do that. Rather than requiring this to be expressed as "obligation not", the NoA language contains a separate language construct, prohibition, for this case. A prohibition does not motivate the generation of a goal or action, but it acts as a kind of "filter" in the plan selection process.
- **Permissions** allow the achievement of a state of affairs or the performance of an action. NoA introduces the language construct permission for this purpose.

In the design of the NoA language, specific care has been taken of two issues: (a) that norms are often "active" and relevant to a norm-addressee only under specific conditions, and (b) that there are dependencies between norms. For example, the fulfillment of an obligation to achieve a state of affairs could permit an agent to perform some action as soon as that state of affairs is achieved. Therefore, the concept of "norm activation" is introduced into the NoA language. Each normative statement contains two conditions: an *activation* condition and an *expiration* condition. With that, it can be clearly determined under what circumstances or conditions norms are operative or "active". Essential information carried by a normative statement in the NoA language is therefore

(a) a *role specification* to determine the norm-addressee,
(b) the *activity specification*,
(c) an *activation condition* and
(d) an *expiration condition*.

For obligations, activation and expiration conditions determine when an agent has to fulfill an obligation. For permissions, activation and expiration condition determine a "window of opportunity" for the agent to act – if a permission is active, it explicitly allows the achievement of a state or the performance of an action. However, if a permission is not activated or expired, it does not mean that the achievement of a state of affairs or the performance of an action is automatically "forbidden". In the same way, an active prohibition forbids the achievement of a state of affairs or the performance of an action, whereas a deactivated prohibition does not mean that this achievement of a state or performance of an action is automatically "allowed". For NoA, a clarification of this undefined situation is needed. This clarification comes into place by establishing certain relationships between norms held by the agent. The following initial basic assumption can be taken:

- *Implicit-permission-assumption*: If an agent has the capability to perform an action then it has an implicit (or default) permission to do so.

Therefore, without an explicit legal context, an agent would be allowed to do what it is capable of doing. It has complete personal freedom to act. With the introduction of norms comprising a legal context (for example, in the form of a contract), the agent will maybe experience restrictions to its freedom. A newly adopted explicit prohibition will *override* and explicitly restrict, partially or completely, the agent's default freedom (or implicit permission). In NoA, an explicit prohibition is regarded "stronger" than the implicit permission that an agent gains from having the capability to act in this way. If, instead, an explicit permission would be introduced on top of the implicit permission, then this new explicit norm would just restate a normative situation that is already in place.

If now, on top of an explicit prohibition, a new permission is introduced, a decision is needed: which of the two norms is now relevant? In terms of NoA, two explicitly introduced norms such as a prohibition and a permission are regarded as having equal influence on the agent's normative state. NoA handles this situation by ranking norms according to the time at which they have been adopted by a NoA agent – the ranking takes place according to the "adoption-time-assumption":

- *Adoption-time-assumption.* If there exists an adopted norm for the achievement of a state of affairs or the performance of an action and a new norm is adopted for exactly the same state or action, then the new norm "overrides" the previous norm – norms are ranked (or "stacked") according to their "arrival time".

With this assumption, the newly adopted permission overrides (temporarily, if activation/expiration conditions are used) this prohibition. For NoA, it can be stated:

- If an agent is explicitly forbidden from performing an action then it is normally not permitted to do so, regardless of whether it has the capability. If activation/expiration conditions are observed, the prohibition occurs only when it is active.
- Explicit prohibitions can be overridden by newly adopted explicit permissions. Taking activation/expiration conditions into account, permissions put prohibitions temporarily out of action.

An n-stage overriding mechanism is, therefore, employed in NoA. To illustrate NoA's norm interpretation with an example, consider an agent that has the ability to query an information source. Without any restrictions in place, it would be able to access the data unhindered. Suppose that a policy or norm is established that explicitly prohibits this agent from obtaining access to this information resource. This agent should not access the resource, but, following a special agreement with the owner, it may temporarily obtain a permission to download a specific document. As soon as this download has taken place, the permission expires and the original prohibition regains its power to determine the normative state of the agent.

2.1.1 Specification of Norms

A familiar example is used to illustrate the specification of norms: a simple blocks world scenario. Figure 1 shows a scenario with five blocks and a robot arm as the agent "BlockMover".

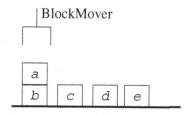

Fig. 1. A simple Blocks World Scenario

Obligations are motivators of a NoA agent. They motivate such an agent to act in a certain way, either to achieve a goal or perform an action, expressed by keywords `achieve` and `perform`. In the example illustrated in figure 1, it is assumed that the agent BlockMover has the obligation to clear block b, expressed by following normative statement:

```
obligation(BlockMover, achieve clear(b),not clear(b),clear(b))
```

This example shows the outline of a normative statement containing specifications for a norm addressee, the activity specification itself and the activation and expiration condition. The activity specification within this obligation requires the agent BlockMover to achieve a specific *state of affairs*, namely clear (b). To fulfill its obligation, the agent has to choose a plan for execution that produces this effect. In addition, the normative statement contains the activation condition not clear(b) and the expiration condition clear(b). This states that this obligation for agent BlockMover becomes active whenever block b (Figure 1) is not clear (stating a kind of maintenance goal [17]). The obligation ceases to be active, as soon as the expiration condition holds. In general, the activation condition indicates when norms become operative, whereas the expiration condition puts a norm out of operation. For obligations, they delimit the period in which the agent must act (possibly giving deadlines for the fulfilment of an obligation). For permissions, this mechanism allows to specify the mentioned *window of opportunity* where this permission is operative.

According to the overriding mechanism of norms described above, the introduction of the following prohibition restricts the agent's implicit freedom to act:

```
prohibition(BlockMover,achieve onTable(a),TRUE,FALSE)
```

A new permission may then, temporarily, overrides this prohibition:

```
permission(BlockMover,achieve onTable(a),on(a,b),
                            clear(b) and onTable(a))
```

This example consists of two normative statements: a general prohibition to put block a on the table (Figure 1), which is always active and never expires, and a permission that expresses that an agent is only allowed to move block a from block b to the table. The permission becomes active as soon as block a sits on top of block b and expires as soon as block a is on the table. With that, the permission temporarily overrides the prohibition.

2.1.2 Specification of Plans

Example specifications of plans for the blocks world scenario will illustrate the crafting of plans. To operate the blocks world as shown in figure 1, it is assumed that the agent "BlockMover" is given following prefabricated plans (see figure 3): plan stack to stack blocks, plan unstack to put blocks on the table, plan shift to move blocks on top of other blocks to an empty block and plan move to move a block to a currently occupied position. Plans are both used for the achievement of a specific state of affairs (an effect) or are simply performed, when the performance of an action is required.

The layout of a plan specification reflects this fact. As figure 2 shows, one obligation uses the construct achieve clear(b) to motivate a state-oriented activity, whereas the second obligation uses perform shift(a, b, c) to motivate an action-oriented activity. The statement achieve clear(b) initiates the search for a set of plan instantiations that could be executed to achieve the effect clear(b).

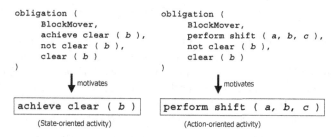

```
obligation (                      obligation (
    BlockMover,                       BlockMover,
    achieve clear ( b ),              perform shift ( a, b, c ),
    not clear ( b ),                  not clear ( b ),
    clear ( b )                       clear ( b )
)                                 )
```

↓ motivates   ↓ motivates

```
achieve clear ( b )      perform shift ( a, b, c )
```

(State-oriented activity)   (Action-oriented activity)

Fig. 2. Activity Generation

```
plan stack ( X, Y )                    plan unstack ( X, Y )
    preconditions(ontable(X),              preconditions(on(X,Y))
                  clear(Y))                effects(ontable(X),
    effects(on(X,Y),                               not on(X,Y),
            not ontable(X),                        clear(Y))
            not clear (Y))         {
{                                          achieve clear(X);
    achieve clear(X);                      primitive doMove(X,"Table");
    primitive doMove(X,Y);         }
}
plan shift ( X, Y, Z )                 plan move ( X, Y, U, Z )
    preconditions(on(X,Y),                 preconditions(on(X,Y),
                  clear(Z))                              on(U,Z))
    effects(on(X,Z),                       effects(on(X,Z),
            not on(X,Y),                           not on(X,Y),
            clear(Y),                              clear(Y),
            not clear(Z))                          not on(U,Z))
{                                      {
    achieve clear(X);                      achieve clear(X);
    primitive doMove(X,Z) ;                achieve clear(U);
}                                          achieve not on(U,Z);
                                           primitive doMove(X,Z);
                                       }
```

Fig. 3. Plans formulated in the NoA Language

Instantiations of the plans `unstack`, `shift` and `move` would provide this effect. The statement `perform shift(a,b,c)` directly determines an instantiation of plan `shift`. For this case, a plan instantiation is chosen according to the plan signature – the plan name with the parameter list. A plan declaration, therefore, serves both cases: state-oriented and action-oriented activity

2.2 Architecture

The NoA architecture provides an executor for plan and norm specifications. The main elements that influence the behaviour of a NoA agent are (a) a set of beliefs, (b) a set of pre-specified plans and (c) a set of norms. Plan specifications contain declarations of all the effects a plan would have during execution. Agents will select plans for execution according to one of these effects, with all the other effects becoming side-effects of such an execution. This plan selection will take place when agents are motivated to pursue a specific "activity": either to achieve a state of affairs or to perform an action.

Activities motivated by changes in the set of beliefs can be described as *internally motivated activities*. But NoA agents introduce norms as an additional element of influence to their acting and obligations represent *external motivators*. Changes in the set of beliefs may result in a request for the agent to pursue a specific activity.

Norms have to be active to take an influence on the behaviour of an agent. Activated norms influence the behaviour of an agent in two ways:

- by motivating the generation of a goal that must be achieved or an action that has to be performed (the distinction between state and action [18] is maintained), these are externally motivated activities, and
- by being used in a special "norm filtering" step within the execution cycle of the NoA architecture by restricting the options of the agent in fulfilling its responsibilities.

The execution of a NoA agent is therefore determined by active obligations that motivate activity and by the complete set of currently active norms that determine what plan options are allowed or forbidden to be used, or if the choice of a plan option would counteract existing obligations. Plan specifications contain preconditions (see figure 3) and a plan is instantiated as soon as these preconditions hold. In the same way, norms become active when their activation conditions hold. It depends on the current set of beliefs, what norms are activated and what plans are instantiated. The set of instantiated plans is the behavioural repertoire currently available to an agent. Like the set of active norms, this set of plan instantiations changes if the set of beliefs held by the agent changes.

When an activity is motivated by an activated obligation, a plan instantiation must be found for execution. The effects of such a plan instantiation should not counteract existing norms. The NoA architecture therefore introduces a special norm filtering step into the plan selection process.

Figure 4 shows details of the NoA execution architecture. Activation and instantiation of norms and plans is done by a Plan Instantiation/Norm Activation element. This is essentially an implementation of a Rete network [6]. Plan specifications and newly adopted norms are compiled into this activation network. Changes in the set of beliefs will be recognized by this activation mechanism and lead to the mentioned instantiations and activations. Activated obligations result in the generation of an activity, either a goal or an action. A so-called "Activity Monitor" is provided to pursue such an activity. It supports the plan selection and execution of plans and the satisfaction / performance of sub-goals / subsidiary actions. Activity Monitors operate concurrently, providing a separate thread of control for each activity. The execution cycle within this monitor has following steps:

- Plan Instantiation Selection. In case that a goal (state of affairs) motivated by an obligation must be satisfied, a set of currently available plan instantiations is chosen according to one of their effects. If the motivated activity is the performance of a specific action, one of these plan instantiations will be chosen directly.
- Norm Filter. Active prohibitions and permissions are applied to this set of plan instantiations to filter out those that would produce effects that are forbidden.

- Plan Choice. One of the plan instantiations must be chosen for execution. In case of the performance of an action, only one plan instantiation would be available, if not filtered out by the previous step.
- Plan Execution. The execution of a plan can have various outcomes: performing a primitive action affecting the world, updating beliefs or establishing a sub-goal or subsidiary actions.

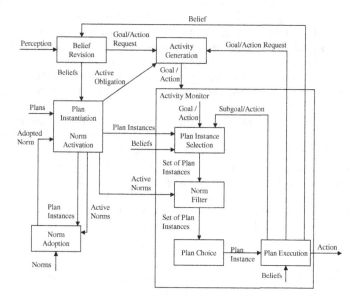

Fig. 4. NoA Agent Architecture

Plans that are chosen as options for goal achievement, are checked against the currently active set of norms. The norm filter has to decide which plans must be filtered out. In its most simplest form of implementation, this would be all the plans that would produce effects that are prohibited according to the currently active norms. More sophisticated norm filters would introduce deliberation to allow NoA agents to handle norms in a maybe more sophisticated or "relaxed" way.

Figure 4 also shows a mechanism for the adoption of new norms. For a new norm, aspects of consistency with existing norms have to be investigated. The adoption mechanism therefore needs information about the current normative state of an agent: its currently active norms and its currently available behavioural repertoire (instantiated plans). If a norm can be adopted, it will be compiled at runtime into the activation mechanism (Rete network) of the architecture. Issues and problems of norm adoption will be outlined in more detail in the following section.

3   Norm Adoption and Consistency

For NoA agents, norm adoption is an ongoing activity. Agents engage in the negotiation and execution of a new contract and, therefore, have to adopt norms stated in such a contract. When an agent adopts a new norm, problems of consistency with its current set of norms can occur. The adoption of an obligation by a NoA agent to achieve a state of affairs, which itself is maybe not forbidden, could lead to the selection of a plan with *side-effects* that are prohibited to be brought about.

In NoA, a specific active obligation will motivate the selection and execution of a specific plan instantiation and prohibitions / permissions currently active will restrict / allow the actual deployment of this plan instantiation. It depends on the set of beliefs currently held by the agent, what norms are active and what plans are instantiated. In detail, the normative state is determined by following concepts: (a) the agent's current beliefs, (b) the agent's current capabilities expressed by a set of instantiated plans, (c) the set of capabilities currently allowed by active permissions and (d) the capabilities currently obliged and / or forbidden by active obligations / prohibitions. States of affairs are achieved by deploying those capabilities in the form of instantiated plans that are currently allowed.

The adoption of a new norm can change the normative state of an agent. A new permission can allow certain capabilities to be deployed by the agent that previously have been forbidden from being used. In the same way, new prohibitions introduce restrictions on the agent's behaviour. Permissions and prohibitions create a specific normative situation in terms of the actions or pre-specified plans to be deployed. For new obligations to be consistent with the current set of norms, only those plan instantiations can be chosen with effects that are not forbidden states of affairs. To describe this aspect in more detail, following notation is used:

- PLANS, the set of currently instantiated plan declarations (or capability specifications)
- O is the set of currently active obligations, F the set of currently active prohibitions and P the set of currently active permissions
- The set S_O describes those states of affairs obliged by currently active obligations contained in the set O, whereas the set T_O describes actions obliged by currently active obligations contained in the set O. Accordingly, the sets S_F and S_P and the sets T_F and T_P describe states of affairs prohibited / permitted and actions prohibited / permitted by currently active norms.
- The function effects(p) providing the set of effects of a plan instantiation
- The function neg_effects(p) providing a set containing for each element in effects(p) a negated version of this element.
- The function options(o) with $o \in O$ providing the subset of plan instantiations of the set PLANS that are options to fulfill the obligation o – either to achieve the required state of affairs or to be performed as the required action

The function effects(p) provides the set of effects of a plan instantiation. Effects of a plan instantiations change the truth condition of propositions expressing the current state of the world. For example, the declaration of plan unstack contains the effects ontable(X), not on(X,Y) and clear(Y) (see figure 3). An instantiation of such a plan declaration would have obtained bindings for the variables X and Y in these effect specifications. To support the discussion in this paper, a separate function is established to allow a reference to states of affairs that are the negation of states appearing within the set of plan effects. The function producing this set is called neg_effects(p). According to the overriding mechanism of NoA for colliding prohibitions and permissions, the set of *currently* forbidden states would be $S_F \setminus S_P$, stating that only those prohibitions are relevant to an agent that are not currently overridden by a prohibition. In the same way, $T_F \setminus T_P$ is the set of *currently* forbidden actions.

In the following sections, aspects of norm adoption are discussed in more detail. Activation and expiration conditions of norms are omitted, which means that such a norm is immediately active and never expires. The re-introduction of these conditions and its implication for consistency issues is discussed in a subsequent section

3.1 Adoption of an Obligation

Obligations are motivators for agents to act. The adoption of a new obligation could motivate an agent to behave in a certain way that counteracts existing norms. The agent finds itself in a specific normative state determined by the set of currently held beliefs, the set of activated norms and the current set of instantiated plans, PLANS, as its current repertoire of behaviour. The violation of existing norms by an obligation can only be observed via the effects of those plan instantiations that can be chosen to fulfill this obligation. The execution of such plan instantiations therefore has an impact on the *consistency* of the set of norms currently held by the agent. It can be stated:

- The execution of a plan instantiation $p \in$ PLANS, with $p \notin T_F \setminus T_P$ (p is not a currently forbidden action), is consistent with the current set of active norms of an agent, if none of the effects of p is currently forbidden and no effect counteracts any obligation ($S_F \setminus S_P$ is the set of those forbidden states that are not permitted by an overriding permission, S_O is the set of obliged states of affairs):

consistent (p, S_F, S_P, S_O)   iff

$$S_F \setminus S_P \cap \text{effects(p)} = \varnothing \qquad (1)$$
$$\text{and} \quad S_O \cap \text{neg\_effects(p)} = \varnothing$$

The adoption of an obligation therefore can lead to inconsistencies. Under specific circumstances, conflicts necessarily occur. The term "Strong Inconsistency" determines these circumstances. "Strong Consistency" determines a situation where no conflict can occur. "Weak Consistency" determines a situation where the addition of an obligation possibly leads to an inconsistency. Definitions are given in the following.

3.1.1 Strong Inconsistency
The adoption of a new obligation introduces "Strong Inconsistency" into a set of currently active norms, if there is *necessarily* a conflict. With the adoption of a new obligation, a plan instantiation p has to be found to either achieve a state of affairs demanded by this obligation or to perform p directly as the required action. If o denotes the adopted obligation and options(o) is a function that returns the set of plan instantiations that are options for fulfilling this obligation, then "Strong Inconsistency" occurs under following condition:

strong_inconsistency(o, S_F, S_P, S_O, T_F, T_P) iff

$$\forall p \in \text{options}(o).\ p \in T_F \setminus T_P \ \vee \ \neg\, \text{consistent}(p, S_F, S_P, S_O) \qquad (2)$$

If a new obligation is added, then inconsistency occurs, if whatever plan instantiation is chosen, the plan instantiation p is either currently forbidden or produces effects that are forbidden or would counteract existing currently active obligations.

As an example, suppose that the following norms are contained in the current set of active norms of agent BlockMover: a prohibition to move block a from block b to the table and an obligation to clear block b:

```
prohibition(BlockMover,achieve ontable(a),TRUE,FALSE)
obligation(BlockMover,achieve clear(b),TRUE,FALSE)
```

Referring to the situation of blocks world example in figure 1, the agent BlockMover can move block a only between blocks c, d and e, any other move would violate norms. The obligation motivates the selection of plan shift (plan unstack produces in one of its instantiations the effect clear(b) as well, but violates the prohibition, therefore will be filtered out). Suppose that plan shift(a,b,c) is executed, resulting in the current state of the blocks world as depicted in figure 5.

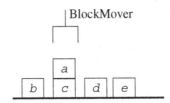

Fig. 5. Blocks world scenario according to the current set of norms

Now, suppose that a new obligation o_1 (see below) is introduced. Issues of consistency have to be investigated. To perform unstack(a,c), an appropriate plan instantiation has to be chosen. This choice will influence the consistency of the set of norms. Assuming that the current situation is that depicted in figure 5, an instantiation of plan unstack would have ontable(a), not on(a,c) and clear(c) as effects. The effect ontable(a) counteracts the prohibition shown above. No other plan can be chosen in that case, therefore the adoption of this obligation will put the set of norms in the state of strong inconsistency.

Obligation o_1:

```
obligation(BlockMover,perform unstack(a,c),TRUE,FALSE)
```

3.1.2 Strong Consistency

A set of norms is strongly consistent, if there is *necessarily* **no** conflict. Again, a plan instantiation p has to be found to either achieve a state of affairs demanded by this obligation or to perform p directly as the required action. If o denotes the adopted obligation and options(o) is a function that returns the set of plan instantiations that are options for fulfilling this obligation, then "Strong Consistency" occurs under following condition:

$$\text{strong\_consistency}(o, S_F, S_P, S_O, T_F, T_P) \text{ iff} \tag{3}$$
$$\forall p \in \text{options}(o). \, p \notin T_F \setminus T_P \, \wedge \, \text{consistent}(p, S_F, S_P, S_O)$$

If a new obligation is added and activated, then consistency is preserved, if whatever plan instantiation is chosen, the plan instantiation p is not forbidden and does not produce effects that are forbidden or would counteract currently active obligations.

The example from the previous section is reused here. According to existing norms, it is assumed that block a has been moved onto block c (which is reflected in figure 5). To guarantee strong consistency, there must be no possibility of a conflict. An example for an obligation that preserves strong consistency would be the following:

```
obligation(BlockMover,achieve on(a,d),TRUE,FALSE)
```

To achieve the state prescribed by this obligation, the plans `stack`, `shift` and `move` are available. According to the current situation depicted in figure 5, only plan `shift` would be instantiated with the effects `on(a,d)`, `not on(a,c)`, `clear(c)`, `not clear(d)`. The plan instantiation to be chosen for this obligation does not produce any effects that would conflict.

3.1.3 Weak Consistency

A set of norms is weakly consistent, if there is at least one option open to the agent in which there is no conflict. If o denotes the adopted obligation and options(o) is a function that returns the set of plan instantiations that are options for fulfilling this obligation, then "Weak Consistency" occurs under following condition:

weak_consistency(o, S_F, S_P, S_O, T_F, T_P) iff

$$\exists p \in \text{options}(o) \text{ s.t. } p \notin T_F \setminus T_P \ \wedge \ \text{consistent}(p, S_F, S_P, S_O) \tag{4}$$

As long as there is at least one plan instantiation p that can be chosen without being forbidden as an action and without producing any of the forbidden states as an effect and does not counteract any obligations, weak consistency occurs.

Again, the previous blocks world scenario is used to show an example. If following obligation is introduced,

```
obligation(BlockMover,achieve clear(c),TRUE,FALSE)
```

then instantiations of the plans `unstack`, `shift` and `move` could provide the required effect. According to the current situation of the blocks world, plans `unstack` and `shift` are instantiated. Following table shows these instantiations:

- `shift (option 1): on(a,b), not on(a,c), clear(c), not clear(b)`
- `shift (option 2): on(a,d), not on(a,c), clear(c), not clear(d)`
- `shift (option 3): on(a,e), not on(a,c), clear(c), not clear(e)`
- `unstack (option 4): ontable(a), not on(a,c), clear(c)`

All four options would provide the required effect. Only option 2 and option 3 would be plan instantiations that are not violating currently active norms. As there exists at least one plan instantiation that preserves consistency, the adoption of this norm and its subsequent activation puts the set of currently active norms in a state of weak consistency. Strong consistency cannot be achieved because there are plan instantiations that violate existing norms with their effects.

3.2 Adoption of a Prohibition

Prohibitions are not motivators for activities, they introduce a restriction on the behaviour of an agent. They are therefore taken into account in the norm filtering process. When a prohibition is adopted, inconsistencies with currently active obligations can occur. This inconsistency would take place if the prohibition forbids what a currently active obligation demands. The agent therefore has to determine, if it still can meet its obligations in case of the adoption of a new prohibition. There are following possible outcomes in case of the adoption of a prohibition:

- the set of currently active norms remains in its current state, which can be strong / weak consistency or strong inconsistency
- The set of currently active norms is transferred or "downgraded" into a weaker state of consistency, which can be weak consistency or strong inconsistency

A prohibition can be considered introducing inconsistency, if it produces a state n which at least one active obligation becomes strongly inconsistent.

3.3 Adoption of a Permission

Permissions may override prohibitions. Permissions can "upgrade" the consistency state of a set of norms. There are following possible outcomes in case of the adoption of a permission:

- the set of norms remains in its current state, which can be strong / weak consistency or strong inconsistency
- the set of norms is transferred or "upgraded" into a stronger state of consistency, which can be weak / strong consistency

As an example, it is assumed that the prohibition

```
prohibition(BlockMover,achieve ontable(a),TRUE,FALSE)
```

is overridden by following permission:

```
permission(BlockMover,achieve ontable(a),TRUE,FALSE)
```

As activation and expiration conditions are set to TRUE and FALSE respectively in both cases, the newly adopted permission will permanently override the original prohibition. Introducing explicit activation and expiration conditions, the permission would determine a "window of opportunity" where the originally forbidden state is allowed to be achieved.

4 Discussion

The previous sections presented aspects of consistency and norm adoption within the NoA agent architecture. As outlined, an agent can be at different levels of consistency, which are strong inconsistency, weak consistency and strong consistency. The adoption of a new norm can transfer an agent into a weaker state of consistency (with the adoption of a new obligation or prohibition) or back into a state of stronger consistency (with the adoption of a new permission). It is assumed here that agents adopt norms one by one, each newly adopted obligation changes the state of the world by the execution of a selected plan instantiation. The new state of the world results from the effects of this selected plan instantiation. This new state of the world is then the basis for the next norm adoption. Based on the current set of beliefs, the current set of active norms and the current set of plan instantiations, the agent can investigate how the adoption of a new norm would affect its consistency level. From the current situation, it can "look ahead" and estimate what its consistency level would be by analyzing all possible outcomes of such an adoption. This is called a "single look-ahead" in the context of NoA, because only the immediate possible future can be estimated. It is not known to the agent if it can hold or improve its consistency level beyond the situations that have been investigated. This estimation shows a specific consistency level based on the current state of the world, which results in a characteristic set of plan instantiations. This set of plan instantiations determines with their effects, what the consistency level will be when the norm is adopted at that moment.

Activation and expiration conditions are the part of normative statements that determine under what circumstances norms are active and therefore relevant to an agent. To simplify the discussion so far, these conditions have been set to TRUE and FALSE, indicating that a norm is immediately activated and never expires. Such a simplification serves well in the explanation of consistency. The use of activation and expiration conditions introduces an additional complication for an agent's estimation of the consistency level of its set of norms after a supposed norm adoption. It depends on the state of the world which norms are active (their activation condition holds and their expiration conditions does not hold). Therefore, it cannot be expected that the complete set of norms is active at the moment when the agent intends to adopt a new norm. With that, potential conflicts are not identifiable and predictable any more with a single look-ahead. To fully investigate any conflicts, the agent would have to establish a complete plan with all plan instantiations (preconditions hold) and norm activations (activation conditions hold, expiration conditions do not hold) in place. This plan then has to be executed without any deviation and the world would have to change its state according to the planned sequence.

The establishment of a complete plan and its exact execution in real world applications is rendered difficult due to unexpected changes in the world. The intention for NoA agents is to be situated in a real, changing world. NoA is therefore based on a reactive planning architecture. As outlined, an automatic consistency check of norm specifications using activation and expiration conditions is a complex problem. To introduce such an automation, three options are available:

1. Use the NoA language in its full expressiveness in terms of norm specification, providing the specification of obligations, prohibitions, permissions, distinguishing states and actions and using activation / expiration conditions. In that case, consistency checks are impractical, as the system cannot make any predictions regarding plan instantiation selection / execution for activated obligations. The strategy would be to pre-design sets of norms (contracts) in a consistent fashion and allow the execution to fail, if the consistency level is downgraded during execution.
2. Use the NoA language in its full expressiveness, but ignore activation / expiration conditions and estimate the change of the consistency level by obtaining information about all the outcomes of a norm adoption (the "single look-ahead" described above). Due to activation / expiration conditions, this look-ahead is not accurate because subsets of norms are maybe not activated in the current situation and therefore potential inconsistencies between norms are not visible.
3. Reduce the expressiveness of the language, remove activation / expiration condition. With that, norms are permanently active and the single look-ahead check produces reliable results. Adopted sets of norms (contracts) will be consistent.

By providing mechanisms for determining consistency during norm adoption, NoA agents become informed about their current normative state and can, therefore, react to such changes. It allows them to make a decision to either adopt or not adopt a norm. If an agent does not have a choice to deny the adoption of an obligation imposed by an authority, it can, at least, consider further actions.

5 Related Work

The central focus of this paper is to investigate norm adoption with automated norm consistency checking. Research into normative agents is, therefore, relevant related work in which these ideas should be placed in context. The foci of this research are:

- *Norm adoption.* Under what conditions would an agent adopt a norm?
- *Norm consistency.* Is the set of adopted norms consistent?
- *Norm influence.* How do norms influence the behaviour of an agent?
- *Norm violation.* Under what circumstances would an agent violate a norm?

Dastani and van der Torre [3] present a mature theory of norms and a decision procedure for selecting a consistent and maximal set of norms. Obligations, in their model are characterized as conditional statements of the form "if this state of affairs holds, perform this action" and "if this action is performed, perform this action". A domain theory is also represented as conditional statements of the form "if state p holds, then q must hold" and "if action a is done then p is the result". With this model, a BOID agent searches for the maximal set of norms that are consistent. These ideas are an influence to the work presented in this paper, but our approach differs in a number of respects. We are concerned with how the consistency of a norm (that refers to the achievement of a state of affairs or the performance of an action) may be checked against a set of plans and a set of prior norms within the context of a practical reasoning agent. Broersen et al. [1] describe the BOID agent architecture, which uses obligations in addition to the attitudes beliefs, desires and intentions. Agents have to resolve conflicts between their attitudes. Different types of conflicts between these attitudes are discussed and conflict resolution types as orders of overruling between the attitudes are described. In contrast to BOID, NoA agents can have conflicting norms. Lopez *et al.* [15] present a proposal for agents that make a decision whether or not to adopt a norm, which includes issues such as the attitude of the agent towards norms, or the consistency of a norm with the agent's currently adopted goals. Castelfranchi *et al.* [2] present an abstract picture of the types of norms that could influence the agents behaviour, including norms that have the potential to generate goals and norms as preferences over decisions of the agent.

Contract management and execution plays a central role in the NoA agent architecture. The NoA language as a means to specify contracts is influenced by the work of Jones and Sergot [10,11] and Pacheco and Carmo [19]. They investigate the modelling of complex organisations and organisational behaviour using normative models. The contract specification language put forward by Pacheco and Carmo includes role specifications, deontic characterisations for these roles, statements of representation, the attribution of roles to agents and the relations between roles. The contract specification language described in this paper uses similar concepts with following extensions: specific normative statements called "sanctions" assigned to an authority role (as specified in [14]) and the explicit consideration of activation and expiration conditions for normative statements in a contract, to clearly specify the time window during which a normative activity is operative. In addition, this contract specification reflects the clear distinction between actions and states as proposed by Norman & Reed [18].

6 Conclusion

In this paper, we have focused on issues of consistency of sets of norms adopted by a practical reasoning agent. Of particular interest is the "level of consistency" that occurs if an agent adopts a new norm. In this paper, three levels of consistency are described: "strong consistency", "weak consistency" and "strong inconsistency". An obligation may be strongly inconsistent, weakly consistent or consistent with a set of norms (obligations, permissions and prohibitions). Prohibitions and permissions can change the agent's consistency level. Using this classification of levels of consistency, an agent may make reasonable decisions on whether or not to adopt a new norm. Such an analysis of consistency is essential for contracting agents, where the contracts under consideration are represented by sets of obligations, prohibitions and the privileges or permissions of a party involved. This provides such an agent with the means whereby it can, at least, make a judgement as to whether the contract "on the table" is consistent with its prior obligations [12]. With the ability to represent and reason about and act according to norms, the NoA agent architecture provides a solution for automated contract management and a technology for the development and deployment of norm-governed agents.

References

1. Broersen, J., Dastani, M., Hulstijn, J., Huang, Z., van der Torre, L. (2001). The BOID architecture: conflicts between beliefs, obligations, intentions and desires. *Proceedings of Autonomous Agents 2001*, pp. 9-16.
2. Castelfranchi, C, Dignum, F., Jonker, C., Treur, J. (2000). Deliberate normative Agents: Principles and Architecture. In *Intelligent Agents VI*, LNAI 1757, pp. 364-378. Springer-Verlag.
3. Dastani, M, van der Torre, L. (2002). What is a normative Goal? In *Proceedings of International Workshop on Regulated Agent-based Social Systems: Theories and Applications*. AAMAS Workshop.
4. d'Inverno, M., Luck, M. (1998). Engineering AgentSpeak(L): A formal computational model. *Journal of Logic and Computation*, 8(3):233-260.
5. Firby, R.J. (1987). An investigation into reactive planning in complex domains. In *Proceedings of the National Conference on Artificial Intellgence* (AAAI-87), pp. 809-815.
6. Forgy, C.L. (1982). Rete: A Fast Algorithm for the Many Pattern / Many Object Pattern Match Problem, Artificial Intelligence 19, pp. 17-37.
7. Georgeff, M. P., Lansky, A. (1987). Reactive Reasoning and Planning. In *Proceedings of the National Conference on Artificial Intellgence* (AAAI-87), pp. 677-682.
8. Ghallab, M., Howe, A., Knoblock, G., McDermott, D., Ram, A., Veloso, M., Weld, D., Wilkins, D. (1998). PDDL – The Planning Domain Definition Language, Tech Report CVC TR-98-003/DCS TR-1165, Yale Center for Computational Vision and Control.
9. Huber, M.J. (1999). JAM: A BDI-theoretic mobile agent architecture. In *Proceedings of the Third International Conference on Autonomous Agents* (Agents'99), pp. 236-243.

10. Jones, A.J.I., Sergot, M. (1992), On the Characterisation of Law and Computer Systems: The Normative Systems Perspective, In J.-J.Ch. Meyer, R.J. Wieringa (editors), *Deontic Logic in Computer Science: Normative System Specification*, Wiley.

11. Jones, A.J.I., Sergot, M. (1996), A Formal Characterisation of Institutionalised Power, *Journal of the IGPL*, 4(3), pp. 429-445.

12. Kollingbaum, M.J., Norman, T.J. (2002). Supervised Interaction - Creating a Web of Trust for Contracting Agents in Electronic Environments. In C Castelfranchi & W Johnson (eds), *Proceedings of the First International Joint Conference on Autonomous Agents and Mulit-Agent Systems* (Bologna, Italy), ACM Press, New York, pp. 272-279.

13. Kollingbaum, M.J., Norman, T.J. (2002). A Contract Management Framework for Supervised Interaction. *UKMAS 2002*, Liverpool, December 2002.

14. Kollingbaum, M.J., Norman, T.J. (2003). Supervised Interaction - A Form of Contract Management to create Trust between Agents. *Trust, Reputation and Security: Theories and Practice*, LNAI 2631, Springer-Verlag.

15. Lopez, F., Luck, M., d'Inverno, M. (2002). Constraining autonomy through norms. In *Proceedings of the First International Joint Conference on Autonomous Agents and Multi-agent Systems*, pp. 647-681.

16. Machado, R., Bordini, R. H. (2001). Running AgentSpeak(L) agents on SIM_AGENT. In d'Inverno, M., and Luck, M., eds., *Working Notes of the Fourth UK Workshop on Multi-Agent Systems* (UKMAS 2001), 13-14 December. St. Catherine's College, Oxford.

17. Norman, T.J., Long, D.P. (1995). Goal Creation in motivated Agents. In M.J.Wooldridge, N.R. Jennings (eds.), *Intelligent Agents*, LNAI 890, Springer-Verlag.

18. Norman, T. J., Reed, C A. (2001). *Delegation and responsibility*. In C Castelfranchi & Y Lesperance (eds), *Intelligent Agents VII*, LNAI 1986, Springer-Verlag, pp. 136-149.

19. Pacheco, O., Carmo, J. (2001). A Role Based Model for the Normative Specification of Organized Collective Agency and Agents Interaction, *Journal of Autonomous Agents and Multi-Agent Systems*, 6(2):145-184, Springer-Verlag.

20. Rao, A. S. (1996). AgentSpeak(L): BDI agents speak out in a logical computable language. In Agents Breaking Away. In W. Van de Velde and J. W. Perram (eds.): *Proceedings of the Seventh European Workshop on Modelling Autonomous Agents in a Multi-Agent World*, LNAI 1038, pp. 42-55, Springer-Verlag.

21. Wooldridge, M.J. (2002). An Introduction to Multi-Agent Systems. Wiley.

A Tool for Integrated Design and Implementation of Conversations in Multiagent Systems

Martin Dinkloh and Jens Nimis

Universität Karlsruhe (TH), Institute for Program Structures and Data Organization (IPD)
Am Fasanengarten 5, D-76128 Karlsruhe, Germany
Tel.: +49 721 608-7337
Fax: +49 721 608-7343
{dinkloh,nimis}@ipd.uni-karlsruhe.de

Abstract. Multiagent systems form a promising paradigm for software development in complex application domains, but unfortunately tend to be complex systems themselves. The existing gap between analysis and design of multiagent systems and their implementation leads to an increased programming effort. In this paper, we present a graphical tool which tries to bridge this gap by integrating the design and implementation of agent conversations. The tool is implemented, as a plugin, for the integrated development environment Eclipse. Its use follows a conversation programming workflow which supports Agent UML and finite state machines as graphical notations. It is shown how the in-memory representation based on the description language cpXML, is automatically translated into source code for the multiagent framework JADE.

1 Introduction

Since the early 1980s the multiagent system (MAS) field has been a very active and highly interdisciplinary research area, driven by the hope that these systems will be able to cope with complex application domains which resist a treatment with ordinary systems. This has led to a deep grasp of conceptual aspects of MAS and to many research prototypes in a wide range of domains. In the recent years, the wish to deploy MAS in industrial settings has been the driving force for development of standards for MAS such as the FIPA standard [1]. This process was accompanied by the development of several standard conforming MAS frameworks, which have now reached a high level of maturity.

Nevertheless, there are still few known large scale industrial applications. One main reason for this is that MAS themselves, like the application domains they must cope with, tend to be very complex. This complexity results in several drawbacks in comparison to ordinary systems, such as difficult error handling, insufficient transparency and increased development effort.

Standards and frameworks can be seen as a first step to reduce these drawbacks. However, for industrial application of multiagent technology there are still many practical issues open to enable developers to implement a MAS based on their analysis and design results. The gap between analysis and design on one side and implementation on the other side for object oriented software development is bridged by extensive tool support.

M. Dastani, J. Dix, A. El Fallah-Seghrouchni (Eds.): PROMAS 2003, LNAI 3067, pp. 187–200, 2004.

Consequently in addition to the further work on standardized MAS frameworks it seems promising to enhance the tool support for them. As infrastructure and low-level communication issues are covered by the frameworks, there are three main development tasks that could be supported by a tool. Firstly, the implementation of the agent internals could be supported, but they are strongly interrelated with concrete agent architectures that are not standardized and not part of the majority of frameworks. The second time consuming task is the implementation of ontologies in which the agents communicate. For this task there exist a number of tools to choose from, which are even capable of transforming the designed ontologies into code for MAS frameworks [2].

The task addressed by the tool presented here is the design and implementation of agent conversations, i.e. of the protocol for the exchange of messages on a high semantic level. The role of conversations in MAS is crucial, as they are the origin of their social ability, which is one of their commonly accepted qualities. The importance of conversations is underlined by the significant role they play in most well-known development methods, including Gaia [3], MaSE [4], PASSI [5], or MASSIVE [6].

Outline. The remainder of this paper is organized as follows. First, related work is covered in Section 2. In Section 3 the use of our tool is demonstrated in the form of a conversation programming workflow. Subsequent sections build up on this workflow. Accordingly, in Section 4 we show how the common AUML notation for conversations can be mapped to finite state machines, which is the representation we have chosen for the presented tool. This is followed by a discussion regarding how the representation can be adopted by a tool (Section 5). The generation of the implementation based on the designed finite state machines is described in Section 6, while Section 7 presents the system architecture of the tool itself. Finally, we conclude the paper in Section 8.

2   Related Work

Several related approaches to develop tools supporting the design and implementation of multiagent systems are mentioned in current computer science literature. These approaches can be separated into two groups:

Tools coupled to MAS frameworks are bundled with a framework that they exclusively provide support for. Hence they cannot be used in any other environment. Examples of tools coupled to MAS frameworks include:

ZEUS [7] is a Java based open-source project, developed by British Telecom, consisting of a MAS framework with a runtime environment, runtime visualization tools and visual development tools.

ADK [8] is a commercial product developed by Tryllian. It contains the same components as ZEUS, but additionally includes an extensive security concept and the unique feature of true code mobility.

Modeling Suites with source code generation provide tool support from the modeling perspective. After an abstract modeling step, these suites provide the possibility to transfer the results to an implementation in one or many target MAS frameworks. Examples of modeling suites with source generation code include:

PASSI [5] (a Process for Agent Societies Specification and Implementation) leads through 12 steps, in which 5 models in UML are developed. It is implemented in a Rational Rose plugin, which allows for partial semi-automatic translation into JADE source code.

An extension to JADE called SmartAgents is presented in [9]. It is complemented by a plugin for Microsoft Visio, which allows for semi-automatic source code generation for SmartAgents, based on a UML state chart diagram. The Visio stencils are extended to represent so-called Hierarchical State Machines (HSMs), which mainly add nesting capabilities to UML state chart diagrams.

3   Conversation Programming Workflow

The use of the presented tool follows the conversation programming workflow shown in Fig. 1.

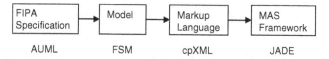

Fig. 1. Conversation programming workflow

It starts with specification of the conversation policy in Agent UML [10]. Next this specification is transferred into a model, based on a finite state machine (FSM). It is necessary to introduce a language which provides the textual representation necessary for a well-defined, serializable, in-memory representation of the model in addition to structured data exchange. cpXML [11], described more thoroughly later, was chosen for this purpose. To ensure extendibility, robustness and interoperability of the model implementation, a model framework is employed. To enable multiple MAS frameworks, a separate code generator module creates a template of the conversation building block for the respective MAS framework. In this work we chose JADE [12] for a first implementation.

4   Translating a Conversation Policy in AUML into a FSM

Agent UML facilitates the visual development of multiagent systems, with an emphasis on agent conversations. It was first specified in [13], which is deprecated due to its age, as well as [14] and is now in the process of further development among others [15]. The latter is concerned mainly with interaction diagrams for conversation modeling, which arguably forms the most interesting part, despite other aspects additionally covered. Interaction diagrams mainly extend the Object Modeling Group's (OMG) definition of UML sequence diagrams with the ability to express explicitly, without relying on condition statements, concurrency in the sending of messages. It can express that from n possible messages n are concurrently sent (thick line), 0 to n concurrently (diamond) or exactly one out of n (diamond with cross) (see Fig. 2).

The Foundation for Intelligent Physical Agents (FIPA) uses AUML interaction diagrams and an informal semantic description in the specification for conversation policies (CPs), which are called interaction protocols (IPs). Because of the intuitive notation and the fact that the FIPA Standard is well established among MAS Frameworks, we chose AUML, in our design, to model the CPs. Other common approaches to model agent conversation are Colored Petri Nets (CPN) and finite state machines (FSM). While CPNs support modeling and qualitative analysis of complex interactions, as shown in [16], FSMs suffer from their missing support of concurrency and factorization. Nevertheless this representation is used in several approaches, such as e.g. in the MAS framework KAoS [17].

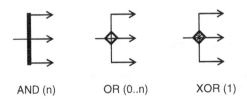

AND (n)   OR (0..n)   XOR (1)

Fig. 2. AUML interaction notation

In the presented approach FSMs were chosen as a model for the tool because of the direct support from the target MAS framework JADE, which provides a so-called FSMBehavior. As it is shown in the next section, this representation also translates directly into the selected textual description language cpXML. In order to use both graphical notations, AUML must be converted into an FSM representation. Below, the algorithm used is first described informally and then semi-formally using the example of the IP *FIPA-ContractNetProtocol*.

Based on the FIPA Specification of the ContractNet Protocol, we process the AUML protocol diagram in the following manner: Each activity bar is divided into one or more sections, which will subsequently be mapped to a state in the finite automaton. The division is done chronologically, from the top to bottom of the diagram. Send message events always form a common section with all receive message events occurring after the last send message event. If there are additional receive message events remaining, they will be divided into single subsections by default. Should they originate from a common XOR (diamond with cross) branch (see Fig. 2), they can also be grouped into a common section. The message flows, which are depicted as arrows in the AUML protocol diagram, become transitions in the finite automaton. In Fig. 3, the resulting states are placed next to the corresponding activity bar sections. The segregation of the sections is represented by parenthesis.

After connecting the states with transitions, in a manner analogous to the message flows in the AUML diagram, the FSM in Fig. 4 results.

In the specification of the *FIPA-ContractNetProtocol* in addition to the AUML diagram other requirements are described in the text: The sending of not-understood messages and the so called *FIPA-Cancel-Metaprotocol*:

Every received message is responded to by a not-understood, if the comprehension of the message failed. In this case, the protocol is cancelled for the corresponding participant. In an FSM, this is realized by adding a transition to the abort state ABORT to every state except the initial state. The automaton after performing this step is shown in Fig. 5.

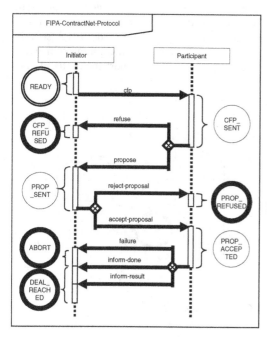

Fig. 3. Mapping of states

Fig. 4. Finite automaton for FIPA-CNP (1)

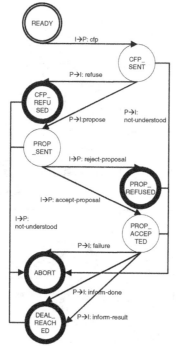

Fig. 5. Finite automaton for FIPA-CNP (2)

In the final step, the FIPA-Cancel-Metaprotocol can be integrated in the finite automaton. In Fig. 6, the state label * means that the state is mapped to all states of the subordinate automaton. This corresponds to the requirement of the FIPA specification, that the Cancel-Metaprotocol must be executed from the initiator in every state. Exceptions are the final states, since it is not possible to abort the protocol after it has already been terminated.

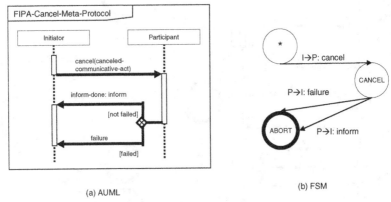

(a) AUML   (b) FSM

Fig. 6. FIPA-Cancel-Metaprotocol

The Cancel-Metaprotocol can now be integrated in the finite automaton, as can be seen in Fig. 7. As described above, there are transitions into the CANCEL state from every state the initiator sends in.

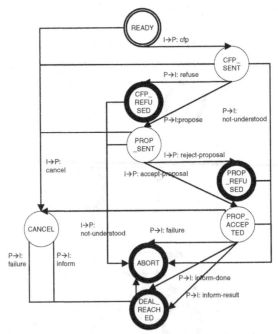

Fig. 7. Finite automaton for FIPA-CNP (3)

The pseudocode in Fig. 8 shows the algorithm informally, described above in a semi-formal description, which can be directly implemented.

```
// FIPA-ContractNet-Protocol
For all roles:
  For all activity bars:
    // Group the message arrows in:
    For all arrows:
      If current arrow send-arrow or exists send-arrow
      further down
        Create group with all receive-arrows up to
        and including the next send-arrow
      Else // receive-arrow
        If it does not originate from same XOR
          Create new group
        Else
          Create new group or build common group
          with next receive-arrow (design decision)
For all groups:
  Create a state and name it arbitrary, but uniquely
For all arrows:
  If branch:
    For each branched arrow:
      Create a transition between the states
      corresponding to start and end role of the arrow
      Name the transition with
      "start role -> end role: label of the arrow"
  Else:
    Create a transition between the corresponding
    states of the start- and end role
For all states:
  If there are no outgoing transitions mark as
  final state
  If there are no incoming transitions mark as
  initial state
// Not-understood
Create a state and call it "ABORT"
For all states:
  If state neither initial nor final state:
    For all incoming transitions:
      Remember different (start role, end role) pairs
      For all pairs:
        Create transition from current state
        to "ABORT" state
        Label it
        "start role -> end role: not-understood"
// FIPA-Cancel-Metaprotocol
Create a state and call it "CANCEL"
For all states:
  If neither initial nor "ABORT" state nor "CANCEL"
  state:
    Create a transition from this State
    to "CANCEL" state.
Create a transition from "CANCEL" state
to "ABORT" state and name it
"Participant -> Initiator: failure"
Create a transition from "CANCEL" state
to "ABORT" state and name it
"Participant -> Initiator: inform"
```

Fig. 8. Semi-formal algorithm description

5   Describing the FSM in cpXML

As previously mentioned, in order to adopt the FSM model in the tool, it is necessary
to introduce a language which provides a textual representation. This makes it possible to derive a well-defined, serializable, in-memory representation of the model.
Therefore several description languages with conversation support, like e.g. DAML-S
[18], BPEL4WS [19], and cpXML [11] were evaluated. cpXML was chosen because
it does not restrict the type of messages and allows multilateral conversations.

Conversation XML (cpXML) was introduced, by IBM's Conversation Support for
Webservices Team, in the fall of 2002. The reference implementation aims to extend
Java Connection Architecture (JCA) with conversation support that follows a specified policy. JCA provides J2EE applications with access to enterprise information
systems (EIS) over a resource adapter (RA), which abstracts from the EIS proprietary
interface. Therefore it introduces three components in the J2EE application server.
The conversation support implementation provides a conversation manager to communicate with the conversation adapter (CA), analogous to the EIS RA. Each CA can
restrict the ongoing conversations dynamically by loading conversation policies in
cpXML. These can be held with other conversational resources. The latter do not
necessarily have to be other CAs, but may also be other types of conversational resources, such as MAS. This versatility makes the whole approach very interesting in
the current debate regarding how to connect Webservices and their compositions with
MAS.

Conversation Policy XML (see Fig. 9) is defined in an XML schema which starts
with naming and defining the roles by which the participating parties can be identified. The XML Schema's main content is the list of states, which themselves contain
the transitions originating from them. One of the states is marked as the initial state.
In addition to containing transitions for sending messages, a state can also contain
transitions, as occurs with a timeout and nesting of other conversation policies. This
can be achieved by a `LoadChild` element, containing the name of the nested CP and
a mapping of the roles to the roles of the nested protocol. In this case, `ChildReturn-
Transition` elements must specify based on the return values of the subprotocols
where to branch to.

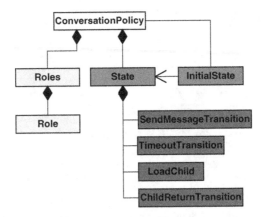

Fig. 9. cpXML class diagram

In this work, cpXML is used as an in-memory model of the conversation description, as described in detail in Section 7. cpXML could also be used to serialize the CP in a standardized way, but currently the tool only supports XMI serialization. The translation from the graphical representation into an FSM is done in the following way: A cpXML representation of the FSM from the previous step can be derived by a list of roles, a state entry for each state, and the appropriate initial state. For each FSM transition, a `SendMessageTransition` element is added to the state from which it originates. Fig. 10 illustrates the graphical user interface of the tool. It shows a conversation following the ContractNet protocol as a finite state machine and as an abstraction of its corresponding cpXML representation.

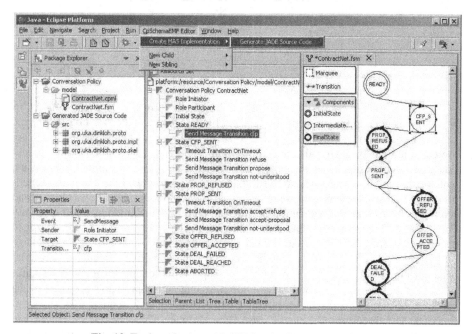

Fig. 10. Tool screenshot with FSM and cpXML representation

6   Generating JADE Behaviors as See-Next-Action Cycles

This section covers how cpXML conversation descriptions can be converted into a behavior for the MAS framework JADE [12]. The JADE building block generator is encapsulated in a separate system component, which could be easily exchanged for other target MAS frameworks. How a JADE conversation behavior is built up internally is covered first as a foundation for the later description of how this internal structure is generated from the cpXML model.

In Section 4 an algorithm with which AUML diagrams can be translated into the cpXML model, was introduced. The output of the algorithm was a finite automaton, which is now to be converted into a building block for the MAS framework JADE. The resulting FSM therefore is mapped onto the well-known abstract agent architecture [20], consisting of three functions and one database (see Fig. 11). In the see function, sensor input to the agent is converted into an internal representation. From this, and the previous state, the `next` function determines the new state of the agent. This corresponds to its beliefs and intentions. Accordingly, the action-function executes an action dependent on the contents of the database. This architecture is intentionally abstract and does not consider any specific type of agent. For software agents considered in this work the main sensor input is the reception of messages, and the set of actions is limited to the sending of messages.

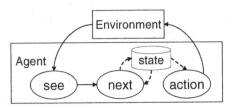

Fig. 11. Abstract agent architecture [20]

The MAS framework JADE, used as the target platform here, has the concept of behaviors as concurrently executed threads, which exchange data over objects of type `DataStore`. Although JADE is written in Java, it introduces behaviors and does not use conventional Java Threads, because of their complicated inter-thread communication and coordination. The package `jade.core.behaviours` contains behaviors, which can be used as templates to write other behaviors, control the execution scheduling (once, cyclic, sequential, parallel or as a FSM), communication (receive and send) or synchronization (execution in time intervals and execution at a certain time). For the FSM behavior any behavior complying to the most basic behavior template can be registered as a state. Additionally, there are four behaviors in the package `jade.proto.states`, which contain prepared functionalities (execute a particular behavior put in the `DataStore`, receive a message, reply to a message and reset states in an `FSMBehavior`). Finally there are complex interaction protocols prepared in the package `jade.proto` for the protocols ContractNet, Query, Request and Subscription. The last three protocols make use of the template `AchieveRE` (RE = Rational Effect) behavior, which encapsulates the initiator, sending a speech act followed by the answer of the participant.

In the abstract agent architecture the `see` function is responsible for the reception of messages. JADE uses the prepared behavior `MsgReceiver` for this purpose. When sending messages, the message to be send is an answer in all states, excluding the initial state. Thus, the behavior `ReplySender` of JADE is used for this purpose. In the initial state, the `SimpleBehaviour` template is used instead.

The business logic that processes the received input is encapsulated in methods of the states, in which they are needed. Thereby a clear distinction into functionalities is provided and a systematic development of the business logic is made possible. Additionally, the methods can be understood more easily in the maintenance phase of the software lifecycle. Since the methods can have identical names for all MAS frameworks, no further knowledge of the originalities of the respective framework are required. Thereby an additional level of abstraction is provided.

The building block generator creates a behavior for each role of the interaction protocol as a subclass of the `FSMBehaviour`. The classes for all different states are implemented directly into these classes, in the case of the ContractNet protocol, for example, these would be `StateREADY`, `StateCFP_SENT` etc.. When calling the constructor of the respective class, the finite automaton is created at the time of instantiation by adding states and transitions to it. One of the states needs to be marked as the initial state. Before it can be deployed, the developer has to fill the behavior with its business logic. In order to do so, he creates subclasses of the generated classes and overwrites the methods provided for this purpose. Which methods he has to overwrite depends on the classification of the state according to one of the following five categories:

1. initial sending:
   `prepareInitialMsg(), chooseKey(), chooseTransition()`
2. initial receiving:
   `chooseKey(), chooseTransition()`
3. intermediate sending:
   `prepareMsg(), chooseKey(), chooseTransition()`
4. intermediate receiveing:
   `chooseKey(), chooseTransition()`
5. final:
   `lastAction()`

The method `chooseKey()` selects the key which is used to store the receive message in the `DataStore`. `chooseTransition()` selects the transition, which should fire after the corresponding state execution has terminated. `prepareInitialMsg()` prepares the message(s) to be sent in the initial state as `prepareMsg()` does this for the intermediate states. `lastAction()` executes a final action before the whole protocol is terminated.

7   The Tool as an Eclipse-Plugin

Crucial for the acceptance of a programming tool is the embedding in the Integrated Development Environment (IDE). Therefore we decided to choose a framework for embedding our tool, which provided as much flexibility as possible. Since Java is the language most MAS frameworks are implemented in, several IDEs were evaluated.

The chosen development platform Eclipse [21] was developed by OTI, which was later purchased by IBM. IBM then contributed it to the Open Source Consortium Eclipse.org, of which many companies including SAP, Borland, OMG, Oracle and Rational Software are part of. Eclipse is a platform, which contains a very powerful Java IDE and itself is written in Java. As opposed to the direct competitor Netbeans from Sun, Eclipse is based on the graphical toolkits SWT and JFace, as opposed to AWT and Swing. It can be modularly extended by so-called plugins, which can provide functionality to other plugins via extension points.

The Eclipse platform provides a solid base with the Eclipse Modeling Framework (EMF) and Graphical Editing Framework (GEF). As described above, the IDE itself is communicated with via the interface from the Java Development Tooling (JDT) eclipse plugin.

The Eclipse Modeling Framework (EMF) allows building of an in-memory representation of a model. The framework itself contains classes which provide serialization, change notifications, and integration with the MVC model used in SWT/JFace. Additionally, a source code generator is provided to extract the model from an XMI file, a Rational Rose class diagram, annotated Java source code or an XML Schema. The latter was used to create an in-memory representation of the cpXML model as well as a simple tree-based editor. To allow for editing of the conversation policy in its FSM representation, a graphical editor based on the Graphical Editing Framework (GEF) was added. Fig. 12 depicts the components of the system architecture.

In order to provide a tight integration with the development environment, the source code is created directly in the Java model of the so-called Java Development Tooling (JDT) of Eclipse, which provides the Java IDE on the Eclipse platform. Several templates were defined, which contain place holders and markers in order to be able to customize them. These are replaced, respectively extended, with items directly taken from or derived from the conversation model.

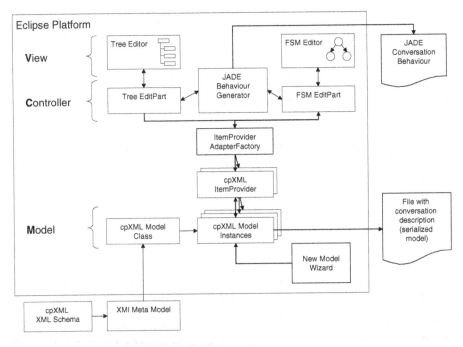

Fig. 12. System architecture

8   Conclusion

MAS promise to be able to cope with complex application domains, but unfortunately tend to be complex systems themselves. The gap between analysis and design of MAS and their implementation leads to an increased development effort. The presented work tries to bridge this gap by integrating the design of MAS conversations and their implementation in a graphical tool.

We illustrated how conversations modelled in AUML can be mapped to finite state machines, the model building the basis for our tool. This model was adopted, in the tool, using cpXML as the language for the in-memory representation of the conversations. We discussed how an implementation for the target MAS framework JADE can be derived from cpXML descriptions of the designed conversations. Finally, we presented the system architecture of the tool as an Eclipse plugin.

By using this intuitive visual tool as a plugin for a professional development environment, the programming of MAS conversations is significantly simplified.

In the future, we plan to integrate direct AUML support into our tool, in order to allow the developer to choose between FSMs and AUML for graphical representations. Another extension we are currently working on is a plugin for ontology modelling. The combination of both plugins would facilitate parameterization of conversations with patterns for the message contents, thus supporting the developer in two important programming tasks.

Acknowledgements

The work done for this paper was partially funded by DFG – Deutsche Forschungsgemeinschaft (German Research Foundation) contract no. Lo 296/17-2 within the National Research Initiative 1083.

References

1. Foundation for Intelligent Physical Agents (FIPA). Repository of FIPA Specifications. http://www.fipa.org/repository/ (2003)
2. van Aart, C.J., Pels, R.F., Giovanni C., Bergenti F.: Creating and Using Ontologies in Agent Communication. In Proceedings of the Workshop on Ontologies in Agent Systems. Bologna (2002)
3. Wooldridge, M., Jennings, N.R., Kinny, D.: The Gaia Methodology for Agent-oriented Analysis and Design. In: Proceedings of the First International Conference on Autonomous Agents and Multi-Agent Systems (2000) 285–312
4. Wood, M., DeLoach, S.A.: An Overview of the Multiagent System Enginnereing Methodology. In: Ciancarini, P., Wooldridge, M. (eds.): Proceedings of the First Int. Workshop on Agent-Oriented Software Engineering. Lecture Notes in Computer Science, Vol. 1957. Springer-Verlag, Berlin (2000)
5. Cossentino, M., Potts, C.: A CASE tool supported methodology for the design of multi-agent systems. In: Proceedings of the 2002 International Conference on Software Engineering Research and Practice (SERP'02). Las Vegas (2002)
6. Lind, J.: Iterative software engineering for multiagent systems: the MASSIVE method. Lecture Notes in Computer Science and Lecture Notes in Artificial Intelligence, Vol. 1994. Springer-Verlag, Berlin (2001)
7. Nwana, H., Ndumu, D., Lee, L., Collis, J.: ZEUS: A Tool-Kit for Building Distributed Multi-Agent Systems. In: Applied Artifical Intelligence Journal, Vol. 13 (1), (1999)
8. Tryllian b.v.: ADK Homepage. http://www.tryllian.com/technology/product.html (2003)
9. Griss, M.L., Fonseca, S., Cowan, D., Kessler, R.: Using UML State Machine Models for More Precise and Flexible JADE Agent Behaviors. In: Proceedings of the Third Int. Workshop on Agent-Oriented Software Engineering. Lecture Notes in Computer Science and Lecture Notes in Artificial Intelligence, Vol. 2585. Springer-Verlag, Berlin (2002)
10. Foundation for Intelligent Physical Agents (FIPA): FIPA Contract Net Interaction Protocol Specification, SC00029H. http://www.fipa.org/specs/fipa00029/ (2002)

11. Hanson, J., Nandi, P., Levine D.W.: Conversation-enabled Web Services for Agents and e-Business. In: Proceedings of the International Conference on Internet Computing (IC-02), CSREA Press (2002)
12. Bellifemine, F., Poggi, A., Rimassa G.: JADE: a FIPA2000 compliant agent development environment. In: Proceedings of the Fifth International Conference on Autonomous Agents, ACM Press (2001)
13. Odell, J., Van Dyke Parunak, H., Bauer, B.: Representing Agent Interaction Protocols in UML. In: Proceedings of the First Int. Workshop on Agent-oriented Software Engineering (AOSE 2000). Springer-Verlag, Berlin (2001) 121-140
14. Foundation for Intelligent Physical Agents (FIPA): FIPA Interaction Protocol Library Specification, XC00025F. http://www.fipa.org/specs/fipa00025/ (2003)
15. Foundation for Intelligent Physical Agents Technical Committee Modeling: FIPA Modeling: Interaction Diagrams, Working Draft. (2003)
16. Mazouzi, H., Seghrouchni A. E., Haddad S.: Open protocol design for complex interactions in multi-agent systems. In: Proceedings of the First International Joint Conference on Autonomous Agents and Multiagent Systems, ACM Press (2002)
17. Bradshaw, J.M.: KAoS: An Open Agent Architecture Supporting Reuse, Interoperability, and Extensibility. In: Proceedings of the Tenth Knowledge Acquisition for Knowledge-Based Systems Workshop, Alberta (1996)
18. Ankolekar, A., Burstein, M., Hobbs, J., Lassila, O., Martin, D., McDermott, D., McIlraith, S.A., Narayanan, S., Paolucci, M., Payne, T., Sycara, K.: DAML-S: Web Service Description for the Semantic Web. In: Proceedings of the First International Semantic Web Conference. Lecture Notes in Computer Science, Vol. 2342. Springer-Verlag, Berlin (2002)
19. Curbera, F., Goland, Y., Klein, J., Leymann, F., Roller, D., Thatte, S., Weerawarana, S.: Business Process Execution Language for Web Services, Version 1.0. Edition 2002-07-31 (2002)
20. Wooldridge, M.: Intelligent Agents. In: Weiss, G. (ed.): Multiagent Systems - A Modern Approach to Distributed Artificial Intelligence. MIT Press (1999)
21. Eclipse.org Consortium: Eclipse Homepage. http://www.eclipse.org (2003)

SPACE: A Method to Increase Tracability in MAS Development

Bruno Mermet, Gaäle Simon, Dominique Fournier, and Marianne Flouret

Laboratoire d'Informatique du Havre, Le Havre, France
Bruno.Mermet@univ-lehavre.fr

Abstract. This paper deals with a method and a model called SPACE allowing to design multiagent systems. Their main interest is to introduce tools to design and to validate the produced system at the same time. First, the main steps of the proposed method are described. Then, the different components of the SPACE model are defined. Finally, two case studies (on a BDI model and on a graph colouring problem) show how the method and the model can be applied.

Keywords: MAS development method, agent model, graph colouring

1 Introduction

For the last decade, in order to answer to the growing interest for multi-agent systems (MAS) development, several methods, models and tools have been proposed [17, 22, 14]. Among them, there are some methods [26, 12], agents models [20, 8], MAS models [16] and MAS development environments like Madkit, Jade, Zeus... [15, 21, 19]. Our research focuses on the design of a MAS development method coupled with a model allowing, at the same time, validation, verification or even system proof. Generally, already proposed methods do not provide enough necessary elements to do this task. Moreover, we want the method to be a real guide for the developer to help him to analyse and to break up the global goal of the MAS so as to obtain the structure of the MAS, the different agents, their goal and their behaviour. Most of existing methods propose only a set of models which can be used to express different aspects of the MAS but do not really propose guidelines to apply these models to the problem which must be solved by the system. Finally, we wish the method to be coupled with models in order to be able to directly implement specifications obtained by the method. Unfortunately, models proposed by the existing methods can not often directly be used to implement the system in a MAS development platform.

In [23], we have described a first development of our method dedicated to optimisation problems. This method is summarised in the paper. Starting from an informal problem specification, we show how to obtain the specification of a set of agents allowing to solve this problem. For this process, we introduce specification tools such as variants which will be used, in the future, to help to verify properties of the developed system. Moreover, this method allows to associate a goal to each agent whose behaviour is described by an automaton.

M. Dastani, J. Dix, A. El Fallah-Seghrouchni (Eds.): PROMAS 2003, LNAI 3067, pp. 201–220, 2004.
© Springer-Verlag Berlin Heidelberg 2004

As for other methods, using this method allows to produce an operational-isable specification of each agent of a system. In existing methods, this speci-fication can be expressed in different formalisms like A-UML, Gaïa... In every cases, it must be transformed into an operational specification which can then be executed. We propose a model which can be used to make this task easier. This model, called SPACE (Structure, Perception, Action, Comportment and Envi-ronment) can be seen as an interface between agents model, like BDI, Aalaadin, Vowel [20, 8, 3]... used to characterise agents behaviour, and their corresponding implementation in a MAS development environment (figure 1). For example, the BDI model can be expressed using SPACE model [13]. Once the SPACE specification of the agents has been obtained, their implementation becomes an automatic task. Indeed, with the SPACE model, we provide a direct translation into several MAS development environments like MadKit. So, the SPACE model has been designed to be used both to specify agents produced by our method and to implement agents produced by other methods and expressed in higher-level models.

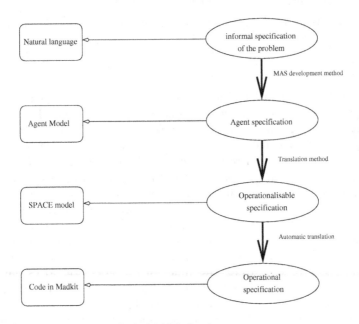

Fig. 1. Global MAS development process

Using SPACE model allows the developer to avoid the coding step into the MAS development environment language he wants to use. Moreover, a SPACE specification of an agent gives the most declarative operational view as possible of this agent. This property gives the basis to potentially future validations of the agent implementation by reasoning on its specification in SPACE. Last but not least, this model must allow to control the consistency of the agent specification.

Indeed, we propose a MAS validation process in four steps:

1. Inner consistency verification of each agent model:
   the SPACE model described in this paper, must provide tools to do this verification. For example, it must be checked that all variables used by the agent perceptions are defined in the agent model.
2. Inner consistency verification of the MAS model:
   this verification must not only take into account all the agents models but also relations between agents and the number of instances of each agent model. Suppose for example that a given agent, instance of A model, can make its job only if n agents, instances of a second B model, are created. Our model must allow, in this case, to verify that the MAS can always create these n instances of B model.
3. Agents behaviour validation:
   the problem, here, is to be able to answer to the following question: "does the agent really act as the developer wanted to?". In other words, does the effective behaviour of the agent fit to the specified behaviour?
4. System behaviour validation:
   for this validation, the question to which an answer must be given is the same as the previous one but at a different scale: the entire MAS. As a consequence, this validation allows to verify that the global behaviour of the system fits to the system behaviour the developer wanted to obtain.

The inner consistency verification is an aspect that as already been taken into account in the model and that is presented in the paper. Our research is currently focused on agent behaviour validation. It is one of the reasons of the creation of the SPACE model. Indeed, we need a model that has enough formal materials for validation. We are now working on the validation process itself, that is to say, specifying how to combine specific properties we have put in SPACE in order to perform the validation.

The first part of the paper is dedicated to the description of the method we propose. Then the SPACE model is presented. After these two first parts, two kinds of applications are presented. The first one shows how BDI specifications can be expressed with SPACE. The second one shows how the method and the model have been used to build a multi-agent system for the graph colouring problem whose main principles and constraints are briefly presented.

2   Method

The goal of our research is to provide a method and also tools to help the analysis and design of MAS.

As presented in the sequel, the method is based on a top-down approach which warrants the progress of our system towards a *satisfying* solution.

2.1   Usage Conditions

The method defined here must be used to solve global problems which can be specified by a set of local constraints (LC). A more restrictive usage condition is that this method is dedicated to problems for which a trivial (but probably bad) solution exists.

Of course, for non NP-hard and non distributed problems for which a sequential algorithm is known, using agents (and so our method) is rarely a good solution because communications and synchronisations introduced by MAS make the program less efficient [25].

An example of a target problem for our method is the graph colouring problem which consists in colouring a graph with a minimal number of colours in such a way that two connected nodes do not have the same colour. This application is presented in section 4.

2.2   The Method

Global variant. The first thing to do is to define a variant characterising the problem that the system must solve. A variant is a notion often used to prove termination of algorithms. A variant is a variable defined on a totally ordered structure that must decrease at each iteration and that has a lower bound. These two properties imply the termination of the iterations.

Local decomposition. The second step is perhaps the hardest one: the global problem has to be expressed in terms of local sub-problems. This consists in dividing the solution of the problem into several parts with respect to LC. These parts are not necessarily disjunctive. Each part is associated to a local sub-problem. The resolution of each of these sub-problems must help to solve the global problem. The ideal case is a sub-problem whose resolution is a necessary condition for solving the global problem. However, this is not always the case. An other possibility is a sub-problem whose resolution makes the global variant decrease.

Agentification. Once the global problem has been decomposed, we still do not have agents. Of course, a first idea could be to assign each local problem to an agent, but this is not always possible. Indeed, to agentify a problem:

- each sub-problem must be assigned to an agent;
- each property of the problem (piece of data) must be assigned to an agent.

However, each agent perceives only a local part of the environment. Moreover, an agent being autonomous, no other agent can modify directly its properties. These two constraints are called *the locality principle*. So, if the resolution of two sub-problems needs to modify the same property, assigning two problems to two different agents is impossible. A first solution could be to assign properties to the environment instead of agents. This is an easy solution, but this makes the environment a central resource for the MAS, limiting the benefit of the distribution.

A better solution is to change the structure of the local problems so that the modification of a property occurs only in the resolution of one sub-problem. So, each property modification is controlled by one and only one agent. Other agents that need to get the value of this property must have the agent owning the property in their accointance set and can know its value by message passing. Subproblems resulting from this restructuring are called Property Oriented Sub-Problems (POSP) in the sequel.

This step is necessary (it provides the agents and the accointance relations of the MAS) and not so difficult to realize as it is shown in this article for the graph-colouring problem.

Agents Behaviour

General behaviour. Each POSP is assigned to an agent. So, the general behaviour of each agent is very simple:

- if its problem is solved, it does nothing (it could also help other agents). The agent is *satisfied*;
- otherwise, it tries to find a solution to its problem.

For the global problem, we introduced a variant. We have to do the same for each POSP in such a way that each time a local variant decrease, the global variant does not increase. These variants allow to control the progress of each POSP solving.

Each POSP can be divided into sub-goals whose resolution makes the local variant decrease. Then, an unsatisfied agent chooses a sub-goal and tries to solve it.

When a sub-goal has to be solved, there are two cases:

- either it can be solved by the agent: the agent can then choose a new goal;
- or the agent cannot solve it.

There are two reasons making a subgoal unable to be solved:

- either there is a blocking situation: an other agent prevents the active agent to apply one of its strategies;
- or the agent doesn't know what to do to solve the subgoal in the given situation.

In the second case, the agent chooses an other goal or waits for a modification of the situation. In the first case, the agent attacks an obstructing agent. This behaviour follows the eco-agent's one [7]. The attack mechanism is simulated by sending an aggression message. An agent under attack has to flee so that the blocking situation disappears, but preserving the local constraints LC. Note that the fleeing behaviour can increase the local variant. If the agent cannot flee, it ignores the attack.

In order to help us specifying agents behaviours, we used the formalism of transducers [1]. This formalism can also be used to specify behaviours of other kinds of agents [18]. Thus, we define the general behaviour of an eco-agent by a transducer as detailed in [23].

The method described in this part helps MAS developers to determine and specify the set of agents (and also their goals and behaviour) which are necessary to solve the initial problem. The next part describes a model allowing to design these agents from an implementation point of view.

3   The SPACE Model

In this part, we present the different elements of the SPACE agent model. As explained before, this model is designed in order to be a good compromise between a purely executable agent specification about which it is not possible to reason and a more formal specification not really implementable. We try to obtain an almost runnable agent specification while keeping the most declarative description as possible. As a consequence, the resulting specification can be considered as an operational one: we provide not only models but an operational semantics describing the effective operation of the agent from these models.

In SPACE, an agent is represented by three complementary models and a structure: the perceptions model, the actions model, the behaviour model and the inner structure.

These different elements are described in the following paragraphs. They are of course not independent from each other. That's why they must satisfy a set of consistency rules which are also described in further section (3.6).

3.1   Perceptions Model

This model describes the set of perceptions of the agent, that is to say, whatever is likely to modify the actions the agent may do. There are four different perceptions which can be divided into two kinds:

- Message perceptions: they occur when a message is received from another agent. There are two kinds of messages associated to such perceptions:
  - information messages: an Information Message Perception (IMP) is associated to each kind of information messages,
  - request messages: a Request Message Perception (RMP) is associated to each kind of request message,
- Variables Perceptions: they represent the agent view of some variables. They are also divided into two kinds of perceptions:
  - Environment Variables Perceptions (EVP),
  - Inner Variables Perceptions (IVP).

Variables perceptions (EVP/IVP). These perceptions are connected to inner and environment variables. The environment in which the agent is living is considered as a set of variables. The environment evolution implies changes on the values of the variables. A priori, an agent has only a partial and biased view of the environment. The prey-predator model is a good example of the difference between the environment and its perception by an agent. A predator only knows a part of the grid on which it moves. This vision is also biased because it depends on the agent interpretation. By this way, it is easy to take into account the point of view of the agent in its behaviour. Thus, some elements of the environment may be considered differently according to the goal of the agent. For example, let us consider weather variables like wind, hygrometry and temperature. Using these variables, an agent can have a perception about the current weather. In an airport, assuming the wind blows slowly, an agent in charge of planes take off can discern propitious conditions. Even though, simultaneously, another agent dedicated to control of a wind farm would estimate the weather conditions are bad.

An Environment Variable Perception associates a particular value to a subset of values of significant environment variables for the agent. It allows to design the agent point of view on the environment. Considering again the three weather variables, the perception "weather" could have four values: nice, very nice, bad and very bad. Thus, when the wind speed is lower than 15 MPH, the hygrometry fewer than 100% and the temperature between 20°c and 25°c, the weather perception shall be nice.

Inner variables perceptions rely on the same principles, but they are not based on the same kind of variables. As it will be presented later, an action performed by an agent rely on perceptions. As a consequence, we decided to introduce inner variables perceptions in order to allow the agent to perform actions according to its own life cycle (its state, its goals, ...), and not only in reaction to environment variations. Inner variables perceptions are very important ones because they allow to define proactive behaviours. To define such perceptions, it is assumed that an agent maintains some variables during its life. Generally, these variables are connected to the problems and goals it has to achieve. They are designed to manage some aspects of the agent behaviour. If we consider again the agent in charge of the wind farm, it shall have at least two variables indicating the number of wind turbines and the number of running ones. Each inner variables perception allows the definition of significant subsets of variables values which could modify its behaviour. The agent in charge of the wind power plant shall have a perception "free turbines" with the value corresponding to the difference between the total number of turbines and the number of running ones.

Formally, the table 1 describes the 5-tuple (N, C, V, T, F) defining variables perceptions.

Table 1. EVP and IVP

Name	Type	Role
N	String	Name of the perception
C	{EVP, IVP}	Kind of the perception
V	{variables}	Set of significant variables
T	{values}	Set of potential values
F	Function	Function from V to T describing the value of the perception according to the value of the concerned variables.

Information Messages Perceptions (IMP). These perceptions are based on the information messages. These messages contain information sent to the agent (the receiver). An information message is considered as a set of variables. Receiving these variables may modify a subset of receiver's inner variables. Yet, every values are not necessarily useful to the receiver. An IMP allows to define which elements of the message are relevant for the receiver. The information message also provides the way to read and use the information it contains.

These perceptions are defined by a 6-tuple (N, C, S, V, T, F) given in the table 2.

Table 2. IMP

Name	Type	Role
N	String	Name of the perception
C	IMP	Kind of the perception
S	Class	Message structure (name and type of each variable)
V	{inner variables}	List of inner variables the perception may modify
T	{true, false}	true if the message of class S is in the mailbox; false otherwise
F	Function	Casting function from S to V describing how to modify inner variables according to the value of the message.

Request Messages Perceptions (RMP). These perceptions rely on request messages. These messages allow the sender to ask for information/action to the receiver. As for information messages, these information may be represented by values of variables. So, if the receiver decides to take the request into account, the request message must be saved in the inner structure of the agent in order to be processed later.

RMP are defined by a 6-tuple (N, C, S, F, T, A) detailed in the table 3.

Table 3. RMP

Name	Type	Role
N	String	Name of the perception
C	RMP	Kind of the perception
S	Class	Structure of the request message
F	Function	Function defined on S and inner variables with values in {true, false} specifying if the request must be taken into account or must be ignored
T	{true, false}	true if the message of class S is in the mailbox; false otherwise
A	Action	Action responding to the request (by a message sending or not). The associated event (§ 3.2) must determine when the agent is able to answer.

This is worth noting that the sender may be (and will often be) a field of the message. This allows the receiver to determine, for instance, which agent it must send the answer to, or what sort of relationships it has with the sender.

3.2   The Actions Model

The action model allows to describe the entire set of actions the agent is able to do. It also allows to describe each action, to describe conditions in which it can be performed (precondition), and also to describe properties (on inner or environment variables) always having to be checked after its execution (postcondition). Actions may consist in reactive behaviours (for instance, in response to a Request Message) or in proactive ones (i.e. depending on inner variables related to the current goal of the agent). We can notice that sending messages is considered as specific actions. The associated precondition describes, in this case, the time when the agent can send the message.

An action is then defined by a 3-tuple (Pre,M,Post) described in table 4.

Table 4. Actions

Name	Type	Role
PRE	Event	Precondition. Precondition are specified by events (see below)
M	Method	Describes what the action does.
POST	{properties}	Postcondition expressed as a set of properties. A property is a constraint over one or more inner environment variables.

Definition: An *event* is a (named) function defined on values of one or more perceptions or events, with result in B = {True, False}. This notion allows to specify a significant special context for the agent behaviour, i.e. in which it can implement specific actions.

For example, if an agent wants to play tennis, several conditions have to be checked. To express them, an event "tennis condition" will be defined. This event takes into account values of perceptions as "weather" (see § 3.1) and "free partner". Thus, this event will be "true" if the "weather" perception value is "nice" or "very nice", and if the "free partner" perception value is "true".

In a more proactive context like the pray-predator problem, a predator shall hunt if and only if it is hungry. As a consequence the hunting action may depend on an event relying on an inner variable perception using a variable evaluating the feeling of hunger of the agent.

3.3   The Behaviour Model

A part of the agent behaviour is formalised by specific automata which are transducers.

A transducer is defined by a 6-tuple t = (Σ, γ, Q, I, F, δ) such that:

− Σ is a finite input alphabet,
− γ is a finite output alphabet,

- Q is a finite set of states,
- I ⊆ Q is the set of initial states,
- F ⊆ Q is the set of final states,
- $\delta \in (Q \times \Sigma \times Q \to \gamma)$ is the application associated to transitions.

To adapt this tool to specify the agent behaviour, we made specific choices concerning the part assigned to each state and the labels associated to the transitions [23]. Within the framework of our model, the agent automaton is in fact the representation of a decomposition of its goals. More precisely, a goal (or sub-goal) is associated to each state. A transition between two states p and q is labelled by a couple (E,A) where E is an event which can occur when the agent decides to leave p. If E occurs, the agent executes the action A and tries to reach the goal q. We give below the state and transition patterns with more details.

A state p is defined by a 7-tuple (N,L,M,Ve,Vs,V, π) such that:

- N is a string labelling the state,
- L={(E,A)} is an ordered list of couples (event,action). Notice that an action A can be performed only if the associated event E is true.
- M is a method, possibly neutral, which sorts actions of L if a specific order is needed,
- Ve is the set of input variables, i.e. variables the agent can read when it tries to reach the goal p,
- Vs is the set of output variables, i.e. the ones it can modify during its stay in state p,
- V is the variant of the goal p,
- π is the choice policy of transitions (ordered list) starting from state p when several events are true at the same time.

Transitions are defined by a 4-tuple (Ed, Ea, E, A). Such a transition shall be fired when the current state is Ed and when event E is true. The action A will then be run and the current state becomes Ea.

3.4   Inner Structure of the Agent

The inner structure of the agent contains a set of variables which represent, in real time, the evaluation the agent can do of its own situation. In fact, it corresponds to its knowledge of itself. In this structure, there is a list of known agents and a memory of received requests. There are also inner variables, especially those which interact with IVP and IMP.

The list of known agents shall be linked with a qualitative judgement about the kind of relationship (friends, enemies,...). This could be taken into account, for example, in the management of RMP decision process. Last but not least, the inner structure includes the behaviour automaton, and a reference to the current state in which the agent is.

3.5   Operational Semantics

The basic behaviour of the agent is described by the automaton. The agent's behaviour in a given state depends whether a method is associated to it or not. If no method is associated to the state then the list L of pairs (event E, action A) is processed sequentially else the list L is processed in the order given by this method. For each pair (E,A), the agent first evaluates the event E. This event relies on perceptions Pi that are also evaluated at this moment. The evaluation of messages perceptions implies the checking of the agent mailbox at this moment too (messages corresponding to the perceptions which are found at this moment are removed from the mailbox). Messages that do not concern the perceptions Pi are preserved but not processed. If this event E is true, the action A triggers (and is not executed if E is evaluated to false). Notice that many actions may depend on the same event. For instance, the list L could look like { (e1, a1), (e2, a2), (e1, a3) }. So, the event e1 will be evaluated twice. It may be true the first time, and be false the second one. We can make another remark: if the action a3 must be performed only if a1 was performed, then the event associated to a3 must not be e1 but a new event e3 associated to an IVP relying on an inner variable set by the action a1 to tell it was executed.

Once all the pairs of the list L associated to the current state have been processed, the agent analyses if the goal associated to the current state is reached (has the variant reached its lower boundary ?):

- if the goal is completed, one of the transitions whose original state is the current one must be fireable (a fireable transition is a transition whose associated event is true). The events associated to all the transitions starting from the current state are evaluated, and therefore the perceptions they are based on. Thus, a list of fireable transitions is built. A transition is chosen among the elements of this list, with respect to the defined policy (a random choice by default). Then, the action of the chosen transition is executed and the incoming state of the agent becomes the final state of this transition.
- If the goal is not completed, the events associated to all the transitions starting from the current state are evaluated as described above.
  - If there is at least one fireable transition, one is chosen as in the former situation, the action is executed and the incoming state is reached.
  - Otherwise, the agent executes again the current state. When the agent reaches its final state, it stops.

3.6   Consistency Rules

In the SPACE model, an agent is represented by 3 models: the perceptions model, the actions model and the behaviour model. These three models are not only complementary, but also interconnected. So, consistency rules have to be defined between these models to determine if an agent is consistent. They are presented in the following. These rules have consequences on the inner structure which are also detailed.

Structure/Perceptions consistency: there is only one simple consistency rule between these two models concerning the definition of the variables: all the variables named in the perceptions (IMP and IVP) must be defined in the inner structure. The existence of this single rule comes from the obvious split of the model.

Perception/Event consistency: events must rely on perceptions defined in the perception model or on other events described previously in the actions model. To determine if an event occurs, values of perceptions or events it relies on must be specified. These values must be in the type of the perception result for a perception or in true, false for an event.

Event/Automaton consistency: all the transitions of the automaton must be labelled by an event defined in the actions model. The precondition of the action to perform must be the event associated to the transition. Moreover, when the goal associated to a state s is reached, at least one of the events associated to the transitions whose initial state is s must be true.

Automaton/Action consistency: the action A of each RMP (taking into account the answer to a request message) must belong to the actions associated to the states or to the transitions.

Actions/Inner Structure consistency: the free structure of the actions makes general consistency rules impossible to define. However, we can notice that each action must preserve the definition domain of every inner variable it may modify.

4   SPACE as an Intermediate Model: Application to BDI Specifications

BDI agents rely on three essential characteristics: their beliefs, their desires and their intentions. Beliefs correspond to how the agents percieve their environment and their inner state. In our model, beliefs of BDI agents can be easily translated into perceptions.

Desires correspond to the set of goals an agent may have. In SPACE, the behaviour of an agent being described by an automaton whose states are associated to goals, the set of desires of BDI agents will correspond to the set of states of the automaton.

Finally, intentions correspond to the current goal and eventually to an intention about next goals or actions. The current goal is represented, in SPACE, by the current state. Intentions about next goals and actions can be modelized by inner variables. The latter must be taken into account by the events associated to transitions.

The typical algorithm describing how a BDI agent works is presented in figure 2.

This algorithm can also be easily translated into SPACE. The option generation corresponds to the calculus of the perceptions associated to the transitions starting from the current state. The choice of the option and the updating of the

```
initial state();
repeat
   options := options - generator(event_queue)
   selected_option := deliberate(options)
   update_intention(selected_option)
   execute();
   get_new_external_events();
   drop_successful_attitudes()
   drop_impossible_attitudes();
end repeat
```

Fig. 2. BDI agent algorithm

intention of the agent correspond to the choice of the transition if several are fireable. The executed statement is similar to the standard behaviour of SPACE agents when they are in a given state. Let us notice that it is not necessary to translate the *get_new_external_events()* function because required events are automatically evaluated before executing actions. As well, the deletion of successful goals is a consequence of the automaton structure. Indeed, solving a goal implies the evaluation of the transitions coming from the state associated to this goal. By this way, the current state, and as a consequence the current goal, of the agent change. Finally, the deletion of impossible attitudes can be taken into account by adding an inner variable indicating when a goal is impossible. Then, transitions ending in the state associated to this goal must evaluate this variable. By this way, main concepts of BDI models can be translated into a SPACE models.

5   Application to Graph Colouring

5.1   The Graph Colouring Problem

We describe in this part the application of the method and the model presented before to a graph colouring problem. The *general problem* is to colour the nodes of a graph with a minimal number of colours without two neighbour nodes having the same colour (*LC*).

The problem of graph colouring being NP-hard, algorithms looking for optimal solutions are numerous [5] but rarely useful for real-size problems. We can refer to [6, 9–11] for various methods trying to solve this problem, and more precisely to [2, 24] for ants algorithms.

The essential characteristic of our solution is that it starts with a correctly coloured graph but not optimal as far as the number of colours is concerned. For instance, a trivial initial solution consists in assigning a different colour for each node. As the time goes, our algorithm tries to suppress colours, keeping a correct coloured graph. So, the more our algorithm will work, the more pertinent the proposed solution will be.

For details about graph definitions and properties, it can be referred to [4] for example. Here are given the main ones used in the sequel. We denote $G = (N, E)$ an oriented (resp. non oriented) *graph* with N and E two sets such that elements of E are ordered (resp. unordered) couples $(u, v) \in N^2$, and $N \cap E = \emptyset$. The elements of N are *nodes*, those of E are the *edges*. Two nodes u, v of G are *neighbours* if $(u, v) \in E$. $V(u)$ will denote the set of all neighbours of u.

Let $C(u)$ the colour associated to a node u, and $C(V(u))$ the set of colours of u neighbours. The k-colouring of a graph $G = (N, E)$ is the attribution, to each node, of a colour among k such that, for each edge (u, v) of E, $C(u) \neq C(v)$.

A graph is k-*colourable* if a k-colouring can be applied[1]. The smallest k such that G is k-colourable is the *chromatic number* of G and denoted $\chi(G)$.

In the following, we will consider a k-coloured graph.

For this application, we have to define two new specific notions concerning nodes. The *local chromatic number* of a node u is $lcn(u) = max\{|C|, \forall C$ clique of G $/u \in C\}$. The *current chromatic number* of u is $ccn(u) = |\{c(u)\} \cup \{c(v)/v \in V(u)\}|$. Then, a node u *satisfies its lcn* if and only if $lcn(u) = ccn(u)$.

The following properties are used to implement our solution.

Theorem 1. *Let $G = (N, E)$ be a graph. For all node $u \in N$, if G is correctly coloured, then $ccn(u) \leq lcn(u)$.*

Theorem 2. *Let $G = (N, E)$ a graph, and let $\chi(G) = n$. For each node $u \in N$, we have $lcn(u) \leq n$.*

Remark 1. Let us notice that, despite these two theorems, even if all the nodes of a graph satisfy their *lcn*, the chromatic number of the graph can not always be reached. There are also some graphs which can not be coloured such that each node satisfies its *lcn*.

5.2   Application of the Method

Global variant. The goal is to make decrease the number of colours of the nodes of a graph which is the chosen global variant. The lower bound of this variant is the chromatic number of the graph.

Local decomposition. The previous property is decomposed into subproblems for each node. Each node tries to change the colours of its neighbours in order to make the local variant decrease. This variant corresponds to the node *ccn* whose lower bound is the node *lcn*.

Agentification. The previous decomposition does not follow the locality principle. Indeed an agent should modify the colour of another agent. So, each *POSP* consists in the colour modification of a node. The new associated local variant is the tuple of the *ccn* of the neighbours of the node. Then, each *POSP* is assigned to an agent called a *node agent*. It can be reached by solving a set of subgoals.

---

[1] For $k \geq 3$, decide whether a graph is k-colourable or not is NP-hard.

A subgoal consists in decreasing the *ccn* of a given neighbour. Notice that as each node agent has at least one neighbour, so its neighbours will make its *ccn* decrease.

Agents behaviour. When the *POSP* assigned to an agent is not satisfied (that is one of its neighbours has a *ccn* greater than its *lcn*), it has to choose a colour:

- existing in the graph;
- making the *ccn* of the neighbour *n* decrease;
- being different from the colours of its neighbours.

As a node agent can only see (and communicate with) its neighbours, to find a colour verifying the two first items enumerated above, it asks to its neighbour u the colours of its neighbours, which gives a first set $C(V(u))$, the colours set of the neighbours of u.

To verify the third point, the active agent a first asks to its neighbours their colours and constructs the set $C(V(a))$ of these colours. Then it chooses a colour among the new set $S = C(V(u)) \backslash \{C(V(a)) \cup C(a)\}$ [2].

If a node agent u can not change its colour, necessarily, the set $C(V(u))$ is a member of the set $C(V(a))$. In such a case, u attacks one of its neighbours whose colour is in the set $C(V(u))$. If it is attacked, it flees, trying to take an other colour. It chooses a colour among the neighbours' ones of its neighbours, which is not a colour in its neighbours' colours.

Two other agents have to be created for coordination and implementation reasons. The topological agent creates the initial graph, node agents with their characteristics (e.g. list of neighbours, initial colours), and a drawer agent giving a graphic view of the graph updated when colours change.

5.3   Application of the Model

In this part, we partially describe the node agents of the graph colouring problem presented above with the SPACE model. In this section, names of inner variables, actions, events and perceptions are respectively suffixed by _ *V*, _ *A*, _ *E* and _ *P*.

The behaviour model. The global behaviour of a node agent corresponds to an eco-agent one [7] which is formalised by a transducer described in [23]. The main goal of an agent is to decrease its own *ccn* as much as necessary. If it is impossible, it can attack an obstructing neighbour agent. An attacked agent can flee by changing its own colour. For instance, we detail the state of the transducer corresponding to an attack. In this state, the agent begins to evaluate if the attack is possible. If it is the case, the agent determines a target agent among its neighbours. Then, it sends an attack message to it. Finally, it analyses its mailbox and updates its goals list. Here is the description of this state in the SPACE model.

---

[2] The new colour must be different from the previous one, that is why $C(a)$ is removed from possible colours.

- N = "attack state";
- L = ((true;setAttackTo1_A); (true;canIAttack_A);
  (attacking_E;determineTarget_A);
  (targetExists_E;attackTarget_A); (true;readMailbox_A);
  (true;setupGoal_A); (true;setAttackTo0_A));
- M = void;
- Ve = {neighboursNumber_V; neighbours_V;
  neighboursColour_V; neighboursNeighbourColour_V};
- Vs = {neighboursAttacked_V; goals_V; attack_V};
- V = attack_V;
- π = {attacked_E > satisfied_E > unsatisfied_E};

Some of the actions or variables used above are described further in the paper.

The inner structure. Hereafter is given a part of the inner structure of a node agent.

- myCCN_V : integer;
- myColour_V : Colour;
- currentState_V : integer;
- neighboursNumber_V: integer;
- neighbours_V: list of Agents;
- neighboursColour_V: array of Colours indexed by neighbours numbers;
- neighboursCCN_V: array of ccn values indexed by neighbours numbers;
- neighboursNeighbourColour_V: set of Colours. This is the set $C(V(a))$ described in 5.2.
- goals_V: list of Goals;
- attack_V: {0; 1};
- neighboursAttacked_V: set of (Agent; Colour).
- fleeSuccess_V: {true, false} (flag indicating whether the last flee attempt succeeded).

The Perceptions Model

Information Messages Perceptions. For a node agent, we define four IMP as described below:

1. **Current Chromatic Number Receipt**
   - N: CCNReceipt_P
   - C: IMP
   - S: CCNMessage class with two attributes sender(*Agent*) and ccn(*int*)
   - V: {neighboursCCN_V[sender]}
   - F: neighboursCCN_V[sender]:=ccn
2. **Colour Change Receipt**
   - N: ColourChangeReceipt_P
   - C: IMP

- S: ColourChangeMessage class with two attributes sender (*Agent*) and colour (*Colour*)
- V: {neighboursColour_V[sender]; myCCN_V}
- F: neighboursColour_V[sender]:=colour;
  myCCN_V := 1 + card(neighboursColour_V);

3. **Neighbours Neighbour Colour Receipt**
    - N: NeighboursNeighbourColourReceipt_P
    - C: IMP
    - S: NNCMessage class with two attributes sender (*Agent)* and colourSet (*Set of Colours*)
    - V: {neighboursNeighbourColour_V}
    - F: neighboursNeighbourColour_V := colourSet

Request Messages Perceptions. For each node agent, we define two RMP called *Attack Receipt* and *Neighbours Colour Request.* We only detail the first one below. An attack is taken into account only if the agent is not currently fleeing or if it has just failed to flee.

- N: **attackReceipt_P**
- C: RMP
- S: fleeRequestMessage class with one attribute sender (*agent*)
- F: (currentState_V != "fleeState" or (currentState_V == "fleeState" and fleeSuccess_V == false));
- A: flee_A (described later).

Inner Variables Perceptions. We only give one of them called *CurrentState_P* that allows the agent to have information about its current state.

- N: **currentState_P**
- C: IVP
- V: {currentState_V}
- T: state
- F: currentState_V $\mapsto$ currentState_V (identity function).

The actions model. First, we need to define the three following events:
stateAttack_E is an event that is true if the current state is the attack state:

$$stateAttack\_E : \{currentState\_P == attack\}.$$

underAttack_E is an event that is true if the agent received a *fleeRequestMessage*:

$$underAttack\_E: \{attackReceipt\_P == true\}$$

neighboursNeighbourColourReceipt_E is an event that is true if the agent received a NNCMessage:

neighboursNeighbourColourReceipt_E:
{neighboursNeighbourColourReceipt_P == true}

Here are now two examples of actions relying on these events:
setAttackTo1_A:

- PRECONDITION: stateAttack_E
- METHOD: attack_V := 1;
- POSTCONDITION: attack_V == 1

Another kind of action is a response to a request message. This is for instance the case of the *flee_A* action. By this action, the agent tries to change its colour. It searches a colour among the set of the colours of the neighbours of its neighbours (*globalnnc*) and that is not a colour of its own neighbours.

flee_A:

- PRECONDITION: underAttack_E;
- METHOD:
  globalncc: *set of colours of all neighbours of neighbours*
  neighboursNumber: *number of remaining awaited answers*
  globalnnc := ∅
  broadcastMessage(NeighboursColourRequestMessage);
  neighboursNumber := card(neighbours_V);
  while (neighboursNumber ≠ 0) {
      neighboursNeighbourColour_V = ∅;
      while(! neighboursNeighbourColorReceipt_E);
      globalnnc = globalnnc ∪
                  neighboursNeighbourColor_V;
  }
  globalnnc = globalnnc -
                  (myColour_V ∪ neighboursColour_V);
  if (globalnnc ≠ ∅) {
      myColour_V = choice(globalnnc);
      fleeSuccess_V = true;
      broadcastMessage(ColorChangeMessage(me, myColour_V));
  }
  else
      {fleeSuccess_V = false;}

- POSTCONDITION: true;

6   Conclusion and Future Work

The method we presented in this paper helps to design a multiagent system to solve a given problem. It gives guidelines to decompose problems for agentification. The goal of the SPACE agent model is to help to specify, and then to implement resulting agents, while keeping some essential properties. Indeed, our aim is to design a model so as to be a good compromise between a purely executable agent specification and a too formal one not really implementable helping both to implement and to validate the agent behaviour. These two goals, nearly conflicting, are not both reached in other models such as Metatem [12] or Gaïa [26] for example, in which many aspects are either too or not enough formal. Specifications of agents in Metatem are hard to write because expressed in temporal logic. Moreover, no proof obligation rule is defined. In Gaïa, essentially built to give a method, many aspects are not formal enough to make a system validation possible. For instance, there is no semantics specifying how many roles taken into account by a unique agent work together. Our requirements about SPACE imply the existence of variants, accurate descriptions of perceptions, actions and events, but also consistency rules allowing to verify the inner consistency of the model when applied to a particular agent specification.

The first outlook of this work is to provide multiple implementations of SPACE in different MAS development platforms in order to make the model easily usable. Secondly, we would try to integrate SPACE in the complete chain from the definition of a problem to an efficient MAS solving it. More precisely, the goal is to extend the method in order to produce an agent model expressed with SPACE. This step is necessary because of the richness of the model induced by its declarative aspect. This method must also provide tools allowing to exploit the different components of the SPACE model in order to check and validate agents and then the MAS. Application of the method to problems with no trivial solution should also be studied. Further steps will be to search an adaptation of these tools to other kinds of problems.

References

1. V. Jay D. Olivier C. Bertelle, M. Flouret and J.-L. Ponty. Automata with multiplicities as behaviour model in multi-agent simulations.
2. F. Comellas. An ant algorithm for the graph colouring problem. http://citeseer.nj.nec.com/112038.html.
3. Y. Demazeau. Voyelles, 2001.
4. R. Diestel. *Graph Theory*. Springer-Verlag, New-York, 2000.
5. dimacs92. Clique and coloring problems, a brief introduction, with project ideas, 1992. ftp://dimacs.rutgers.edu/pub/challenge.
6. Raphaël Dorne and Jim-Kao Hao. A new genetic local search algorithm for graph coloring. In Agoston E. Eiben, Thomas Bäck, Marc Schoenauer, and Hans-Paul Schwefel, editors, *Parallel Problem Solving from Nature – PPSN V*, pages 745–754, Berlin, 1998. Springer. http://citeseer.nj.nec.com/dorne98new.html.
7. A. Drogoul. *De la simulation multi-agents à la résolution collective de problèmes: une étude de l'émergence de structure d'organisation dans les systèmes multi-agents*. PhD thesis, Univ. Paris VI, 1993.
8. J. Ferber and O. Gutknecht. Aalaadin: a meta-model for the analysis and design of organizations in multi-agent systems, 1998.
9. G. Ribeiro Filho. Improvements on constructive genetic approaches to graph coloring. http://citeseer.nj.nec.com/242708.html.

10. G. Ribeiro Filho and G. Lorena. A constructive genetic algorithm for graph coloring, 1997. http://citeseer.nj.nec.com/filho97constructive.html.
11. G. Ribeiro Filho and G. Lorena. Constructive genetic algorithm and column generation: an application to graph coloring, 2000.
    http://citeseer.nj.nec.com/filho00constructive.html.
12. M. Fisher. A survey of concurrent metatem - the language and its applications. In D.M. Gabbay and H.J. Ohlbach, editors, *Temporal logic - Proceedings of the first international conference*, pages 480–505. LNAI, 1994.
13. M. Flouret, D. Fournier, B. Mermet, and G. Simon. Formalisation des agents: du modèle conceptuel au modèle opérationnel: le modèle space. Technical report, Laboratoire d'Informatique du Havre, 2003.
14. Tony Garneau and Sylvain Delisle. Evaluation comparative d'outils et d'environnements. In *JFIADSMA*, pages 281–284. Hermes, 2002.
15. O. Gutknecht and Jacques Ferber. La plateforme madkit et l'outil de conception sedit. In *Systèmes Multiagents: Méthodologie, technologie et expériences, JFIADSMA00*, pages 281–284. Hermes, 2000.
16. Jomi F. Hübner, Jaime S. Sichman, and Olivier Boissier. Spécification structurelle, fonctionnelle et déontique d'organisations dans les sma. In *Systèmes Multiagents et Systèmes Complexes, JFIADSMA02*, pages 205–216. Hermes, 2002.
17. Carlos Iglesias, Mercedes Garrijo, and José Gonzalez. A survey of agent-oriented methodologies. In Jörg Müller, Munindar P. Singh, and Anand S. Rao, editors, *Proceedings of the 5th International Workshop on Intelligent Agents V: Agent Theories, Architectures, and Languages (ATAL-98)*, volume 1555, pages 317–330. Springer-Verlag: Heidelberg, Germany, 1999.
18. Bruno Mermet. Formal model of a multiagent system. In Robert Trappl, editor, *Cybernetics and Systems*, pages 653–658. Austrian Society for Cybernetics Studies, 2002.
19. H.S. Nwana, D.T. Ndumu, L.C. Lee, and J.C. Collis. Zeus: a toolkit for building distributed multi-agents systems. *Applied Artificial Intelligence Journal*, 13 (1/2):129–185, 1999.
20. A. Rao and M. Georgeff. Bdi agents from theory to practice. In *Technical note 56*. AAII, 1995.
21. G. Rimassa, F. Bellifemine, and A. Poggi. Jade - a fipa compliant agent framework. In *PMAA'99*, pages 97–108, 1999.
22. Arsène Sabas, Sylvain Delisle, and Mourad Badri. A comparative analysis of multiagent system development methodologies: Towards a unified approach. In Robert Trappl, editor, *Cybernetics and Systems*, pages 599–604. Austrian Society for Cybernetics Studies, 2002.
23. Gaële Simon, Marianne Flouret, and Bruno Mermet. A methodology to solve optimisation problems with mas; application to the graph colouring problem. In *AIMSA*. LNAI, 2002.
24. A. Vesel and J. Zerovnik. How good can ants color graphs? *Journal of computing and Information Technology - CIT*, 8:131–136, 2000.
    http://citeseer.nj.nec.com/443529.html.
25. Michael Wooldridge and Nicholas R. Jennings. Pitfalls of agent-oriented development. In Katia P. Sycara and Michael Wooldridge, editors, *Proceedings of the 2nd International Conference on Autonomous Agents (Agents'98)*, pages 385–391, New York, 9–13, 1998. ACM Press.
26. Michael Wooldridge, Nicholas R. Jennings, and David Kinny. The gaia methodology for agent-oriented analysis and design. *Autonomous Agents and Multi-Agent Systems*, 3(3):285–312, 2000.

Author Index

Lecture Notes in Artificial Intelligence (LNAI)